Behind The Veil

By
Abd El Schafi

PIONEER BOOK COMPANY

PO Box 284
Caney, KS 67333

First Printing 1996
Second Printing 2000
Third Printing 2001
Fourth Printing 2002

Table of Contents

Table of Contents

Section One

The Veil of Human Rights

Introduction

This book has a motive as well as an objective. The motive is simply a genuine intense love for our Muslim brothers. The objective is to capture the personal interest of Moslems and direct their thoughts to their temporal and eternal security.

Therefore, this book is dedicated first to individual Moslems one by one, including Muslim clergymen and the leaders of Islamic nations. This book is dedicated to all those who desire to worship the One real God in a way acceptable to Him which will fill their hearts with light, peace, and joy.

Moreover, this book is also dedicated to all Europeans and Americans who have converted to Islam in order to reveal to them Islam's origin and roots. Such converts will not have scrutinized ancient Arabic references for Muslim scholars; they have believed what has been told them by contemporary Muslim propagandists. In fact, the material in this book will prove new to those Westerners as well as to a vast majority of Arabic Moslems themselves. As a result of reading this book, we pray that they will all start to re-evaluate the Islamic religion and to re-examine the claims of Muhammad's prophecy.

In addition to these groups, this book is also dedicated to all the thinkers and all researchers in the field of religion, particularly in these days when more attention is being paid to Moslems, Islam and to God in general.

Of course, this book is also dedicated to preachers of the Gospel who invite all people everywhere to come to salvation. Therefore, this book is dedicated to all Christians who sing, "Shine Jesus shine, fill this land with the Father's glory," to be used by the power of the Holy Spirit.

The Sources and References of this Book

Muslim scholars are the sole authority that have the right (as well as the ability) to discuss the issues of Islam, to explain the verses of the Qur'an and to depict the life of Muhammad, his wives, and his companions. Therefore, we have relied **completely** on the reference books or Muslim scholars whether the contemporary scholars in Al-Azhar (Egypt), Saudi Arabia and the rest of the Islamic universities in Islamic nations, or the great, ancient Muslim scholars agreed upon in Saudi Arabia, Al-Azhar and the rest of the Muslim world. In fact, contemporary scholars **command** every researcher and every student in the field of Islam to refer to the writings of the great, ancient scholars. We must conclude then that these ancient scholars are the only ones in the field of Islamic studies, including Qur'anic exposition, Islamic law (Sharia), the life and sayings of Muhammad, and Islamic history.

Such ancient Muslim scholars include Al-Bokhary, Moslem, Ibn Hisham, Ibn Kathier, Al-Baydawy, Al-Tabarie, Jalalan, Al-Mahallie, and Al-Siewtie, Ibn Al-Athier, Ibn Hazm, Ibn Teimeia, Ibn Khaldoon and Al-Zama-khsharie as well as the four great Jurisprudents: Al-Shafaie, Abu Hanifa, Malek, Ibn Ons and Ibn Hanbal since the vast majority of all Moslems follow one of these four creeds. In fact, these scholars rely mainly on the life and sayings of Muhammad as well as the teachings and sayings of his companions, such as the four successors Khaliefa Abu Bakr, Omar, Ottoman, and Ali. They also relied upon Ibn Abbas, Muhammad's cousin who was rightly depicted as the Qur'an Expositor and the most knowledgeable concerning the inspired writings of Muhammad.

As a matter of fact, all Muslim researchers (as well as common Moslems) know those scholars. For Moslems, these scholars are similar to Paul, Peter, John, Matthew, Mark and Luke and all they represent for Christians. Actually, Moslems rely on the writings of these ancient scholars since such scholars are the pillars of Precept (Sunah).

Islam is based on the Qur'an and on Precept (Sunah), and not simply on the Qur'an. This is confirmed unanimously by all contemporary scholars. Anyone who does not believe in Precept (Sunah) cannot be reckoned as a Muslim according to all authorities. Precept (Sunah) includes primarily the sayings and life of Muhammad as well as exposition of Qur'anic verses and the reason for these verses being revealed to him.

Al-Siewtie, the well-known Muslim scholar, stated that the angel, Gabriel, revealed the Precept (Sunah) as well as the Qur'an to Muhammad. Therefore, many rules in Islamic Law are followed by all Moslems simply because they originate from the sayings of Muhammad as well as his life—despite the fact that such rules have not been mentioned in the Qur'an.

The Contents of this Book

This is a two-volume work. Each book contains three sections. The first five sections deal with Islam, the Qur'an, the biography of Muhammad and his companions, his disciples and his wives. The last section (Section 6) deals with Christianity and Christ, in some detail. Yet, at the end of the first book, some facts about Christianity will be mentioned briefly.

In the first section, the reader will discover that all Muslim scholars and historians agree that (according to Islamic law) the Muslim who leaves Islam and converts to another religion or to no religion is to be sentenced to death unless he repents and returns to Islam within a few days. So said Muhammad and so said all the Muslim successors (Khaliefa).

The first section deals with human rights—rights that are lost completely in Islam. We will see clearly how Muhammad compelled (by the sword) Arabs to accept Islam or be killed, as is stated plainly in verses of the Qur'an. This book will help you see how Islam spread among Arabs and in other cities and countries such as Damascus, Jerusalem, Jordan, Egypt, Palestine, Iraq, Iran, all the countries of North Africa, India, and China. In fact, Muhammad and his successors (Khaliefa) had but three options for the surrounding nations: convert to Islam, pay tribute, or be killed, as is plainly presented in verses of the Qur'an according to all Muslim scholars and historians. So the objective of the first section is to remove one of the veils that covers the face of Islam by claiming that Islam respects human rights and freedom of religion.

The second section of this book aims at removing the second veil of Islam for Islam calls itself the religion of equality and social justice. Upon reading this chapter, even the Muslim will discover that Islam is the religion of **inequality**—between men and women, Moslems and non-Moslems, and even between a man and his own brother—in a shameful obvious way because Islam believes in slavery. It is inevitable that the reader be astonished to realize the disgraceful, lowly position of women in Islam and in the eyes of Muhammad.

Humiliating non-Moslems is another example of injustice which is based upon Islamic Law, the sayings of Muhammad and verses from the Qur'an, according to all Muslim scholars. Moreover, we will see that Muhammad owned dozens of slaves whose names can be mentioned. In addition, he was a slave merchant who bought, sold and rented out his slaves **especially** after he claimed himself to be a prophet and after migrating from Mecca to Yathrib (according to Ibn Kaim AL-Gozieha).

The third section gives a circumstantial account of the Qur'an, the book of Moslems, and its teachings. Not only does the Qur'an tell mythical stories (such as that of a war between King Solomon supported by Hoopoe against the ants' kingdom), but also is full of numerous errors (especially scientific ones) such as locating the site of sunset in a fixed area of the earth. These are the main issues covered in the first book of this set.

As to the second book of this two-volume set (to be published following shortly upon the first), it will be dedicated to depicting the life of Muhammad and his companions; i.e., his disciples, successors (Khaliefa) and his wives. Even the Muslim reader will be astonished to learn how cruel and brutal Muhammad was as he tortured his captives with fire, then killed them and took their wives as bond maids and wives for himself as well as for his companions. Had anyone dared to write defamatory poetry about him, the poet would have been assassinated whether a centenarian or a nursing mother.

The reader will see clearly Muhammad's uncontrollable forbidden sexual lusts, including his desire to marry the wives of his companions. So he claimed that verses of the Qur'an were revealed to him to satisfy his desires and to allow him to marry those wives after they had been divorced from his companions just for that purpose. Moreover, sexual perversion was one of the characteristics of Muhammad. He desired, and married such young girls as Aisha, whom he married when she was six years old and he was fifty-one. One day he saw a young girl playing, he desired her and pledged to marry her if she reached her age of maturity while he was still alive! Yet he died before she grew up for he was sixty years old when he made that pledge. In fact, this is a portrait of Muhammad's life.

Following Muhammad's death, his companions fought each other in relentless, savage wars. Competing for authority and out of deeply rooted hatred, Muhammad's relatives and closest friends sacrificed and slaughtered one another. Muhammad's wife, Aisha (together with Talha and Al-Zobair) led the wars against Ali Ibn Abi Taleb, Muhammad's cousin. Consequently, Ali Ibn Abi Taleb together with Muhammad's closest companions fought Maaweia, one of those who had been trusted to write down the Qur'an for Muhammad. Then Ali killed thousands of his faithful followers (led by Al-Khawareg) in a few hours despite the fact that they had fought Aisha and Maaweia with him.

Othman Ibn Affan, the third successor (Khaliefa), who married two daughters of Muhammad successively, was killed by famous companions and relatives such as Muhammad Ibn Abu Bakr Al-Sediek and Ammar Ibn Yaser at the instigation of Aisha, Amr Ibn Al-As and others. These are only a few examples of the astonishing deeds of those to whom paradise was promised. Not only did Muhammad describe his companions as the best nation, but the Qur'an also praised them. All these historical facts are agreed upon by all Muslim scholars and historians according to the references which will be mentioned in detail.

No wonder that we see Moslems these days fighting with each other. In fact, these wars and hostilities spring from the heart of the teachings of Islam since it calls for the use of force to combat wrongdoing, as Muhammad's relatives did with one another. It was Muhammad who said that "...whoever sees an abomination must straighten it with his hands." Saddam Hussein repeated and relied upon this saying of Muhammad in his attack on Kuwait's ruling family. Muslim brotherhood in Egypt depended upon this saying when they killed Anwar El Sadat. Why not, if Ali Ibn Abi-Talib attacked Mowaeia! A great Muslim even killed Othman, the third caliph and Muhammad's relative, and one of the Qur'anic writers who was promised paradise by Muhammad.

In the last section, Section 6, the fundamental principles of Christianity will be highlighted, and the way of salvation and abundant life will be outlined. Also, the most important questions raised by our Muslim brothers will be answered.

Our Hopes and Expectations

We believe this book will prove to be of great interest to the religious world as it highlights essential facts about Islam, the Qur'an, Muhammad, his companions and his wives for the first time. Therefore, we hope for and expect a spiritual revolution and drastic change in the Islamic world as a result of the publication of this book and its translation into different languages. In fact, it will require countless knees to bow before our great living God for the fulfillment of our expectations.

We will persevere in fasting and prayers that our One true God will lead millions of Moslems to the fountain of living waters —waters of joy and salvation, for this is the call of our God in the Bible.

> "Ho! Everyone who thirsts, Come to the waters .... Listen diligently to Me, and eat what is good, And let your soul delight itself in abundance" (Isaiah 55:1-2).

> Christ invited everyone to come to Him as He said:

> "Come to Me, all you who labor and are heavy laden, and I will give you rest" (Matthew 11:28).

Praise God, for God is love!

When we say that Islam does not believe in human rights and does not recognize the individual's freedom, many people object. Also, when we claim that the wars which Muhammad and his successors waged were offensive wars to spread Islam by force, to plunder the abundance of the countries, to seize the properties of the lands and to capture women and children, we encounter multitudes of people who express their astonishment and disapproval.

Because of this disbelief, we are going to confine ourselves to two subjects, and our only source of information will be great Muslim scholars.

Chapter One
The Apostate
Relinquishing the Faith

Regardless of whether the Muslim embraces Christianity (as is happening today with millions of the Indonesians) or becomes an atheist, Islamic law declares that he must be killed. Also, anyone who rejects any of the basic ordinances of Islam or insults the prophet or the Qur'an (as Salman Rushdie did) will be regarded as an apostate and must be killed. It is well-known that all Muslim scholars agree upon these points without exception. They also avow that the prophet Muhammad said it, and they practice it with those who relinquish Islam and become apostate. The scholars also teach that this is what all the Caliphs (Muhammad's successors) did after him. Contemporary scholars declare without any shame that the Muslim's freedom to change his faith is non-existent and is not recognized by Islam.

Contemporary Scholars

The Azhar University in Egypt

It is well-known that Egypt is the largest Arab/Islamic country in the world. The University of Azhar has been regarded through the years as the Mineret (light) of Islam for the entire Islamic world. The Legislative committee at the Azhar issued "The Bill of Legalistic Penalties. This book has been sent to all the Mosques in the West accompanied by a descriptive memorandum for these laws. The legislative committee

11

requested Muslims to implement these penalties and comply
with Islamic law. This bill was written both in Arabic and in
English. It deals with the penalties imposed by Islamic law such
as amputation of the thief's hand and the scourging of the wine
drinker. However, we would like to deal here with the penalty
for the apostate who relinquishes the Islamic faith.

Provisions Specific to Apostasy

The "Bill of Legalistic Penalties" says (p.12),

> "A person guilty of apostasy (man or woman) shall be put
> to death if repentance is not made within the period
> allowed which shall not exceed sixty days. Repentance of
> a person who commits apostasy more than twice shall not
> be accepted.

> "An apostate is that Muslim who has renounced the faith
> of Islam irrespective of his adoption of another creed.

> "The crime of apostasy is committed in the following
> ways:

> 1. making an explicit statement or committing an act
> definitely indicating renunciation of Islam,

> 2. denial of essential tenets of the faith,

> 3. bringing into ridicule through word or action, the
> Gracious Koran."

On page 30, we find this explanatory note:

> "The ordained penalty for apostasy is based on the Sunah.
> The prophet, peace be on him, said, 'One who changes his
> faith is to be killed' (al Bukhari). It is also narrated by Al
> Dar Qutni that when a woman called Umm-Marwan had
> renounced Islam, the Prophet ordered that if she failed to
> repent she should be put to death. The rightly guided
> Caliphs continued this practice. It is fully known that
> Abu-Bakr the truthful fought against those who had
> deserted from the religion of Islam and killed many. The

> Gracious Companions were of the same view, and a
> consensus emerged on this issue."

These are the verdicts of the contemporary Azhar scholars. They are the most knowledgeable people in the laws of the Islamic traditions of Muhammad and the actions taken by his successors.

The Scholars of Saudi Arabia

In one of his speeches which was published by the Tunisian newspapers, the former President of that country assaulted the Qur'an and said it is full of contradictions. He also said that Muhammad was a desert man who wrote myths in the Qur'an. The Saudi scholars wrote a book in which they threatened him. On the cover of the book, the following was printed:

> "From the publications of the Islamic League of the
> Madina Munawwara in Saudi Arabia-9
>
> "The Verdict of Islam: 'To him who alleged that the
> Qur'an is contradictory and includes some myths, who
> described the apostle Muhammad to imply that he was
> inflicted with vices or one who attacked his message...'

In page 13 of this book, Sheikh 'Abdul-'Aziz, along with all the Sheiks of Saudi Arabia, said:

> "The verdict of Islam is to sentence to death anyone who
> commits such things. Thus the president Abu Raqiba must
> haste to repent."

They assured him (pages 14 and 15) that all Muslim scholars have agreed that anyone who does these things must be killed. They said this is also the opinion of the head of the four major Islamic schools. The major Islamic schools are the Shafi'i, Malik, Abu Hanifa, and Ahmad. It is well-known that the former president of Tunisia did not change his liberal opinions regarding Muhammad and the Qur'an which he mentioned in his speeches.

It is public knowledge in Tunisia that it is forbidden for a man to marry more than one woman. Thus, Western society should not have been surprised when Khomeini ordered the execution of Rushdie because this is the opinion of all Muslim scholars as well as the heads of the four leading schools.

The Egyptian State Assembly: The Highest Judicial Authority

On August 6, 1977, the most prestigious newspaper in Egypt, al-Ahram, published the following statement:

> "The state assembly has approved a bill to enact the penalty for apostasy. The apostate who intentionally relinquishes Islam by explicit declaration or decisive deed must be put to death. Apostasy is established by one confirmation or by the testimony of two men. The apostate is forbidden to administer his properties. He will be given 30 days to repent before the execution of the sentence of death. But if one converted to Christianity was 10-14 years old, he will only be scourged fifty times."

This law **has not been implemented** in Egypt up to now. This is because of the objection of some liberal, enlightened writers such as Mustafa Amin who published an article in the Akhbar newspaper during the same month, in which he said,

> "We have to think one thousand times before we approve such a law because any divine religion does not need a gallows to protect it. It does not need a sword to cut off the necks of those who disagree with it."

Mustafa Amin is a very famous person in all the Arab world for his noble character, knowledge, and boldness, but he does not know (or maybe he does know) that the religion of Islam surely does need a gallows to protect it because the law of apostasy is an Islamic law.

The most astonishing part of the statement of the Egyptian state assembly is this: "The apostasy is established by the testimony of two men." Yet it is possible that two Muslim men may come forward and testify that they heard such-and-such a Christian man saying, "I am converted to Islam and I testify that Muhammad is the apostle of God." They may say that while actually the man has never made that claim. Still, the testimony of the Muslim witness will be accepted. In this case, that poor man has no choice but either to embrace Islam or be put to death.

It is a detestable law which is rejected by the Egyptian government (they do not implement it) though many Muslims in Egypt have already become Christians. This is because the government is a secular government and not an Islamic one, but the government is subject to increasing pressure, day after day, from the terroristic Islamic forces.

What Happens To Muslims in Egypt Who Become Christians

In January of 1986, the Egyptian authorities arrested eight people (males and females) whose ages ranged from 20-30 years. The charge was that they had embraced Christianity several years before. Eight months later, they were released from jail after their story was publicized in many of the Western newspapers and magazines. What is important to us here is that while the eight Christians were in prison, a Muslim leader wrote to the government demanding that they execute them—not just keep them under arrest. On the second of July 1986, "The Islamic Light" newspaper which is published by the Ahrar party (the freemen party), said in an article titled, "Point of Absurdity":

> "Two things we find absurd. The first one is that the Egyptian church is demanding their immediate release and has contacted the International Amnesty Committee to convey its indignation for the imprisonment of eight people because of their apostasy from Islam. The second thing which we call absurdity is that the Egyptian government was content to arrest them only. It was supposed to execute Islamic law upon them; namely, death

if they do not repent. The government must make this clear to all the world and be proud of this law because it is God's verdict. "

Maybe such a verdict honors this newspaper, but it does not honor the Egyptian government. It does not even honor her to hold them in jail; that is why she released them.

This is not **God's** verdict, my friend. God is love and respects man's decisions. God wants to set you free from your delusions in order to bring you to the light of the truth. What really amazes us is the common impression that God is vindictive like the law would imply. What adds to our amazement is that the name of the newspaper is "The Journal of Light" and the name of your party is "The Party of the Freemen." What light and what freedom are these? This Islamic law is a shame.

The United States—Land of Freedom and Human Rights— and the United Nations

The Muslim Youth in New York publish a weekly Islamic magazine called al-Tahrir ("Liberation"). In its issue of February 5, 1983, the chief editor wrote an article under the title, "The Symptoms of Apostasy in the Islamic Society". On page 15, he said:

> "The apostate is not only the person who relinquishes Islam and embraces another religion, but the symptoms of apostasy are many, and those who practice them are regarded as infidels and apostate and deserve to be killed. The symptoms of apostasy are: when the ruler does not govern by God's law (most of the Muslim rulers do that), or when the ruler derides some aspect of the religion or one of the Islamic laws as the ex-president of Egypt, al-Sadat, did when he said that the dress of the Muslim women is like a tent.

> "Another symptom of apostasy is that a Muslim believes in the Qur'an only and rejects tradition; namely, the sayings and deeds of Muhammad (the Sunah) and attacks

the apostle Muhammad by any insult or criticism of the Qur'an. Also among the symptoms of apostasy is the promotion of mottoes which may contradict the Qur'an, such as the mottoes of nationalism, patriotism, and humanism! Anyone who calls for these mottoes is regarded as an infidel and an apostate and deserves to be killed if he does not repent. Also, anyone who believes in Masonianism. "

We respond by saying that the writer is right according to the Islamic tenets, but what is the view of the American police of these claims and of this newspaper, especially since many Iranians and Arabs in the U.S. have become Christians and American citizens. They are under the threat of death in accordance with the Islamic law.

The Former Scholars

Without exception, all the former scholars agree on depriving any person the right of freedom to change his religion and they call for the death penalty for anyone who does so. I have chosen the most important and famous scholars—those who are acknowledged by all Muslims.

The Imam al-Shafi'i

In his book, "The Ordinances of the Qur'an" (part 1, p. 289), he remarks:

> "If someone becomes a Muslim then apostatizes, he would be asked to repent; if he does not repent, he should be killed."

> The Shafi'i is one of the four founders of the jurisprudence schools who (the Saudi scholars said) have agreed that the apostate must be put to death.

Ibn Hazm

In Vol. 4, p. 316 of his volume, "The Sweetened" (Al Muhalla), Ibn Hazm says:

"Any of the infidels who said, 'There is no God but God, and Muhammad is the apostle of God', he became a Muslim obligated to Islamic laws. If he rejected that later on, he would be subject to death. But if he was one of the people of the Book (namely, from the Jews or Christians), in order to become a Muslim, he must say, 'I have embraced Islam.' Then he becomes a Muslim obligated to the Islamic laws. If he rejected them, he would be killed."

Ibn Timiyya

This famous scholar, who is called Sheikh al-Islam, says under the title of the law pertaining to the apostate,

"The Muslim who does not pray must be ordered to pray; if he refuses to pray, he must be put to death, because he would be an infidel and apostate, according to the scholars and Imams, even if he said that Muhammad is the apostle of God, and even if he was convinced of the purposes of prayers" (Vol. 35, pp. 105-106).

In Vol. 32, pp. 276 and 279, he addresses this matter, namely, the killing of one who abandoned prayers. Then he speaks to husbands:

"If a wife abstain from praying, she would be asked to repent. The husband may scourge her to repent, otherwise she must be killed."

It is well-known that the majority of Muslims do not pray the daily five prayers, especially the wives who do not have enough time to do so. Thus, in this case, if the husband is a true Muslim, he would beat his wife to force her to pray, and if she declined to obey he must condemn her to death. God, have mercy upon us!

This judgment is not the verdict of Ibn Timiyya only, but (as he frequently claimed), it is a verdict which all the scholars and Imams recognize. Actually our research has led us to believe Ibn Timiyya's claim. In part 11, Vol. 8, Ibn Hazm in his book, "al-Muhalla" ("The Sweetened", p. 378), repeats the same words and declares to us that this is also the opinion of the Shafi'i and

Malik, both of whom emphasize that the one who abandons prayers and does not repent must be killed. Sahih of Muslim (Vol. 1, p. 267) indicates that this is also the view of 'Ali Ibn Abi Talib. Yet Abu Hanifa has a slightly different opinion. He says that the one who ignores prayer will not be killed but must be scourged until he repents. If he does not repent, he must be continuously, beaten even if he dies under the punishment.

From the Inception of Islam

Sayings of Muhammad and His Successors

Prophet of Mercy and Freedom

We have already seen how the scholars of the Azhar based their resolution concerning the death penalty of the apostate on Muhammad's saying: "Who relinquishes his faith, kill him." This is quoted on the authority of Ibn 'Abbas as it is recorded in Sahih of al-Bukhari (part 9, p. 19). Not only al-Bukhari but the following scholars also ascribe this famous statement to Muhammad.

• Ibn Hazm, pp. 129 and 401, part 8 Vol. 11

• Ibn Hisham, p. 284, part 3, of Muhammad's biography, al rawd al-Anaf.

• Ibn Qayyim al-Jawziyya, p. 45, part 5 of his book Zad al-Ma'ad in which he asserts that Muhammad uttered these words and condemned anyone who relinquished his faith.

Other statements by Muhammad Related to this Issue:

In a very famous declaration, Muhammad defines three cases in which a Muslim must be killed:

> "The blood of the Muslim is not lawful [to be shed] except in three cases: Infidelity after faith, adultery after marriage, and killing a soul without any right."

What is important to us here is his phrase "Infidelity after faith." If you ask me who claimed that Muhammad said this, I will respond: All former and contemporary scholars, without exception, attest to that.

When 'Uthman Ibn 'Affan, the third caliph and the husband of Ruqayya the daughter of Muhammad, was besieged by some famous Muslim companions of the apostle, he reminded them of Muhammad's sayings and asked them: "For which of these three reasons do you intend to kill me?" and "Am I not the prince of believers?" Yet they killed him. Among those who were involved in his assassination were Muhammad Ibn Abu Bakr El Seddik and 'Ammar Ibn Yasir. (Refer to the Chronicle of al-Tabari Vol. 2, p. 669, and all the books of the Islamic history such as the "Chronicle of the Caliphs" by the Suyuti and Ibn Kathir).

This statement is also recorded in the following:

• Sahih of Muslim Vol. I, p. 267 (the interpretation of Nawawi).

• Sahfi'i, "The Ordinances of the Qur'an", part 2, p. 46.

• Ibn Hazm, part 11, Vol. 8, p. 377 and restated also on p. 400.

• The Sheikh Shaltute in his famous book, "Islam: a Dogma and a Law", p. 322.

• Dr. Afifi 'Abdul-Fattah, in his widespread book, "The Spirit of the Islamic Religion", p. 408.

It is obvious then, that this statement is well documented and unquestionably ascribed to Muhammad. It is also well-known that the Sahih of al-Bukhari has recorded in part 9, p. 18 that:

> "The apostate has to be killed based on God's saying in the Qur'an: 'And whosoever of you turns from his

religion and dies disbelieving..."' (the Chapter of Cow: 217).

Deeds of Muhammad, Prophet of Mercy and Freedom

The Supreme committee of law in the Azhar mentioned that a woman by the name of Um Mirwan relinquished her Islamic faith. Muhammad ordered her to repent or to be killed. Islamic history books record also that when Muhammad conquered Mecca, he sentenced to death all who apostasized or insulted him (refer to the Chronicles of Tabari, part II, p. 160 and Ibn Hisham part 4, pp. 15, 16 in "The Biography of the Prophet").

Muhammad's Companions and Successors: What Did They Do?

Mu'az Ibn Jabal and the Jewish Man

He was one of Muhammad's greatest companions among the "helpers." Even Muhammad himself said, "Learn (to take) the Qur'an from four (people): Mu'adhs Ibn Jabal and ..." (refer to the Bukhari, part 6). The following terrifying incident is recorded in the Sahih of al-Bukhari (part 9, p. 19):

> "Mu'adhs Ibn Jabal went to visit Abu Musa the governor of Yemen. He offered him a cushion to sit on. A man tied with ropes was there. Mu'adh asked Abu Musa: 'What is this?' He answered, 'This man was a Jew, then he was converted to Islam, later he apostatized and turned a Jew again.' Mu'adh said to him: 'I will never even sit down on a cushion until this man is put to death. (This is) the verdict of God and His apostle.' (The governor) ordered him to be killed. (Only after that) Abu Mu'adh sat."

Here we see a Jewish man who was converted to Islam and later was convinced that he made a mistake. Thus, he returned to his old faith and was tied with ropes like an animal. Then

Mu'adh came in and refused to sit down on a cushion unless this man was put to death immediately; so they executed him. Then, and only then, Mu'adh sat, ate and drank with Abu Musa who felt at peace with himself because he believed that he had implemented the command of God and His apostle, Muhammad. His apostle and the lord of the messengers, the prophet of mercy and freedom, said, "Whosoever relinquishes his faith, kill him."

Ali Ibn Abi Talib and Some Christians

This brutal man used to burn apostates whether they were alive or dead. He was the cousin of Muhammad and his son-in-law. He was Muhammad's favorite friend and one of the ten to whom Muhammad granted paradise. Muhammad reared him before and after the death of his father and said that Ali was the best one to judge according to Islamic law.

Now let us see what was recorded about Ali Ibn Abi Talib, the fourth Caliph, who is admired by both the Shi'ites and Sunnis. In his eighth volume, part eleven of his book, "The Sweetened", Ibn Hazm says (page 189),

> "Ali brought apostates and burned them. When Ibn 'Abas received the news he said: 'If it were me instead of (him), I would not have burned them but I would rather have killed them in another way because the apostle of God said: "Whosoever relinquishes his faith, kill him."'"

This same incident is recorded in Sahih of al-Bukhari (part 9, page 19). Ibn Hazm (in the same previous source, p. 190) also relates what 'Ali did to some ex-Muslims who were converted to Christianity. He narrates the following three episodes:

Ibn Hazm says:

> "They brought an old man to 'Ali who was originally a Christian, then embraced Islam, and later reconverted to Christianity. 'Ali told him: 'Maybe you apostatized to Christianity in order to acquire an inheritance, and after that you would come back to Islam.' The (old man) said: 'No.' 'Ali asked him: 'Maybe you apostate to Christianity

in order to get married to a Christian girl and after that you would return to Islam.' The old man said: 'No.' 'Ali told him: 'Then, re-embrace Islam.' The old man said: 'No, not before I meet Christ.' 'Ali ordered him (to be killed). They beheaded him.

"Another Muslim apostasized and became a Christian. 'Ali ordered him to repent but he refused. 'Ali killed him and did not deliver his corpse to his family. They offered him a lot of money (to do so), but 'Ali refused and burned the corpse.

"Another man from the tribe of bany 'Ijl became a Christian. They brought him to 'Ali chained in irons. 'Ali talked to him for a long time. The man said to him: 'I know that Isa (Jesus) is the son of God.' Ali stood up and stepped on him. When the people saw that, they, too, stood up and stepped on him. Then 'Ali told them: 'Kill him.' They killed him. Then 'Ali ordered them to burn him.'"

For God's sake, 'Ali. Is it because the minds of those men (young and old) have been convinced by Christianity that you ordered them to change their convictions? When they refused to do so you tortured them ... or killed them ... or burned them.

'Uthman Ibn 'Affan

He is the third Caliph and the husband of Raqiyya and then om Kalthom, the daughters of Muhammad. He is also one of the ten to whom Muhammad granted paradise. Someone came to 'Uthman and conveyed to him that some people from Iraq had apostasized. 'Uthman wrote to the governor there and ordered him to command them to repent and re-embrace Islam. If they refused to do so, they all were to be killed. Some of them were actually killed because they refused to return to Islam, while others yielded and returned to Islam because of fear (refer to Ibn Hazm, part 11, p. 190).

Abu Bakr and the Wars of Apostasy

All the civilized world along with people of free conscience regard these wars as tyrannical, savage and barbaric. Wars which were waged without any justification. The world will always wonder what the crime of these poor Arab tribes was and what they did that made Abu Bakr, the first Caliph, wage such long and brutal wars against them, killing tens of thousands of people. All Muslims are quick to answer that Abu Bakr was carrying out Muhammad's orders, as he himself claimed, because these Arab tribes deserted Islam as soon as Muhammad died. Therefore, the fight with them was inevitable.

Advanced countries and free human beings do not comprehend or accept this answer which ignores the simplest principles of human rights and personal freedom to believe in the religious doctrine of their choice. If the reader were given the opportunity to read any of the Islamic history books, he would discover by himself the outrageous brutality which was committed in these wars. Multitudes were massacred, and the survivors were forced to re-embrace Islam and pay alms to Abu Bakr El Seddik, the father of A'isha wife of Muhammad. Of course, Abu Bakr was the first to whom Muhammad granted paradise. He said about him, "Abu Bakr is the most favorite to me among men, and his daughter A'isha is the most beloved among women."

The wars of apostasy are taught in all the schools of Arab and Islamic countries for all famous Islamic chroniclers such as the Tabari, Ibn Khaldun, Ibn Kathir and Suyuti recorded them in detail. In the Chronicles of the Tabari (part 2, pp. 258, 272), we read that Abu Bakr used to tell those whom he sent to fight the apostatized tribes:

> "Call them to re-embrace Islam; if they refuse, do not spare any one of them. Burn them with fire and kill them with force and take the women and children as prisoners of war."

Abu Bakr frequently re-iterated these famous words to Muslim warriors 'Umar Ibn al-Khattab used to tell him that some of the tribes had returned to Islam, but they refused to pay him alms. They said that alms should be paid only to Muhammad, though they were ready to return to Islam. Abu Bakr would respond: "By God, if they refrain from giving me a rope which they used to pay to the apostle of God, I will fight them for refusing" (refer to p. 175 of Vol. I of Sahih of Muslim, interpretation of the Nawawi. Also refer to any book about the wars of the apostasy).

There is a most important contemporary book which was published by the Azhar University, entitled, "The khulafa' al-Rashidun" ("The Rightly Guided Caliphs") by Dr. Abu Zayd Shalabi, professor of Islamic civilization at the College of Arabic language. The book was published in 1967. The author presented detailed information about the Wars of Apostasy which covered 20 pages (pp. 41-60). We would like to quote the following here:

> "Abu Bakr sent eleven Muslim generals against eleven cities to fight the apostates. Many were forced to re-embrace Islam. Among those countries were Bahrin which was invaded by al-'Ala' Ibn al-Hadrami, and Yemen which was attacked by Suwayd Ibn Maqrin. Kalid Ibn al-Walid went to fight against Tulayha, the tribe of Bany Asad and its neighboring Arab tribes."

Then, Abu Zayd comments on these wars on page 60:

> "The victories gained by Muslims in the wars of apostasy had one very significant result: These victories deterred anyone who intended to apostatize from Islam."

The point, then, Dr. Shalabi, is that by threat of death, Islam attempted to keep people against their will, in the realm of Islam. Aren't you also ashamed to record in your book, that by means of offensive wars, Islam spread all over the Middle East? Does not that motivate you to re-examine your religion? Your logic is very strange. These wars deterred anyone who intended to relinquish Islam because he would face the same fate which other Arab tribes had faced. Yet the people of Indonesia will not be deterred or intimidated; their civilized government protects them. They come to Christ by the millions and we pray that you, too, will come.

Ibn Hisham

Ibn Hisham, in "Muhammad's Biography "(El Sira El Nabawia, part 4, p. 180), says:

> "When Muhammad died, most Meccans were about to turn away from Islam and wanted to do so. Suhayl Ibn 'Amru stood up and said: 'Anyone who relinquishes Islam, we will cut his head off.' People changed their minds and were afraid."

This was in regard to Meccans, but the majority of the Arab tribes actually turned away from Islam. Abu Bakr fought them. The ruthlessness of Khalid Ibn al-Walid was very apparent. Dr. Abu Zayd said about Khalid Ibn al-Walid that he was the one who gouged out the eyes of apostates.

Still, there are important questions in this regard which beg our attention and they are: Why did the Arabs become apostate after the death of Muhammad? Why did the Meccans intend to turn away from Islam? The familiar answer is that they had embraced Islam under the threat of the sword because Muhammad forced them to choose between Islam or death.

There are two important questions to which a large number of people would like to have answers.

The First Question

How Do Muslims Justify Killing Apostates?

The assassination of an apostate (one who turns away from his faith) is considered to be a breach of freedom of religious belief as well as an obvious contradiction of the International

Declaration of Human Rights (item 18) which most of the Arab countries have signed. What do contemporary Muslim scholars say about this serious matter?

The scholars of Kuwait and Qatar dealt with this question. The weekly Kuwaiti Magazine, "The Islamic Society" in its issue of April 17,1984, p. 26 said:

> "Somebody may say: 'Do you want to deny freedom to people?' We say to him: 'If what is meant by freedom is to disbelieve in God's religion, or the freedom of infidelity and apostasy, then that freedom is abolished and we do not recognize it; we even call for its eradication, and we strive to oppress it. We declare that publicly and in daylight'" (Quoted from Dr. Taha Jabir's article).

Then Dr. Jabir goes on to explain that Islam does not acknowledge this sort of freedom at all; namely, the freedom of apostasy. He then begins (on page 26) to criticize Islamic governments which allow the media means to make apostasy easier, to regard it as a personal right to anyone who seeks it.

The International Declaration of Human Rights

In order to understand the response of Islam to this declaration, let us go to another Arab Islamic country. Dr. Ahmad from Qatar has a response to this declaration. Dr. Ahmad is a contemporary Muslim scholar and a reputed professor of Islamic law at the University of Qatar. In 1981, he published a famous book under the title, "Individual Guarantees in Islamic Law". If we turn to pages 15 and 16 of this book, we find him saying:

> "Item 18 of the International Declaration of Human Rights states that each individual has the full right to change his faith or to relinquish it as he wishes in order to protect the freedom of thought and the freedom of belief. We wonder if this freedom of changing one's faith would be conducive to harm him along with others? Or even if the purpose of changing the faith is to sow the seeds of riots

and spread viciousness in the land or to waver the faith
from the hearts of others?"

What did you mean, Dr. Ahmad, when you said: "Even if
changing one's faith would be conducive to harm one's self?" Is
this your personal point of view or is it the point of view of the
person himself? Why do you impose your personal point of view
on all people—because you think that it is a sound view? You
believe that relinquishing Islam causes harm to the person who
does it, but this is your own conviction. What if somebody else
believes differently and is convinced that to continue as a
Muslim will bring him harm? If for his own welfare, he wants to
be converted to Christianity and to believe in the One who died
for him so that he may live a life of peace, joy, love and holiness,
why do you come to that person and tell him, "We forbid you!
We do not grant you the freedom to change your faith. If you do
that, we will kill you lest you harm yourself!"

Maybe it was for this reason that Muhammad, Ali and
'Uthman killed the apostates and Abu Bakr fought those who
turned away from Islam, killing tens of thousands ... "lest they
harm themselves".

In regard to your statement that the one who relinquishes his
faith will shake faith in the hearts of others: this has nothing to
do with his conviction. It is their problem with their own creed
and not with him. He is seeking his own spiritual welfare and is
persuaded to embrace another religion. Maybe it is better for
those people to doubt their faith or even to have it uprooted from
their hearts, because it may be a mere fruitless illusion which
would lead to destruction.

There **is** something called human rights, Dr. Ahmad. That is, a
man has the right to be freely and intellectually convinced to
embrace the creeds he wants and to worship God according to
his own persuasion. The civilized countries as well as the United
Nations have acknowledged that, ignoring of course, the

command of your prophet: "Whoever changes his faith, kill him!"

You said that the apostate spreads viciousness in the land. Does the one who is converted to the Christianity with its noble spiritual principles included in the Gospel spread corruption on earth, or is it the one who holds to Islam that kills those who change their faith? Christianity is clearly manifest in the Gospel. It calls us to worship the one God and it emphasizes love—even for our enemies. It calls for a life of holiness and peace.

The Second Question

How Can Muslims Deny the Compulsion of Force?

Most often Muslims who really desire to know the truth and who believe that their faith respects man's freedom, cite the Qur'anic phrase, "There is no compulsion in faith" as an evidence to their claim. Those people do not know its meaning as it was interpreted by the Muslim scholars. We have already seen that Islam states that the apostate must be killed, but in order to understand the meaning of "There is no compulsion in faith," refer to the answers of the contemporary and former scholars of Islam.

The Sheikh Muhammad Mutawilli al-Sha'rawi

He is one of the most famous contemporary scholars in Egypt. Millions of people in the Islamic world watch his television programs as he constantly attacks Christianity. He claims that Christians are infidels, and he stirs Muslims in Egypt to attack Christian churches, burn them and kill the infidels. Local Egyptian newspapers and magazines report this, too. I have not met this man nor have I watched his program, but I have read all of his books. In one of his famous books, "You Ask and Islam Answers", I found the following (page 52 of part 2):

"Some ask: How does Islam say that there is no
compulsion in faith, and yet it commands the killing of the
apostate? We say to them: You are free to believe or not to
believe, but once you embrace the faith you are not free
(anymore) and you should be bound to Islam otherwise
you will suffer punishment and the restrictions, among
them is the killing of the apostate; that is, there is no
compulsion in embracing the faith but, if you do, you are
not free to relinquish it."

Sha'rawi's statement is in full conformity with the law of
killing the apostate. It acknowledges the law and validates it. In
his interpretation of this verse, Ibn Hazm, al-Baydawi agrees
fully with the Sha'rawi. A man (be he a Christian or a Jew) is
free to believe or disbelieve; that is, he has the option either to
accept Islam or to pay the poll tax. If he is not religious, he is not
free to choose another religion, but must become a Moslem. Ibn
Hazm remarks that:

"It was truly related to us that Muhammad used to force
the Arab pagans to embrace the faith. He used to give
them the option either to accept Islam or death. That is
forcing people to accept Islam (refer to Vol. 8, part 11, p.
196, "The Sweetened" Al Mohalla)."

What is of greatest significance to us in the Sha'rawi's claim
is that whoever believes in Islam **does not have freedom** to
relinquish it, otherwise he must be put to death.

Chapter Two
Offensive War to Spread Islam

Muhammad and his successors initiated offensive wars against peaceful countries in order to impose Islam by force as well as to seize the abundance of these lands. Their objective was to capture women and children and to put an end to the poverty and hunger from which Arab Muslims suffered. So, Islam was imposed upon Syria, Jordan, Palestine (Jerusalem), Egypt, Libya, Iraq, Iran, all of North Africa, some parts of India and China, and later Spain.

Undoubtedly, the concept of an offensive war to spread the faith is a genuine Islamic concept; it is known as a Holy War for the sake of God. We will see what Muslim scholars have explicitly determined that this is the essence of Islam. They also indicate that if sufficient military power is available to Islamic countries, they ought to attack all other countries in order to force them to embrace Islam, or pay the poll tax and be subject to Islamic rule. Muhammad (as well as all the Caliphs who succeeded him) called for holy wars . All scholars and lawyers acknowledge that.

Those who say that the Islamic wars were always defensive do not understand Islam and have not read sufficient history. It should be evident that offensive wars to spread Islam are the heart of the entire religion of Islam. They embody the meaning of "Striving for the cause of God"—holy war to make the Word of God supreme over the whole world. Our study will be filled

31

with objective quotes from the statements of scholars, along with a throng of true stories.

The Sayings and Deeds of Muhammad and His Companions

One of Muhammad's popular claims is that God commanded him to fight people until they become Muslims and carry out the ordinances of Islam. All Muslim scholars without exception agree on this. Muhammad said:

> "I have been ordered by God to fight with people till they bear testimony to the fact that there is no God but Allah and that Mohammed is his messenger, and that they establish prayer and pay Zakat (money). If they do it, their blood and their property are safe from me" (see Bukhary Vol. I, p. 13).

Scholars understood this claim to mean the waging of offensive wars against unbelievers in order to force them to embrace Islam as individuals or communities. This is exactly what Muhammad himself **did** in carrying out God's commandment to him.

Azhar's Scholars in Egypt

In his book, "Jurisprudence in Muhammad's Biography", the Azhar scholar, Dr. Muhammad Sa'id Ramadan al-Buti says the following (page 134, 7th edition):

> "The Holy War, as it is known in Islamic Jurisprudence, is basically an **offensive war.** *This is the duty of Muslims in every age when the needed military power becomes available to them.* This is the phase in which the meaning of Holy War has taken its final form. Thus the apostle of God said: 'I was commanded to fight the people until they believe in God and his message ...'"

Dr. Buti deduces from Muhammad's statement that this is the concept of offensive war—this is Holy War as it is known in

Islamic jurisprudence. Notice by his statement also that this matter is a duty incumbent on every Muslim in every age. The time will come when East and West, as well as politicians and military personnel all over the world will realize that the real military danger is the Islamic community. When the needed military power becomes available to them, they will wage wars and invade other countries.

In his book,"The Method of Islamic Law", Saudi Scholar, Dr. Muhammad al-Amin clearly indicates:

"No infidel [unbeliever] should be left on his land as it is denoted from Muhammad's statement: 'I was commanded to fight the people...'"

This claim by Muhammad and its generally-accepted meaning are recorded not only by these contemporary scholars in Egypt and Saudi Arabia, but are also quoted in the following sources:

- The Sahih of al-Bukhari, part I, p. 13.
- The Sahih of Muslim, part I, p. 267 (The Interpretation of the Nawawi).
- The Commentary of Ibn Kathir, p. 336
- The Muhalla (the Sweetened), Vol. 4, p. 317
- "The Ordinances of the Qur'an" by al-Shafi'i, p. 51, part II (on the authority of Abu Huraira).
- Mishkat of al-Masabih, part 1, p. 9.

Almost all major Islamic references have quoted this statement because it is one of the most famous sayings of Muhammad which he followed and which he commanded his followers to implement.

Many provocative and painful events were inflicted on individuals and tribes in the course of Muhammad's life. Muhammad, as we will see, used to exhort his followers:

"Invitation first (that is, call them first to embrace Islam).
If they refuse, then war."

In other words, he told his followers not to kill anybody unless you first invite him to embrace Islam. Only if he rejects it, must he be killed. This is evident in the story of Abu Sufyan:

> When Muhammad and his followers were about to attack Mecca to subjugate it to Islam, his adherents arrested Abu Sufyan, one of Mecca's inhabitants. They brought him to Muhammad. Muhammad told him: "Woe to you, O Abu Sufyan. Is it not time for you to realize that there is no God but the only God?" Abu Sufyan answered: "I do believe that." Muhammad then said to him: "Woe to you, O Abu Sufyan. Is it not time for you to know that I am the apostle of God?" Abu Sufyan answered: "By God, O Muhammad, of this there is doubt in my soul." The 'Abbas who was present with Muhammad told Abu Sufyan: "Woe to you! Accept Islam and testify that Muhammad is the apostle of God before your neck is cut off by the sword." Thus he professed the faith of Islam and became a Muslim.

There are many sources which record this story:

- Ibn Hisham, part 4, p. 11 ("Biography of the Prophet')

- "The Chronicle of the Tabari", part 2, p. 157

- Ibn Kathir, "The Prophetic Biography", part 3, p. 549, and "The Beginning and the End"

- Ibn Khaldun, the rest of part 2, p. 43 and on

- Al-Sira al-Halabiyya, Vol. 3. p. 18

- Al Road Al Anf, part 4, p. 90, by Al Sohaily

It is also mentioned and attested to by contemporary scholars such as Dr. Buti in his book, "The Jurisprudence of Muhammad's Biography", p. 277. He repeated it on page 287 because such stories incite the admiration of the Buti and bring him joy. Yet Dr. Buti feels that some people will protest, especially liberals and the civilized international society, who believe that faith in a certain creed ought not to be imposed by the threat of death. Therefore, he said (p. 287) the following:

"It may be said, 'What is the value of a faith in Islam which is a result of a threat? Abu Sufyan, one moment ago, was not a believer, then he believed after he was threatened by death.' We say to those who question: 'What is required of an infidel or the one who confuses other gods with God, is to have his tongue surrender to the religion of God and to subdue himself to the prophethood of Muhammad. But his heartfelt faith is not required at the beginning. It will come later.'"

This is God in Islam, my dear friends—a God who is satisfied with the testimony of the tongue of a person who is under the threat of death. But "the heartfelt faith" will come later! The important thing is to increase the number of Muslims either by threat or by propagation.

Dr. Buti was more than frank, and we would like to thank him for that, yet we would like to tell him that Christianity rejects the testimony of the mouth if it does not stem from faith that is rooted in the heart first. In Christianity, a person has sufficient time to think quietly before he makes his decision, as the Gospel says:

"Let each be fully convinced in his own mind" (Rom. 14:5).

God reveals His attitude in the Bible when He says:

"My son, give me your heart" (Prov. 23:26).

When the Ethiopian eunuch expressed his desire to be baptized, the evangelist Philip told him:

"If you believe with all your heart, you may" (Acts 8:37).

God even rebukes the people of Israel and says:

"These people draw near to Me with their mouths and honor Me with their lips, but have removed their hearts far from Me" (Isa. 29:13).

The story of Abu Sufyan reveals clearly that Muhammad does not care much about the faith of the heart, especially at the beginning, as Dr. Buti suggests. What is really important is that professing faith is a natural response to the threat of death. The threat is very clear: Testify that Muhammad is the apostle of God or you will be beheaded. The story concludes: Abu Sufyan professed the testimony of "truth" immediately.

In his book, "The Biography of the Apostle", part 4, Ibn Hisham says (page 134):

> "Muhammad sent Khalid Ibn al-Walid to the tribe of the children of Haritha and told him: 'Call them to accept Islam before you fight with them. If they respond, accept that from them, but if they refuse, fight them.' Khalid told them: 'Accept Islam and spare your life.' They entered Islam by force. He brought them to Muhammad. Muhammad said to them: 'Had you not accepted Islam I would have cast your heads under your feet'" (refer to page 134, and also see Al Road Al Anf, part 4, pp. 217, 218. You will find the same incident).

We see in this story the main Islamic concept: First, an invitation to accept Islam, then war against those who refuse to do so. This was Muhammad's order to Khalid Ibn al-Walid. It is also noteworthy to examine Ibn Hisham's statement that "they entered Islam by force." Muhammad himself told them later: "Had you rejected Islam, I would have beheaded you and cast your heads under your feet." This was an undisputed threat: Either they accepted Islam or they would have been beheaded.

The brutal irony is that he uttered these words with ruthlessness and relentlessness instead of congratulating them on their new faith. What a strange man who failed to show any love or genuine compassion. His act was an act of a first-class terrorist. He did not congratulate them because he knew that they entered Islam by force. Is this man really the prophet of freedom, compassion, and human rights? Listen carefully. These oppressive attitudes and actions are as clear as the sun on a bright summer day. Muhammad's words are self-explanatory:

> "Had you not accepted Islam I would have beheaded you
> and cast your heads under your feet!"

What human rights! What compassionate, kind, meek and noble characters! Undoubtedly, this alone is enough to uncover the dreadful dark side of Muhammad's character and his religion.

Azhar scholar Dr. Buti adds on p. 263 of his book:

> "The apostle of God started to send military detachments from among his followers to the various Arab tribes which were scattered in the Arab Peninsula to carry out the task of calling (these tribes) to accept Islam. If they did not respond, they would kill them. That was during the 7th Higira year. The number of the detachments amounted to ten."

Would God's help be sought, Oh Muhammad, to fight peaceful tribes whose only crime was that they could not believe that you are an apostle of God? Satan (not God) assists wicked people to commit these things.

No wonder all these tribes so quickly became apostate and relinquished Islam after the death of Muhammad. Abu Bakr Al Sadiq waged the aforementioned wars to force them to re-embrace Islam. Dr. Buti states this in chapter six of his book, under the title, "New Phase of the Mission". He quotes a statement made by Muhammad which proves that those wars were offensive wars. Muhammad said, "From now on, they will not invade you, but you will invade them."

Now let us see what Muhammad's followers did who implemented the same principle:

Ali Ibn Abi Talib

In his book, "The Biography of the Prophet" (part 3, p. 113), Ibn Hisham relates this episode:

> "Ali Ibn Abi Talib encountered a man called 'Umru and told him, 'I indeed invite you to Islam.' 'Umru said, 'I do

not need that.' 'Ali said, 'Then I call you to fight.' (This was the same policy Muhammad used with those who rejected his invitation.) 'Umru answered him, 'What for my nephew? By God, I do not like to kill you.' 'Ali said, 'But, by God, I love to kill you'" (see Al Road Al Anf part 3, p. 263).

It is obvious from the dialogue that 'Umru does not like fighting because he does not want to kill 'Ali while he is defending himself. He wonders, "What for? I do not want to embrace Islam." But 'Ali says to him, "By God I love to kill you," and he did kill him.

We would like to conclude these stories by relating another moving episode which the Muslim Chroniclers recorded. Among them, Isma'il Ibn Kathir in his book, "The Prophetic Biography" (part 3, p. 596), says that Muhammad's followers met a man and asked him to become a Muslim. He asked them, "What is Islam?" They explained that to him. He said, "What if I refuse it? What would you do to me?" They answered, "We would kill you." Despite that, he refused to become a Muslim and they killed the poor man after he went and bade his wife farewell. She continued to weep over his corpse for days until she died of grief over her slain beloved who was killed for no reason.

Dr. 'Afifi Abdul-Fattah

On the cover of his famous book, "The Spirit of Islamic Religion," which was reprinted more than nine times, it says the following, "It has been revised by the committee of Azhar scholars with introductions made by the greatest Muslim professors and judges of Islamic legal courts."

On page 382 Dr. 'Afifi says:

"Islam has approved war so that the Word of God becomes supreme. This is war for the cause of God (Holy War). Muhammad, therefore, sent his ambassadors to eight kings and princes in the neighborhood of the Arab Peninsula to call them to embrace Islam. They rejected his

call. Thus, it became incumbent on the Muslims to fight
them."

On page 384, we read the following:

"Islamic law demands that before Muslims start fighting
infidels (unbelievers), they first deliver the message of
Islam to them. It was proven that the prophet never fought
people before he called them to embrace Islam first. He
used to command his generals to do so also."

Dr. 'Afifi (along with the Azhar scholars who revised his
book) boasts that the prophet never fought anybody before he
called them to Islam first. Those people fail to realize that
human rights emphasize that when you call people to embrace
any religion and they refuse to do so, you must leave them
alone! You are not to fight them in order to force them to accept
the new religion as Muhammad and his followers did.

We did not say that Muhammad did not call them to believe in
Islam first. We acknowledge that, but we blame him because
whenever they rejected his invitation, he fought and killed them
Are these the human rights? Don't you understand, Dr. 'Afifi?
Do Muhammad's teachings make you so blind that you fail to
see the simplest principles of human rights? Do you not respect
man's freedom to believe in whatever he wants? Muhammad had
the right to call people to embrace Islam and to commission
Khalid along with his followers to carry out this task; but he did
not have the right to kill them if they refused to accept Islam.

Dr. 'Afifi says that eight kings and princes declined to accept
Muhammad's mission; thus it was incumbent on the Muslims to
fight them. We ask him: **Why** was it incumbent on them to fight
those kings and princes? Is their refusal to accept Islam a reason
for the Muslims to fight them? "Yes!" This is what all Muslim
scholars say, without exception.

Let the people of the West and of the East ponder these events
which took place in the course of Islamic history and during the
life of Muhammad and after his death. Beware, nations of the

world, for **any strong Islamic country** would implement the
same policy of war to obey God's order and his messenger! !

The Saudi Scholars

In his book, "The Methodology of Islamic Law", Dr.
Muhammad al-Amin says (page 17):

> "God had made it clear to us that (we should) call for
> acceptance of Islam first, then wage war. It is not
> admissible to wage war before extending the invitation to
> embrace Islam first, **as the Qur'an says.** 'We verily sent
> our messenger with clear proofs and revealed to them the
> scripture and the balance, that mankind may observe right
> measure, and he revealed iron, wherein is mighty power
> and uses for mankind and that Allah (God) may know him
> who helps Him and his messengers—Allah is strong,
> Almighty'" (Surah Iron 57:25).

Thus, God's words, "We sent down iron, which has powerful
might", followed His saying, "We have sent our apostles with
signs." This denotes that if the signs and books fail, then unleash
the sword against them, as the Muslim poet said, "The Book
(Qur'an) offers guidance, and he who does not turn away (from
evil) by the guidance of the book will be kept straight by the
squadrons."

The reader may be confused and want to inquire about
Muhammad's policy in spreading his mission. They may
question his orders to his generals and his explicit attitude
towards Abu Sufyan and say, "These attitudes prove to us that
Islam forces people to accept it. The case is not limited to
ignoring people's freedom and confiscating their properties only
or sentencing the apostate to death, but it also calls for slaying
whoever rejects Islam. What is the opinion of the scholar about
that? Is force used as compulsion in accepting this religion?"

The Muslim scholars say, "Yes." There is compulsion used in
accepting Islam, but this applies only to pagans and those who
are irreligious. For Christians and Jews, the orders are to fight

them and subject them to the ordinances of Islam, making them pay a poll-tax. In this case, they are spared death and are allowed to keep their faith. They are not forced to embrace Islam because they have three options—become Muslims, fight, or pay the poll-tax. The irreligious have two options only: death or Islam. This is what the Muslim scholars say, and the Qur'an itself teaches the same.

Ibn Hazm and al-Baydawi

In volume 8, part 11, on page 196 Ibn Hazm remarks decisively,

> "The prophet Muhammad did not accept from the Arab heathens less than Islam or the sword. This is compulsion of faith. No compulsion in faith (or religion) applies only to Christians or Jews because they are not to be forced to embrace the religion. They have the option either to embrace Islam, the sword, or to pay the poll-tax. In this case they can keep their own faith. It was truly said on the authority of the apostle of God that there is no compulsion in the faith.

> "When the sacred months elapse, kill those who associate other gods with God, wherever you find them" (Surah 9:5).

The Imam al-Baydawi offers us (page 58 of his commentary) exactly the same interpretation.

Abu Bakr El Sadiq

In Al Road Al Anf (part 4, p. 240), Ibn Hisham indicates that Abu Bakr (the daily companion of Muhammad and among the first who believed in him) used to converse with Ibn Abu Rafi al-Ta'i and to say to him:

> "God—to whom belong the might and exaltation—has sent Muhammad with this religion for which he fought until people entered this religion by hook or by crook."

This phrase, I believe, is self-explanatory—"by crook".

The Imam al-Shafi'i

In his famous book, "The Ordinances of Qur'an" (page 50 of the second part), the Shafi'i says:

> "The apostle of God defeated the people until they entered Islam by hook or by crook."

Again we have this clear declaration—"by crook". This is what actually happened.

The Qur'an Exposes the Aggressive Nature of Islam

The Qur'anic verses reveal to us the aggressive, hostile nature of the Islamic mission and of Muhammad. The Qur'an includes verses pertaining to fighting against infidels, as well as other verses related to Holy War against Christians and Jews.

Pertaining to the Infidels

> "But when the sacred months elapse, then fight and slay the pagans wherever you find them and seize them, besiege them and lie in wait for them in every stratagem (of war). But if they repent and establish regular prayers, and practice regular charity, then open the way for them for Allah is oft-forgiving, Most Merciful" (Surah 9:5).

How did Muslim scholars and chroniclers interpret this verse in order to understand what Muhammad did after the conquest of Mecca and its occupation?

The Jalalan

In this commentary, which was published by the Azhar in 1983 (page 153), the authors say decisively,

> "The chapter of Repentance was revealed to raise the level of security which the infidels enjoyed because Muhammad had earlier made a covenant with them not to

kill them. After that, this verse was given (9:5) in order to free God and Muhammad from any covenant with the infidels. It gives them four months in which they will be protected, but by the end of the four months (the end of the grace period), the order comes: Kill the infidels wherever you find them. Capture them, besiege them in their castles and fortresses until they are forced to accept Islam or be killed."

As you see, this verse was inspired in order to free Muhammad (and God) from any peaceful and protective covenant which Muhammad made with the people of Mecca, as if the covenant were shameful behavior from which Muhammad (and his God) must free themselves. Nothing remains after that, except the pledge of war and massacre, as Ibn Hisham says later.

Ibn Qayyim al-Jawziyya.

Ibn Qayyim al-Jawziyya's book was published in Saudi Arabia (second edition) in 1981. In part 5, p. 90, this famous scholar tells us the following:

"When the prophet migrated from Mecca to Medina, God ordered him to fight those who fought him only. Then when the chapter of Repentance was revealed, God commanded His prophet to fight anyone who did not become a Muslim from among the Arabs, whether (that person) fought him or not. He did not command him to take the poll-tax from infidels."

This means that Arabs did not have a choice. They either had to embrace Islam or die by the sword. It is obvious then that God (according to the above interpretation) had ordered His prophet to fight anyone from among the Arabs who refused to become a Muslim whether he fought against Muhammad or not. This is overt aggression and unjustified attack against peaceful people.

Ibn Hisham: - Al Sohaily

In his book, "al-Rawd al-Anaf" which is the most famous book about Muhammad's life (part 4, p. 194), we read the following text:

> "When Muhammad conquered Mecca and the Arabs realized that they were not able to wage war against Muhammad, they accepted the Islamic faith. But some of the infidels continued to be as they were. (They used to make pilgrimages also because this practice was in vogue among the people hundreds of years before Muhammad). Then suddenly Muhammad sent someone to announce to the Tribe of Quraysh that no pilgrimage would be allowed for the infidels after that year (9H); none would enter paradise unless he were a Muslim. Muhammad was going to give the infidels a respite for four months, and after that there would not be a covenant except the covenant of the sword and war (lit: piercing and the strike of the sword). After this period, people entered Islam by hook or by crook, and anyone who did not become a Muslim fled the Arabian Peninsula."

Ibn Hisham already quoted Muhammad's famous words:

"No two religions are to exist in the Arab Peninsula"
(pp. 50, 51).

Ibn Kathir, Al-Baydawi-al-Tabari (The Pillars of Islam)

Isma'il Ibn Kathir reiterates the above interpretation on page 336 of his commentary. He also asserts that this verse (9:5) is the verse of the sword which abrogated any previous covenant between the prophet and the infidels. On pp. 246 and 247, the Baydawi borrows Ibn Kathir's explanation and indicates to us the four months which were Shawal, Dhu al-Qu'da, Dhu al-Hijja and Muharram. The Baydawi adds that after the elapse of these four months, the infidels must be taken as prisoners lest they enter Mecca. In this case, they don't have any choice except either to embrace Islam or to be killed. Al Tabari said the same words and the same explanation on p. 206, 207 of his commentary dar-el-Sheroq.

Dr. Muhammad Sa'id al-Buti

We would like to conclude our discussion about this verse by referring to the opinion of one of the most eminent scholars of Azhar and the Islamic world. In his book, "The Jurisprudence of the Biography", he says,

> "The verse (9:5) does not leave any room in the mind to conjecture about what is called defensive war. This verse asserts that Holy War which is demanded in Islamic law, **is not defensive war** (as the Western students of Islam would like to tell us) because it could legitimately be an offensive war. That is the apex and most honorable of all Holy wars" (pp. 323, 324).

Dr. Sa'id, I wish that Westerners would actually believe your statement. I wish that Western people would drop any notion that Holy war is a defensive war. You really astonish me, though, because you regard the offensive war designed to spread the faith to be legal as if you had never heard of an agency in New York called the United Nations or of human rights. You even say that offensive war is "the apex and the most honorable Holy War" among all wars.

Pertaining to the People of the Book

Explicitly and shamelessly, the Qur'an declares (Chapter of Repentance, 9:29),

> "Fight against those who have been given the scripture but believe not in Allah nor the last day, and who forbid not that which Allah has forbidden by His messenger, and who follow not the religion of truth, until they pay the tribute willingly, being brought into submission" (p. 182, English copy by Saudi Arabian scholars).

Muslim scholars have agreed on the interpretation of this transparent verse by which all the Muslim warriors were guided in their offensive, violent wars against peaceful people.

The Baydawi

In his book, "The Lights of Revelation", a commentary on the Qur'an, he remarks,

> "Fight Jews and Christians because they violated the origin of their faith and they do not believe in the religion of the truth, namely Islam, which abrogated all other religions. Fight them until they pay the poll-tax with submission and humiliation" (page 252).

The Tabari

On page 210, the Tabari declares in his commentary that this verse is referring in particular to the people of the Book and has direct relation to the preceding verse (9:28). He said that the reason for the revelation of this verse (9:29) was that God had prohibited infidels from coming to the mosque for pilgrimage any more. They used to come with food and to trade. Muslims said, "Then, where we can get food?" They were afraid of poverty; thus God gave this verse so that they could collect money (the poll-tax)from the people of the Book.

This same interpretation is also found in the "Biography of the Apostle" by Ibn Hisham (p. 104 in part 4), and in the Jalalan. The rest of the scholars agree upon this interpretation. I would like to quote here the text of the two verses (9:28-29) because they really complement each other. The Qur'an says:

> "O ye who believe! Truly the pagans are unclean, so let them not approach the sacred Mosque after this year, and if ye fear poverty, soon will Allah enrich you (if He wills) out of His bounty for Allah is All-Knowing, All-Wise ... fight against the people of the Book ...." (to the end of verse 29).

The Tabari adds:

"The meaning of the Qur'anic statement: '... until they pay the poll-tax with submission and humiliation' (literally: to pay by hand and with forced submission) is that the Muslim will receive the tax imposed on Christians and Jews while he is sitting and they are standing. He will take it from their own hands since the Christian or the Jew should not send the money with a messenger but come himself and stand to pay it to the Muslim who will be sitting. The saying, 'with forced submission', also means with humiliation" (page 210).

The Jalalan (Al Suyti and 'Al Mahally)

On page 156, we find the same words and interpretation stated by the Tabari. Then he adds:

"The order to fight the people of the Book is because they do not prohibit what the apostle had forbidden such as wine."

Then he explains the humiliating procedure by which Christians have to pay the poll-tax—exactly as the Tabari described it.

Ibn Hisham Al Sohaily

In his book, "The Biography of the Apostle" (Al Road Al Anf, part 4, p. 201), Ibn Hisham repeats the above-mentioned quotation and adds,

"The poll-tax is to be paid by the Christian or the Jew forcibly and submissively. It is to spare their lives; that is, they pay it in lieu of being killed because if they did not pay it, they would be killed unless they intended to become Muslims, then they would be exempted from paying it."

The Shafi'i:

Lastly, we would like to refer to the Shafi'i's statement in his book, "The Ordinances of the Qur'an" (part 2, p. 50),

> "The apostle of God killed and captured (many) of the
> people of the Book until some of them embraced Islam,
> and he imposed the poll-tax on some others."

For God's sake, Muhammad! You killed and captured Jews
and Christians, who believe in one God—the followers of Moses
and Jesus—and forced them either to embrace Islam or to pay
the poll-tax!

In the same book and part, the Shafi'i summarizes the entire
situation, whether in relation to infidels or to the people of the
Book. He says,

> "From idolaters and those who associate other gods with
> God, the poll-tax is not to be accepted. Either they believe
> in Islam or be killed, but the people of the Book can pay
> the poll-tax with submission and humiliation whether they
> are Arabs or non-Arabs" (pp. 52,53).

The Shafi'i adds in the same source (pp. 62-64) saying,

> "When the people of Islam became strong enough, God
> revealed the chapter of Repentance and ordained the fight
> against the people of the Book until they pay the poll-tax."

If the reader wonders why, I would remind him of what the
Tabari and Ibn Hisham said—Muslims were afraid of poverty
and they wanted to acquire properties and bounties. Thus the
Qur'an explained, "If you fear poverty, soon will Allah enrich
you if He wills, out of His bounty...Fight... the people of the
Book... until they pay the poll-tax."

Isn't this the same as crimes committed by bandits and
pirates? Yet, this is exactly what Muhammad used to do. On
various occasions, Muhammad himself attacked the caravans (or
he would order his followers to do so) to plunder them.

In short, Islamic law calls for the death penalty for apostates
and forces peaceful infidels (unbelievers)either to accept Islam
or be killed. If they are the people of the Book, they have a

choice either to be killed, to become Muslims, or to pay the poll-tax in humiliation.

Where are human rights? Where is respect for the individual's freedom to choose the faith he wants?

Contemporary Muslim Scholars Concur on the Principle of Offensive War

In addition to the foregoing quotations, I would like to add some statements which may have more bearing for international readers. I will include many other declarations quoted from publications of the Liberation Party in Jerusalem as made by another Muslim scholar.

"The Jurisprudence of the Biography" by al-Buti (7th ed.) published by the Azhar in Egypt

This book was revised by Al Azhar, so it is accepted by all Muslims and is well-known all over the Islamic world. It deals with Muhammad's biography, interprets it and comments on the most famous events of his life. The author states (page 324) that the offensive war is legal. He literally uses these words,

> "The concept of Holy War in Islam does not take into consideration whether (the war is) a defensive or an offensive war. Its goal is the exaltation of the Word of God and the construction of Islamic society and the establishment of God's Kingdom on Earth regardless of the means. The means would be offensive warfare. In this case it is the apex, the most noble Holy War. It is legal to carry on a Holy War."

The implications are plain enough—there is no need for comment. Then he adds on p. 242,

> "Defensive warfare in Islam is nothing but a phase of the Islamic mission which the prophet practiced. After that, it was followed by another phase; that is, calling all people to embrace Islam so that nothing less would be acceptable

from atheists and those who associate other deities with
God than that they embrace Islam. Also, nothing would be
acceptable from the people of the Book except conversion
to Islam or being subjugated to Muslim rule. In addition,
there is the command to fight anyone who attempts to
stand in its way. Now, after the domination of Islamic rule
is in place, and its mission complete, it is meaningless (in
regard to Holy War) to (talk about) defensive wars, as
some of the researchers do. Otherwise, what does
Muhammad's statement mean (as it is related by the
Bukhari), 'They would not invade you, but you invade
them '?"

It is obvious that defensive warfare was a temporary phase in
Muhammad's strategy. After that, a second phase followed
which was offensive war, a legal tool for holy war. In this phase,
people were not left to enjoy their status quo, but were invaded
and they suffered the horrors of the war, though they did not
attempt to start a war or to invade the Muslims. It is as
Muhammad said: "They will not invade you, but you are those
who will invade them." Why? Is it an order to impose Islam on
infidels or to kill them? Or (as is the case with the people of the
Book) are they either to accept Islam, fight a war, or surrender
and pay the poll-tax with humiliation?

This is an explicit declaration and Dr. Buti does not hide the
truth. To the contrary, he boasts of it and asserts that it is wrong
to regard Islamic wars as defensive wars. He insists that this is a
false concept which some researchers have reiterated along with
Western nations in order to halt the Islamic march.

Let the entire world listen to the opinion of one of the most
famous Muslim scholars from the Azhar University as he
demands the resumption of war to conquer the world. He says
(pages 265 and 266),

"The concept by which the mission directed itself from the
beginning of Muhammad's migration to Medina to the
Hudaybiyya treaty, was simply a defensive phase of the
plan. During this stage, the prophet did not initiate an

attack or start an invasion, but after the treaty of
Hudaybiyya, the prophet intended to enter a new, essential
phase in accordance with Islamic law. This was the phase
of fighting those who heard the message but arrogantly
rejected it. This phase, by the act of Muhammad and his
word, has become a legal decree, according to Muslims in
every age until the day of resurrection!"

I wonder, "Why should Muhammad fight them? Is it because
they rejected his faith that he should fight with them?" The
Azhari scholar answers, "Yes, because they arrogantly refused to
believe in him, so he added that this new stage of war; that is,
the phase of fighting unbelievers. This came after the completion
of the defensive period which followed the treaty of
Hudaybiyya. It has become (according to Muslims) legal in
every age until the day of resurrection."

Dr. Buti continues:

"...This is the concept which professional experts of
thought attempt to conceal from the eyes of Muslims by
claiming that anything that is related to a holy war in
Islamic law is only based on defensive warfare to repel an
attack" (page 266).

Many have thought as much, but it is obvious from this
statement that defensive warfare is an attempt made by Western
thinkers to hide from the eyes of Muslims the reality of offensive
warfare. If we wonder why Western thinkers do that, Dr. Buti
answers this question on the same page 266 saying,

"It is no secret that the reason behind this deception is the
great fear which dominates foreign countries (East and
West alike) that the idea of Holy War for the cause of God
would be revived in the hearts of Muslims, then certainly,
the collapse of European culture will be accomplished.
The mind set of the European man has matured to
embrace Islam as soon as he hears an honest message
presented. How much more will it be accepted if this
message is followed by a Holy War?"

Have European, American and Eastern people—as well as the governments of the World—read these obvious words? We have been led to believe that Muhammad and his followers only waged defensive wars. Yet here they declare that **defensive warfare** was a temporary strategy at the beginning of Islam. Six years after Muhammad's departure from Mecca to Medina, a new phase has begun; namely, **offensive warfare**. Muslims are concerned that the popular notion that Islamic wars were nothing more than defensive wars is a deception invented by the people of the West to divert Muslims away from allowing the dream of Holy War to be revived in their hearts. The West is afraid that the Islamic dream would set off a holy, offensive war in order to establish God's state on Earth (an Islamic government) and to make God's word supreme. Then Western civilization would collapse.

There is no need to comment further on these statements, but I would like to tell Dr. Buti something: If the mind set of the European man is potentially ready to embrace Islam, it is because he is not exposed to the reality of Islam or who Muhammad really was. Only such books as ours will remove the Islamic deceptive veils. If real Islam is truly exposed, it will be **eradicated** not only in Europe, America, Asia and Africa, but also in Arab countries as well. People will re-examine the reality of this religion and the prophethood of this Arabic man called Muhammad.

We tell you, Dr. Buti, that powerful foreign countries are not afraid of Arab countries and Islamic states which do not have modem technology because one strong foreign country can annihilate all these countries. If the state of Israel alone is able to exhaust all the Arab countries, how much more can other powerful foreign countries do so? If foreign countries claim that Islamic wars were defensive wars, that is because **they have been deluded** and have believed the deception, but praise be to God for people like you who expose the ugly truth to them.

You have demonstrated to them that holy war in Islam is a **continuing ideal** which will last to the day of resurrection. It is a plan in which it is incumbent on all Muslims to fight (in the cause of God) those who reject Islam. This concept started in the sixth year of the Hegira and continues to the present.

As Dr. Buti endeavors to justify the principle of offensive warfare, he remarks that offensive war is the most noble of all wars and the verses (chapter 9:29 and 9:5) do not leave any room in the imagination for defensive warfare. He addresses his readers,

> "You may wonder now: Where is the wisdom of forcing infidels and their associates to embrace Islam? How could the mind set of the twentieth century understand such matters? The answer is: We wonder where the wisdom is when the state forces an individual to be subjugated to its system and philosophy despite the freedom he possesses? How can it be reasonable for the state to have the right to subjugate its citizens to the laws, principles, and ordinances it enacts, while the creator of all does not have the right to subjugate them to His authority and to convert them from every creed or faith to His religion?" (pages 266 and 267).

I would like to ask you, Dr. Sa'id El Buti, you who are a contemporary scholar at the Azhar University: How can people of the twentieth century understand and accept your logic of imposing a certain religion on a person with the death penalty as the only alternative? Would it not be more reasonable for Muslims to understand and accept the concept of human rights and the freedom to embrace the creed a person wishes to believe, in accordance with his conviction? We take into consideration your circumstances and we understand that you would be likely to defend Islam and the Qur'an. You would be likely to defend Muhammad's behavior, sayings and all that his companions and successors did, but let me tell you that twentieth century thinking rejects your attitude.

On the other hand, who told you that the state and its rulers have the right to impose regulations and systems on their citizens as they wish? Don't you know that the people of modem countries in Europe and America **vote** on the constitution they feel is appropriate for them? They even **elect** their rulers as well as the people's assemblies, such as parliament. The people in these democratic countries have the authority to remove the leaders of the state if they fail to act in accordance with their constitutions which were established by free elections and public vote.

Maybe you are comparing yourself to the governments of underdeveloped countries (like most of the Arab and Islamic countries) which are characterized by the rule of one individual, tyranny, terrorism and the neglect of human rights. Woe to the one who opposes the ruler or dares to change his Islamic religion! Some Islamic countries subject him to Islamic law, and carry out the orders of Muhammad and his successors by sentencing him to death immediately. Other countries are content to put him in jail and torment him for a while.

Dr. Sa'id, what makes you think that God's character is similar to the character of the rulers of these tyrannical states? We pray that the time will come when there is freedom for evangelism and the preaching of the Gospel in the Arab world for the benefit of the Arab people—first and last. We also pray that the rulers of the Arab countries will become like Gorbachev, the former ruler of Russia, who guaranteed religious freedom and opened wide the door of human rights and individual freedom.

God (the only eternal, true God) is not the one who exists in your mind or the one about whom Muhammad preached, but He is the God of love and freedom. He is the God of Christian revelation. The true God is not a God who demands that a poll-tax be paid to Muhammad, or a God of capturing women and children, or of slaughtering the men of peaceful towns if they do not become Muslims. Yours is an imaginary God who does not exist. The true God says,

> "Let the one who thirsts, come. And the one who desires, let him take the water of life freely" (Rev. 22: 17).

He also says,

> "Ho! Everyone who thirsts, Come to the waters; And you who have no money, "Come, buy and eat ... let your soul delight itself in abundance" (Isa. 55:1-2).

Arab Scholars in Jerusalem

"The Book of the Islamic State" by Taqiy al-Din al-Nabahan was published in 1953. It encapsulates the entire issue in simple, plain style and in explicitly few words. It will suffice to quote four self-explanatory paragraphs which need no comment because they are obvious.

On pages 112, 113, and 117, Taqiy al-Din says,

> "The foreign policy of Islamic states must be to carry the Islamic mission to the world by way of holy war. This process has been established through the course of the ages from the time the apostle settled down until the end of the last Islamic state which was ruled by Islamic law. This process has never been changed at all. The apostle Muhammad, from the time he founded the state in the city Yathrib, prepared an army and began holy war to remove the physical barriers which hinder the spread of Islam.

> "He subdued the tribe of Quraysh as a body, along with other similar groups until Islam prevailed all over the Arabian peninsula. Then the Islamic state started to knock at the doors of other states to spread Islam. Whenever it found that the nature of the existing system in these states was a barrier which prevented the spread of the mission, they saw it as inevitable that the system be removed. **So holy war continued as a means of spreading Islam. Thus by holy war, countries and regions were**

conquered. By holy war, kingdoms and states were removed and Islam ruled the nations and peoples.

"The glorious Qur'an has revealed to Muslims the reasons for fighting and the ordinance of holy war and it declares that it is to carry the message of Islam to the entire world. There are several verses which command the Muslims to fight for the cause of Islam. Therefore, carrying the Islamic mission is the basis on which the Islamic state was established, the Islamic army was founded, and holy war was ordained. All the conquests were achieved accordingly. Fulfilling the Islamic mission will restore the Islamic state to the Muslims."

Then he adds on pages 113, 114, and 115,

"If holy war is the established, unchangeable means of spreading Islam, then political activities become a necessity before initiating the fight. If we besiege the infidels, we would call them to embrace Islam first. If they accept Islam, they become part of the Islamic community, but if they reject Islam, they have to pay the poll-tax. If they pay it, they spare their blood and properties, but if they refuse to pay the poll-tax, then fighting them becomes lawful."

Readers, please note that these same words and principles are confirmed **by all the Muslim scholars** who are well acquainted with the saying and deeds of Muhammad and his successors.

On pages 115 and 116 Taqiy al-Din indicates again this historical statement,

"The Islamic system is a universal system, thus it was natural that it would spread, and natural that countries would be conquered. Here the apostle is receiving from Muslims the pledge of 'aqaba the Second, making a pact with him to fight all people. Those Muslims were the core of the army of the Islamic state whose military task was to carry the Islamic mission. The apostle of God had designed the plan of conquest before his death, then after him, his successors undertook the responsibility of implementing this plan when they started conquering the countries. Later, the Islamic conquests followed successively on this basis. People's resistance or rejection does not matter because the Islamic system is for all people in all countries."

Let the reader ponder these words and judge for himself. **"People's resistance or rejection does not matter because Islam is for all people"**; namely, by force, conquest, and war.

But I would like to state here that Christianity is also a universal system, and it is for all people. Christ said,

"Go into all the world and preach the gospel to every creature..." (Mark 16:15).

Anyone who believes will be saved and whoever does not believe, God will judge. Christ did not say, "Go into the world and preach. Whoever believes becomes one of us, and whoever does not believe should pay the poll-tax to the Christian army or be put to death." He did not say that. This is a crucial difference, my dear reader, between Christ and Muhammad, between Christianity and Islam.

The Bloody History of Islam

Having surveyed the incidents which took place during the life of Muhammad, it is appropriate to mention the events which occurred after his death and how the Caliphs who succeeded him carried out the same Muhammadic principle and the Qur'anic instructions The history of Islam talks to us with two bloodied hands—first is the blood of peaceful people who safely inhabited the land until they were invaded by the Muslim armies which marched from the Arab Peninsula after the death of Muhammad. In the name of spreading the religion, they killed millions of people, and in the name of exalting the word of God, they plundered properties and divided the "booty" of women and children among themselves, the same as Muhammad did in the course of his campaigns. These Arab Islamic armies obeyed Muhammad's orders and the Qur'anic commands. They believed that spreading Islam and taking the material abundance came from God. The Qur'an explicitly says,

> "Allah promises you much booty (spoils of war) that you will capture" (Chapter 48:20).

Muslim scholars do not negate these historically confirmed facts, but rather they brag about them, and their books (both old and modern) are filled with the details of these events. They mention them with pride, and they are glad to explain and demonstrate how the Arab Islamic armies attacked all the Persian lands and part of the Byzantine territories and occupied them. They could tell you how these armies took over Syria, Jordan, Palestine, Egypt, Iraq, Turkey, and, of course, Libya and all of Africa until the Muslim army reached the borders of China and the regions of Iran. Even Spain had fallen into their hands for hundreds of years. They proceeded then toward France, but they were stopped in the battle of Tours at the hands of Charles Martel. These wars were offensive wars of the first degree. Islam dominated these countries. Nowadays, all Muslim countries belong to the under-developed third world.

Before we let the Muslim chroniclers narrate to us what happened, it is fit here to clarify a very significant issue about which many people inquire.

The Cross Denounces the Crusades

These were bitter wars led by the princes of Europe for a period of time without any justification except ruthlessness of the heart and faithlessness of those leaders, who (despite their claims that they were attempting to deliver the Christians in the Islamic East from the persecution of the Muslims) were not true believers in Christ or in His teachings. Where in the Gospel do we find any call for war? In this study, we compare Christ with

Muhammad, the Gospel with the Qur'an, the sublime teaching of Christianity with the clear teachings of Islam.

- Did Christ lead any war to spread the faith, to divide the booty and to capture women to enslave them for himself and for his followers?

- Did Christ order His followers to do so?

- Did he order Peter to sheath his sword when he unsheathed it and struck the servant of the Jewish high priest when Christ's enemies hastened to arrest him?

- Did Christ's successor's and disciples wage wars and march into battle to take poll-taxes and to spread Christianity?

These are the conclusive questions which reveal the difference between Christ and Muhammad, between Christianity and Islam. If some Christians came after hundreds of years had elapsed and committed such detestable things, Christ and Christianity would certainly denounce such deeds. On the other hand, the Islamic wars were waged by Muhammad himself, then by his relatives and companions who lived with him day after day and to whom he promised paradise.

The other important thing is that they were executing the unequivocal teachings of both Muhammad and the Qur'an which we mentioned previously in this chapter. We have many books which all talk thoroughly and in detail about the offensive wars. The most famous of these books is "The Chronicles of Al-Tabari, Ibn Khaldun, Ibn Kathir" and "The History of the Caliphs" by the Suyuti. The entire Islamic world relies on these books.

Among the contemporary scholars who rely on these sources and quote from them is Dr. Abu Zayd Shalabi, professor of civilization at the Azhar University. His respected book, "al-Khulafa' al-Rashidun" The Rightly Guided Caliphs", or successors) from which we quoted when we discussed the wars of apostasy, examines these things. We have selected a few quotations from these sources and references because they almost all repeat each other. These events are well-known and confirmed by all Muslims. They are taught in the public schools in all the Islamic countries, especially in the Arab world.

"The Rightly Guided Caliphs" by Dr. Abu Zayd Shalabi

Dr. Abu Zayd Shalabi discusses the Islamic wars which were initiated by the four caliphs who succeeded Muhammad and who, at the same time, are his favored relatives. These caliphs are: Abu Bakr, 'Umar, 'Uthman and 'Ali. Muhammad married 'Aisha, daughter of Abu Bakr, and Hafesa, daughter of 'Umar. 'Uthman married Ruqayya, the daughter of Muhammad, then after her death, he married her sister Um Kalthum. 'Ali was married to Muhammad's youngest daughter, Fatima al-Zahra.

On pages 35-38, Dr. Abu Zayd remarks,

> "Muhammad had prepared an army to invade the borders of Syria. When Muhammad died Abu Bakr sent an army headed by Usama Ibn Zayd and 'Umar Ibn al-Khattab. The army marched towards southern Palestine and invaded some parts of the land, frightened the people and captured some booty."

At the beginning of page 70, Dr. Abu Zayd talks about the Islamic conquests and indicates that at the inception of the year 12 of Hajira, Abu Bakr ordered Khalid Ibn al-Walid to invade Persian lands and to seize the ports near Iraq. Khalid marched with the army, but before he started the war, he sent his famous message to Hermez, one of the Iraqi generals, "Embrace Islam, or pay the poll-tax, or fight." The Hermez declined to accept any of these terms but war. The Persians were defeated in this battle and Khalid seized the booty and sent Abu Bakr one-fifth of the spoils of war, exactly as they were accustomed to send to Muhammad. One-fifth of the booty belonged to God and to Muhammad.

Abu Bakr presented Khalid with the Hermez's tiara which was inlaid with gems. Dr. Abu Zayd says the value of the gems amounted to 100,000 dirham (p. 73). After that, the successful, savage invasions continued against other countries which could not repel the forces of Islam. This Azhar scholar tells us that in the battle of Alees which took place on the border of Iraq, Khalid killed 70,000 people! He was so brutal in his attack that the nearby river was mixed with their blood (p. 75).

On p. 77, Dr. Abu Zayd mentions another country which surrendered to Khalid. Khalid demanded that they pay 190,000 dirhams. When he attacked Ayn al-Tamr in Iraq, its people took shelter in one of the fortresses. Khalid laid siege to the fortress and forced them to come out. He killed all of them mercilessly. They had done nothing against him or against the Muslims except that they refused to embrace Islam and to recognize Muhammad as an apostle of God. The Muslims seized all that they found in the fortress along with forty young men who were studying the Gospel. Khalid captured them and divided them among the Muslims (refer to p. 81).

It is well-known that Khalid Ibn al-Walid was a very brutal, vicious man. His relentlessness made 'Umar Ibn al-Khattab ask Abu Bakr to kill him or at least to depose him because he killed another Muslim in order to marry his wife! Abu Bakr did not listen, but when 'Umar became the second caliph, he deposed him immediately This was 'Umar's opinion about Khalid. Yet, to Muhammad, the prophet of Muslims, Khalid was one of the best among his relatives and warriors.

On page 134, Abu Zayd relates that when Khalid besieged another town called Qinnasrin which belonged to the Byzantine Empire, its people were so afraid that they hid themselves from him. He sent them a message in which he said: "Even if you hide in the cloud, God will lift us up to you or He will lower you down to us." They asked for a peace treaty, but he refused and killed them all. Then he eradicated the town. These are the words of Dr. Abu Zayd which we faithfully relay to you.

Dr. Abu Zayd continues to list the names of the towns and the regions which the Islamic army invaded after the fall of 'Ain al-Tamr. He says:

> "By the end of the year 12, Hajira Abu Bakr became interested in Syria (Al Sham). He issued orders to four of his great generals and designated for each one of them a country which he was given to invade. He assigned Damascus to Yazid, Jordan to Sharhabil, Homs to Abu 'Ubayda and Palestine to 'Umru Ibn al-'As.

We wonder: Are these wars defensive wars or are they definitely offensive wars and unjustified military invasions? Abu Bakr's era ends during the famous battle of Yarmick in which tens of thousands were slain for no reason except to impose religion by force, capturing women and plundering the properties. Muslims claim that Abu Bakr died from eating poisoned food a few months before.

When 'Umar was elected to the Caliphate, he deposed Khalid Ibn al-Walid and replaced him immediately with Abu 'Ubayda.

The Caliphate (ruling period) of 'Umar Ibn al-Khattab

The invasion of Persia

'Umar Ibn al-Khattab sent sa'd Ibn Abi Waqqas to invade Persia. He camped in al-Qaddisia near the river Euphrates. Dr. Abu Zayd narrates for us a very important incident (pages 117-118) which we would like to examine. The author says:

> "Sa'd sent some of his followers (among them the Mu'man Ibn Maqrin to Yazdagird, one of the Persian generals) who asked him, 'What enticed you and brought you to invade us?' (Ibn Maqrin) said to him, 'Choose for yourself either Islam or the poll-tax or the sword.' The Persian general became very angry and said to him, 'Had it not been (the custom that messengers should not be killed), I would have killed you. Go; you have nothing to do with me.'"

Ibn Khaldun confirms this incident in the end of the second volume of his famous history book (pages 94-96). He says,

> "Rustan, the Persian general, said to one of Sa'd's messengers, 'You were poor and we used to provide you with plenty of food. Why do you invade us now?'"

It was obvious that the Persians had never thought to invade the Arabs, but they used to send them plenty of food because of the poverty of the Arab peninsula. Nevertheless, the Arabs seized the opportunity to invade Persia after they realized that the Persians had been weakened by its wars with the Byzantine Empire and their own internal problems. Thus, they repaid compassion with wickedness and goodness with evil. The question which the Persian general Sa'd asked was a logical one, "Why do you attack us? Did we mistreat you?" The answer was also very clear, "You have three options!" Dr. Abu Zayd says on in p. 123:

> "Sa'd seized (after the battle of Qadisiyya) all that was in the treasury of Khusro of money and treasure. It was so plentiful that each Arab horseman received 12,000 dirham."

The Invasion of Damascus

On pages 131 and 132 of the same book, "The Rightly Guided Caliphs," the author indicates,

> "Abu 'Ubayda marched towards Damascus and besieged it for seventy nights. He cut off all supplies while its inhabitants were pleading for help and assistance. Then Khalid attacked the city and massacred thousands of people. (They were forced) to ask for a peace treaty. Abu 'Ubayda turned over the rule of Damascus to Yazid and ordered him to invade the neighboring (cities). He attacked Sidon, Beirut, and others."

The Attack on Jerusalem

On pages 136 and 137, we read about the attack of 'Umru Ibn al-'as on Jerusalem. He besieged it for four months. Then its Christian inhabitants agreed to pay the poll-tax and to surrender to 'Umar Ibn al-Khattab, the caliph. 'Umar made the trip to Jerusalem and laid the foundation of the mosque. With that, the conquest of Syria was accomplished, but as the pestilence (plague) raged, many of the high-ranking generals of the Islamic army died, among them Abu Ubayda, Yazid and Sharahbil.

The Invasion of Wealthy Egypt

On pages 141 and 142, the author narrates how the invasion and occupation of Egypt were accomplished. Among the justifications which 'Umru Ibn al-'As presented to 'Umar which convinced him to allow 'Umru to attack Egypt were the following:

> "Egypt's abundance and yields are plentiful. The conquest of Egypt would gain for the Muslims a foothold in Syria and make it easier for them to invade Africa to spread Islam."

It is important to mark 'Umru's statement that "Egypt's abundance and yields are plentiful." Eventually Egypt and Africa were both conquered.

On pages 145 and 146, the professor of civilization at the Azhar relates how 'Umru besieged the Fortress of Babylon (south of ancient Egypt) for a full month, and that he said to the messengers of the Muqawqis, the governor of Egypt,

> "There is nothing between us and you except three things:
>
> (1) Embrace Islam, become our brethren and you will have what we have and you will be subjected to what we are subjected (in this case they would pay alms to the treasury of the state).
>
> (2) If you refuse that, you are obligated to pay tribute with humiliation.

(3) War.

"The Muqawqis attempted to offer them something different, but they rejected it. At last, after a fight, he accepted the second condition, namely to pay tribute and to be subjugated to Islamic rule. The Muslims entered Egypt. "

On page 147 and 148 Abu Zayd describes the conquest of Alexandria and denies that the Muslims burned the famous library of Alexandria. Yet he admits that many chroniclers have mentioned that 'Umar Ibn al-Khattab ordered 'Umru to burn it entirely.

After the conquest and the occupation of Egypt, the author says (page 151) that 'Umru wanted to secure this conquest from the west by conquering Tripoli of Libya, and from the south by seizing Ethiopia. Thus at the close of the year 21 H. as Ibn Khaldun and Yaqut al-Kindi remarked (that is in the first half of the year 643 A.D. as Ibn al Athir and other chroniclers said), "'Umru marched on with his horsemen towards Tripoli."

On page 153 he adds:

"'Umru besieged Tripoli for a month. It was a well-fortified city. At last a group of Muslims infiltrated the city and fought some of the Byzantines who soon fled. 'Umar entered the city and captured all that was in it, then he assailed the city of Sabra without warning and conquered it by force. He seized all that could be seized from it. Then he sent his army to Ethiopia, but he failed to enter it and suffered great losses. The skirmishes continued until a peace treaty was signed during the time of 'Uthman Ibn 'Affan."

Are these wars considered defensive? What is an offensive war then?

During the Caliphate of ' Uthman Ibn 'Affan

On pages 167 and 168, the book tells us:

"'Uthman ordered 'Abdalla Ibn Abi al-Sarh to invade
Africa, then he sent Abdalla Ibn al-Zubayr. They
slaughtered thousands of the people among them their
king, Jayan, and they captured booty."

These are the words of Dr. Abu Zayd in his famous book,
"The Rightly Guided Caliphs". We have quoted him word for
word. Let the reader ponder these words and judge for himself.
What is the crime of these people, whether in Africa or Syria or
Egypt or in other countries? Muslims say—That was for the
exaltation of God's word. God the compassionate, the Merciful!

The Wars to spread Islam

On pages 66 and 67 Dr. Abu Zayd confesses clearly,

"The thing which compelled Abu Bakr to invade Persia
and the Byzantine Empire **was not to seize their
abundance, but rather to spread Islam.** This claim is
based on evidence that the generals of the Islamic armies
used to call the countries to embrace Islam before they
started fighting them. Khalid Ibn al-Walid sent a message
to the princes of Persia saying:

"After all, accept Islam and you will be safe, or pay the
tribute; otherwise I will come to you with a people who
desire death as you desire drinking wine."

Yes and no, Dr. Abu Zayd. Yes, we accept your confession
that the war was to spread Islam. We agree that spreading Islam
was an essential incentive for war. We are content with **your
unequivocal confession** in regard to this matter. We have
written these pages in order to denote these facts and nothing
more—to prove that Islam was spread by sword and that the
Islamic wars were offensive wars. Your confirmation and
faithful narration of history in "The Rightly Guided Caliphs"
have helped us to prove this fact. Thank you.

Yet, we disagree with you when you claim that material
abundance was not another reason for these wars. We will not
allow you to conceal this obvious fact because you yourself have

unintentionally alluded to it when you listed the reasons for the invasion of Egypt—among them were "the abundance of Egypt and its yields". More than that, ponder what the Qur'an says in Chapter 48 :20:

> "Allah (God) promises you much booty that you will capture" (Qur'an).

Or let us listen to Muhammad's explicit statement in which he (after exhorting his warriors to fight bravely) promised the plunder of the country. Did you forget, Dr. Abu Zayd, what Muhammad said? Let me remind you. Muhammad said,

> "You see, God will soon make you inherit their land, their treasures and make you sleep with their women" (Lit: make their women's beds for you).

These plain, disgraceful words are recorded by Ibn Hisham on page 182 Vol. II, of his famous book, "Al Rod AL Anf", which all the researchers regard as a reliable reference. Thus, when Muslims invaded a certain land incited by the desire to possess the land, treasures, and women, they were actually fulfilling God's promise as it was stated in the Qur'an and in Muhammad's pledge.

"The Beginning and the End," by Ibn Kathir (vol. 7)

We would like to quote a few incidents from this book by Ibn Kathir who is one of the ancient Muslim scholars and chroniclers and a reliable source for all students of Islamic history. On page 2, we read the following,

> "At the inception of the year 13 of the Hajira, Abu Bakr was determined to draft soldiers to send them to Syria in compliance with the words of the Qur'an: Fight... those who were given the Scripture (Chapter 9:9); and also follow the example of the apostle of God who gathered the Muslims together to invade Syria before his death."

He also adds on page 9:

"When Abu Bakr sent Khalid to Iraq, Abu Hurayra, who was one of Muhammad's companions, he used to exhort Muslims to fight by telling them: 'Hasten to the Houris' (fair, black-eyed women)."

Those Houris are the nymphs of paradise who are particularly designated for the enjoyment of Muslims.

"'The Blood of the Byzantine is more delicious', Khalid said!"

On page 10, Ibn Khathir tells us that when the Byzantine leaders rejected Islam or paying tribute, Khalid told them,

"We are people who drink blood. We were told that there is no blood that is more delicious than the blood of the Byzantines."

Such words well suit people like Khalid, Muhammad's beloved friend and relative.

On page 13 we read the following,

"Gregorius, one of the great princes of the Byzantines, said to Khalid: 'What do you call us for?' Khalid answered him: 'That you testify that there is no God but the only God and that Muhammad is His messenger and apostle, and to acknowledge all that Muhammad received from God (namely pilgrimage, fasting of Ramadan, etc.).' Gregorius said to him: 'And if these are not accepted?' Khalid responded, 'Then pay the tribute.' Gregorius said to him: 'If we do not give the tribute?' Khalid said: 'Then war!'"

Ibn Kathir acknowledges (on page 21) that when the Muslims conquered Damascus, they **seized St. John's church** and converted it into the largest mosque in Damascus today (The Umayyad Mosque). On page 55, we read also about the **invasion of Jerusalem.** On page 123, he states,

"Umar Ibn al-Khattab wrote to Abdil-Rahman Ibn Rabi'a ordering him to invade the Turks (Turkey today)."

The Second Invasion of Africa

In page 165 Ibn Kathir records for us that:

"The second invasion of Africa was accomplished because its people broke their pledge. That was in year 33 of the Hajira (The Moslem Calendar)."

Of course, the people of Africa broke the pledge because that pledge was imposed on them by force in lieu of death. Yet Muslims killed thousands of them. Ibn Kathir already mentioned in page 151 that,

"'Uthman Ibn 'Affan ordered 'Abdalla Ibn Sa'd to invade Africa. [He told him] 'If you conquer it take 1/25 of its booty.' 'Abdalla Ibn Sa'd marched towards it at the head of an army of 20,000 soldiers. He conquered it and killed multitudes of people from among its inhabitants until the remnant were converted to Islam and became subject to the Arabs. 'Abdalla took his portion of the booty as 'Uthman told him, then he divided the rest."

How unfortunate were the African people. They were invaded by the Arabs who killed thousands of them, divided the booty, and forced the remnant to embrace Islam. When they broke the pact, the Muslims attacked them again. **But are the black African people the only unfortunate people?** Or are all the people of Jordan, Palestine, Syria, Iraq, Iran, Egypt, Libya, all the Arab tribes, Spain, even the people of China and India, Cyprus and the Kurds, all the unfortunate peoples? All of these are unfortunate nations who became the victims of Islamic Law which detests human rights and persistently ignores their freedom.

The Invasion of Cyprus and the Kurds

Ibn Kathir tells us that in the year 28 of the Hajira, the conquest of Cyprus was accomplished after 'Abdulla Ibn al-Zubayr slaughtered a multitude of people—as usual. Ibn Khaldun also tells the story of the Kurds. In page 124 of Vol. II, he says,

"Muslims met a number of Kurds. They called them to
embrace Islam or pay the tribute. When they refused to do
so they killed them and captured their women and
children, then divided the booty."

As we see, Ibn Khaldun along with Ibn Kathir, al-Tabari and
other chroniclers, ancient and contemporary such as Dr. Abu
Zayd, recorded all the Islamic historical events in detail.
Moreover, on every occasion Arab newspapers allude boastfully
to these memorial episodes of Islamic history and shed light on
these savage, wild offensive wars. For instance, we read in the
prestigious Ahram newspaper which is published in Egypt, the
following,

"During the era of the Caliph 'Umar Ibn 'Abdul-'Aziz,
Ibn Qutayba in the year 88H, he invaded some of the
neighboring countries of Iran such as Bukhara, and
Samarq and marched close to the **Chinese border**" (refer
to the Ahram, Mary 26, 1986, p. 13).

In his book, "The Beginning and the End" (part 9), Ibn Kathir
narrates in detail the history of this belligerent general, Ibn
Qutayba. He records the story of his campaigns and refers to his
biography.

We would like to conclude this chapter with a brief summary
which Taqiy al-Din al-Nabahani presents in his book, "The
Islamic State" (pp. 121 and 122). He summarizes the history of
Islamic offensive wars against the neighboring peaceful
countries by saying,

"Muhammad had begun to send troops and initiate
campaigns against the Syrian borders such as the
campaign of Mu'ta and Tabuk. Then the rightly guided
caliphs ruled after him and the conquest continued. (The
Arabs) conquered Iraq, Persia, and Syria whose faith was
Christianity and which were inhabited by the Syrians,
Armenians, some Jews and some Byzantines. Then Egypt
and North Africa were conquered. When the Umayyad
took over after the rightly guided caliphs, they conquered

the Sind, Khawarizm, and Samarqand. They annexed
them to the lands of the Islamic state."

According to all Muslim chroniclers, it is well documented
that Armenia and Morocco were conquered during the era of
'Abdul-Malik Ibn Marwan. When his son, al-Walid, assumed the
throne, he invaded India and Andalusia.

Also, Dr. 'Afifi Abdul-Fattah, the Muslim scholar,
encapsulates the whole principle in a few explicit,
straightforward words, as he says (page 382 of his famous book
"The Spirit of the Islamic Religion"),

> "Islam has acknowledged war in order to exalt the word of
> God. This is a fight for God's cause."

He also adds in p. 390,

> "Before the Islamic state declares war against another
> state, it should give (the other state) the choice between
> Islam, tribute or war."

We need not say anything more than that. Maybe this is what
Muslims mean when they say, "We believe in human freedom
and man's right to choose according to his own will! We present
him with three options, and he has the right to chose as he
wishes— either to become a Muslim and pay alms to the Caliph
of the Muslims, or pay the tribute and submit to Islamic rule, or
we kill him."

Let the reader ponder the Muslim contradiction that a man has
the right to choose whatever he wants within the Islamic
context of individual freedom.

Conclusion

These are the Islamic offensive wars, my dear reader. We have
already surveyed the Qur'anic verses which were expounded by
both the great ancient and the contemporary Muslim scholars.
We also alluded to the sayings of Muhammad, his own deeds
and his orders to his companions, relatives and successors. We

witnessed the bloody events of Islamic history narrating for us what Muslims did after the death of Muhammad and how they carried out his orders and the commandments of the Qur'an— how they fought with the People of the Book, the Jew and the Christian, until they paid tribute with humiliation and defeat. We have witnessed how they plundered the lands, killed the unfortunate, and captured women and children for no reason.

Moreover, we have already discussed all the matters pertaining to the death penalty of an apostate who dares to relinquish the Islamic faith and to embrace another religion, or to become an atheist. We also referred to an abundance of evidences and interpretations of Muslim scholars along with the deeds and sayings of Muhammad in this respect. He himself gave orders to kill anyone who is an apostate from Islam such as Umm Mirwan as the Azhar and all the Chroniclers denoted, and all those apostates who fled to Mecca.

Regarding offensive wars or imposing the Islamic religion on people by war, Muhammad said: "I was commanded to fight people until they say there is no God but the only God, and Muhammad is the apostle of God, and they perform all the Islamic ordinances and rituals."

We also examined Muhammad's attitude towards the apostate. He made it clear that the apostate must be sentenced to death. He said about those who relinquish Islam: "Whoever changes his faith...kill him!"

Muhammad indicated that is it unlawful to shed the blood of a Muslim except in three cases: Unbelief after belief, adultery after integrity (or being married) and killing a soul without any right. The first case refers to the death penalty of the apostate and the oppression of his freedom and right to embrace any religion other than Islam Those are the clear claims of the Islamic religion as well as of Muhammad, the prophet of Islam, who always uttered at the beginning of every prayer or sermon, the following phrase,

"In the name of Allah—the Compassionate, the Merciful!"

We talked about individual freedom and human rights. This is the prophet of freedom, mercy, tolerance and human dignity!

Has the veil been removed?

Is the deception over?

Judge for yourself.

Section Two

The Veil of Equality and Justice

Muslim propagandists take advantage of the fact that Westerners do not read Arabic and therefore (out of ignorance) do not know the reality of Islamic faith as recorded in the books of Muslim scholars. Therefore, Muslim missionaries roam across Europe and America, East and West, writing a throng of books, declaring with a loud voice: "How great Islam is! It is the religion of social justice, equality, women's rights and dignity." Many naive and superficial people believe these claims and are deceived by this message, but this deceit should end. This veil should be removed.

We have found in Muhammad's sayings (as well as of those of all Muslim scholars – intentionally or unintentionally – that both Islam and Muhammad discriminate between human beings. It matters whether they are males or females, Muslims or non-Muslims. We even find discrimination between Muslims because slavery (as we will see) is an Islamic principle.

Slavery in Islam has regulations and laws which differ from those for freemen, the masters. Actually, Muhammad, his wives, his successors, companions and his relatives owned slaves— males and maids. We can list the names of Muhammad's slaves: men and women, whites and blacks, and we will show that Muhammad himself was a slave merchant especially **after** he claimed to be a prophet.

After reading these pages it should become very evident to all (including the most fanatical and tenacious Muslim) that Islam is a religion of social injustice, inequality, and racial discrimination.

Before we start our discussion, it is relevant to quote one verse from the Holy Gospel which emphasizes equality in Christianity,

> "There is neither Jew nor Greek, there is neither slave nor free, there is neither male nor female; for you are one in Christ Jesus" (Galatians 3:28).

Chapter Three
The Status of Women in Islam

Some mistakenly believe that Islam honors women and dignifies them for the simple reason that they have not read the Qur'anic verses, and the sayings of Muhammad and all Muslim scholars concerning women. Thus they take at face value all the claims of Muslim missionaries in this respect. We seek to excuse those who have converted to Islam and are deceived because no one would expect a religion which claims to be divine (at the same time) to treat women so disgracefully.

We found on the other hand, some thinkers (even among Muslim Arabs) who have realized that women are not treated equal to men in Islam, though only a few of them occasionally dare to claim that publicly. Still, since their knowledge of Muhammad's sayings and the commentaries of the scholars is limited, they present a few examples related only to the subjects of polygamy (marrying four women) and easy divorce. Therefore, we seek to discuss here several issues to clarify the point under discussion and to remove the deceitful veil of Islam concerning women.

The Qur'an Commands Men To Beat Women

While the New Testament commands men to love their wives and even to sacrifice their own lives for their sake as Jesus gave

His life for us (Ephesians 5), we see that the Qur'an plainly and disgracefully commands men to beat their women as soon as they show any sign of disobedience to man's authority and orders. It states in Chapter 4:34:

> "As for these from women, fear rebellion, admonish them and banish them to beds apart and **scourge them**."

Without any exception, all the Qur'anic expositors agree upon the meaning of this verse because it is so obvious. In their famous commentary, page 69, the Jalalan said:

> "Those of you who are afraid of their disobedience which symptoms become evident to you, threaten them with the fear of God and banish them to beds apart and scourge them."

The Zamakhshari reiterates the same opinion (al-Kash-Shaf Vol. 1, p. 524). Both Imam Baydawi (p. 111), and Al-Tobari (p.92) repeat the same explanation. If we also search Ahkamal-Qur'an (the Ordinances of the Qur'an) by the Imam Shafi'i (Vol. 1, p.211), we read:

> "In case of a husband's ill-treatment [of his spouse], the Qur'an permits reconciliation of the spouses and arbitration, but in the case of the wife it allows scourging her."

At the inception of Islam, we come across a very famous incident which all the Muslim chroniclers record (refer to Imam al-Nawawi: Riyad al-Salihin, "The Orchards of Righteous Men", p. 107-108),

> "Umar Ibn al-Khattab came to Muhammad saying, 'Women have dared to disobey husbands.' He allowed their husbands to scourge them. Many women approached Muhammad complaining against their husbands because Muhammad received a verse for the Qur'an which commands their husbands to scourge them."

In the Kash-shaf (the revealer) of al-Zamakhshari (Vol. 1, p. 525), we read the following,

"On the authority of Muhammad (peace and blessing of Allah be upon him), he said: 'Hang up your scourge in a place where your wife (or wives) can see it.'

Also, on the authority of Asmaa the daughter of Abu Bakr El Sedik:

"I was the fourth wife (among four) of al-Zabayr Ibn al-Awwam. Whenever he became angry at one of us he struck us with a hook rod until it was broken."

This hemistich was composed by al-Zabayr:

"If it were not for her children, I would have hit her."

The command to scourge women is repeated in Sahih al-Bukhari, "The Sound Tradition of al-Bukhari" (Vol. 7, p. 100). Ponder for a moment over Muhammad's order to the husband: "Hang up your scourge where your wife can see it." This is intimidation and threat, as if a husband were telling his wife: "Beware of disobedience, for this is the scourge which is ready to fall upon you!"

There is no security or love in Muhammad's words or in the deeds of al-Zobayer Ibn al-Awwam, who was a relative of Muhammad, one of his companions, and one of those models whom every Muslim imitates and vies with all over the world. He was one of the ten whom Muhammad assured of paradise and one of the six whom Umar recommended for the Caliphate. This man used to scourge his wife until the wooden hook was broken, as Asmaa (the daughter of Abu Bakr El Sedik who was one of his four wives) tells us. Is there greater wife abuse than that?

Contemporary Scholars

All contemporary scholars attest to this fact which is obvious in the Qur'an. In the book, "You Ask and Islam Answers" (p. 94 for example), Abdul–latif Mushtahiri says,

"If admonishing and sexual desertion fail to bring forth results and the woman is of a cold and stubborn type, the

Qur'an bestows on man the right to straighten her out by way of punishment and beating provided he does not break her bones nor shed blood. Many a wife belongs to this querulous type and requires this sort of punishment to bring her to her senses!"

In his book, "The Individual Guarantee In the Islamic Law" (p. 63), Ahmad Ahmad, a professor at the college of Law at the University of Qatar, denotes the following under the title of "Family Problems' Solution",

"If a woman is afraid that her husband may turn away from her or detest her, she will hasten to bring understanding and reconciliation. But if the husband is afraid that his wife may rebel against him, he hastens to bring mutual understanding by means of exhortation, then by abandonment of the bed, then by the scourging which deters."

Did you read it?—"By the scourging which deters" This is if the symptoms of disobedience became apparent exactly as the Jalalan, Baydawi, Zamakhshari have said and as the Saudi scholars indicated in AI-Muslimun magazine in its issue of March 17, 1989 (page 12). I can also easily list dozens of references, both ancient and contemporary, which explain this verse (4:34). Actually, it does not need any exposition because it is self-explanatory—"and scourge them." It is evident that Christian countries regard wife abuse as a crime punishable by law because nature itself (as well as the simplest human principle) teaches us that it is not permissible for a man to beat an animal—much less his wife.

Yet according to the Islamic faith and by distinct orders issued by the Qur'an and Muhammad, a man is allowed to scourge his wife with a peaceful conscience because he is carrying out God's command as recorded in the Qur'an. "God the compassionate, the Merciful" and the Glorious Qur'an—and Muhammad, the prophet of mercy and humanity who claimed that he honored women, yet said: "Hang up your scourge where your wife can see it."

The Story of Job and his Wife in the Qur'an

In Chapter 38:44, the Qur'an declares that God has commanded righteous Job to beat his wife. We read:

> "And (it was said unto him), 'Take in thine hand a branch and smite therewith and break not thine oath.'"

All Muslim scholars agree on the exposition of this verse. Both Jalalan (page 383), and Baydawi (page 604) say:

> "When Job's wife was slow (to do something for him) one day, he swore to scourge her one hundred times. God told him, 'Do not break .... oath, but take a bundle of grass in your hand or rods to beat her up with.'"

The Jalalaan say that Job took one hundred sticks and scourged her once. The Baydawi says that Job's wife's name is Liyya, daughter of Jacob or Rahmeh, daughter of Aphraim, son of Joseph.

Who among us would believe this ridiculous story of the Qur'an about Job, the righteous man, who was famous for his patience? Who among us would believe that God encouraged him to beat his wife with a bundle of grass or sticks so that he would not break his oath?

Forcing the Virgin to Marry

Most people believe that this was merely a detestable habit practiced by some Arabs and Muslims who lived in some underdeveloped countries. However, we must realize that this practice has its roots deep in Islamic law and that it is a principle applied by Muslim scholars. Yet, I myself have read this ordinance in the main sources of Islam acceptable to all Muslim commentators. Let us study together the ordinances and the statements of scholars of exposition and the Islamic law.

Ibn Timiyya and Ibn Hazm, Famous Legists

Muslims regard Ibn Timiyya as the Sheikh of Islam. He truly is. He is the author of many huge volumes on various subjects. If we open Vol. 32, pp. 29 and 30, we read,

> "Even if the virgin is an adult, her father may force her to get married. This is in accordance with Malek Ibn Ons, al-Shafi and Ibn Hanbal's."

On page 39, he also states:

> "The young virgin can be forced by her father to get married without being consulted."

This is the verdict of Ibn Timiyya who was joined by some great Legists such as the Shafii, Malek, Ibn Hanbal, and the professors of Islamic law at the inception of Islam in Mecca and Medina. Most Arabs and most Islamic countries embrace their teaching. Actually, if we study Malek Ibn Ons book (Vol. 2, p. 155), we read,

> "A father can force his virgin daughter, his maid-slave and his male-slave to get married."

What is Ibn Hazm's opinion concerning the daughter's marriage? How can we ignore the opinion of the chief Legists of Islam in this respect? It is well known that Ibn Hazm also composed huge volumes of books on various topics on which all contemporary Muslim scholars rely because he is one of the greatest scholars of the Islamic law through the ages. In his sixth volume, part 9 of his book al-Muhalla ("The Sweetened", pp. 458-460), he says,

> "A father may give his consent to have his young virgin daughter married without obtaining her permission, for she does not have a choice, exactly as abu Bakr El Sedick did to his daughter, Aisha, when she was six years old. He married her to the prophet Muhammad without her permission."

Then Ibn Hazm adds:

"Even if she was deflowered (previously married and divorced, or a widow) as long as she is young and has not reached the legal age, her father may force her to marry without obtaining her permission."

As long as she is a virgin or just still young, she can be forced to get married without her consent. These are unequivocal, plain words. "Without her consent", and "does not have any choice." These are cruel, hard words and iniquitous Islamic principles which the free human conscience utterly rejects and detests because it is related to the most important subject in the girl's life, that is, her body and her future.

If enrolling in a certain school or seeking employment for a particular job, even buying a house or a car, should be in accordance with person's choice, how much more should choice control the issue of a girl's marriage? We acknowledge that a girl should consult with her parents in this matter, and their duty is to offer their sound opinions to protect her interest and future, but we cannot understand or even imagine that a father may force her to get married to a man she does not know and has never met. This is Islam!

These are not just mere words. This is actually what happened to the prophet of Islam because Abu Bakr, El Sedick who was Muhammad's friend, wed him to his daughter, Aisha, when she was six years old, though the actual marriage took place when she was nine years old, according to all the Muslim scholars and Chroniclers, without exception. Even Aisha related the story of her marriage, which we will review shortly.

The difference in their ages was 45 years. Muhammad at that time was 54 years old, the age of her grandfather, but what is significant for us now is not the great difference in age, but rather Aisha's marriage without her permission. Even she was taken by surprise when she found out about it.

What about a son? In part nine, page 462, Ibn Hazm stresses that it is **not permissible** for the father to force his son to get married.

The reader may be interested to read the text recorded in Sahih Muslim (Vol. 3, p. 577) with the commentary of al-Nawawi, because this book is a basic, indispensable book. Aisha said,

> "The messenger of God betrothed me when I was six years old and then married me when I was nine years old."

In another story, he married her when she was seven years old. This is a clear text which makes it permissible for a father to make his daughter marry without obtaining her permission. All Muslims consent to that, and she did not have the option of nullifying this marriage which her father planned. This is according to Malek, al-Shafi'i and the rest of Hedjaz legists.

In Sahih Moslem, a similar text is reiterated several times in Sahih al-Bukhari, part 7.

The Temporary Contractual Marriage

What a disgraceful and degrading thing a temporary, contractual marriage is for a woman. This is something which Muhammad made lawful according to all the scholars and chroniclers without exception. What an insult to a woman whom Muhammad stripped of her humanity and dignity in order to become a mere instrument for man's enjoyment. Can contemporary Muslim scholars who would die defending Islam answer this specific question and tell us why Muhammad allowed men to have sexual relationships with women merely for the sake of enjoyment? According to Muhammad's statement, it could be for some money, or a dress, as Muhammad said to his followers, then he could desert her, leaving her without any rights. What is the difference between this and adultery and debauchery? Could Muhammad and the scholars solve this problem by calling it a temporary marriage or marriage of enjoyment?

Muhammad made it lawful for his followers at first, then prohibited it. Then he made it legal again. Therefore, as soon as he died, the most famous Muslim scholars and relatives of Muhammad (such as Abdulla Ibn -Abbas and Ibn Mas'ud) made it lawful It was also in practice during the era of Abu Bakr and Umar, as is recorded in Sahih Muslim.

At present, the Shi'ite sects are accustomed to it and practice it in different parts of the world because the Shi'ite leaders claim it. There are more than one hundred million Shi'ites worldwide. Ibn Abbas, who defends the legality of the temporary marriage of enjoyment and its continued practice, is well known among all the Muslim scholars. He occupied a very esteemed position with Muhammad and the caliphs who used to seek his legal opinion and call him the interpreter of the Qur'an.

Sahih al-Bukbari

In part 7, page 37, we read the following,

> "While we were in the army, Allah's Apostle came to us and said, 'You have been allowed to have pleasure (Muta), so do it.' If a man and a woman agree to marry temporarily, their marriage should last for three nights, and if they want to continue, they may do so."

There is also a very famous story related to us by Ibn Mas'ud and recorded in all the Islamic sources. We will allude to some aspect of it as it as mentioned in al-Bukhari, part 7, pp. 8,9, (also in section 6 of the interpretation of Sura, (chapter), "The Table," p.66- Arabic edition). Ibn Mas'ud said,

> "We used to participate in holy battles led by Allah's Apostle and we had no wives with us. At that time, he allowed us to marry women with a temporary contract and recited to us this verse, 'Oh you who believe, make not unlawful the good things which Allah (God) has made lawful for you'" (5:87).

This famous story is recorded also in Zad al-Ma'ad by Ibn Qayyimal-Jawziyya (part 5, p. 111). In Sahih Muslim, exposition of Nawawi (Vol. 3 pp. 553, 554), he indicated that Muhammad had allowed his followers to have sexual intercourse with women for a dress !

Sahih Muslim

It was proven that contractual marriage was permissible at the beginning of Islam. It used to be practiced during a journey or a raid, or when it was "necessary" and there was a lack of women. In one of Ibn Abu'Umar's episodes, it said that it was admissible at the inception of Islam, especially when "there was a need for it".

Also, we read the following,

> "The contractual marriage was lawful before the campaign of Khaybar; then it became unlawful in the day of the campaign. Then it was made lawful again in the day of Mecca's conquest. After three days, it was prohibited. The episodes concerning the lawfulness (of the contractual marriage) in the day of the conquest are not ambiguous and it is not permissible to forfeit it. There is nothing that may inhibit the repetition of practicing the contractual marriage again, and God is the omniscient, and the scholars have agreed to regard the contractual marriage as a temporary legal marriage, which does not entail any inheritance. The separation occurs as soon as the date of the agreement expires, and it does not require any legal divorce. Ibn'Abbas used to preach its lawfulness" (pp. 553,554 volume 3 Sahih Moslem).

Actually Sahih of Muslim (in the same volume 3) records for us what Muhammad's followers did when he allowed them to practice this. They used to meet a woman who belonged to one of the tribes (children of Amir) and attempt to seduce her by offering her either a dress or some dates or flour (p. 556). They spent three days with the harlot. Also sahih of Muslim describes for us in detail some moral scandals of which Muhammad approved. It also recounts that Muhammad himself used to bring the women to his followers or send a heralder to proclaim that it is permissible to sign contractual marriages (p.555 Vol. 3).

Ismail Ibn Kathir

In his famous book, "The Prophetic Biography", he tells us the following in part 3:

> "The prohibition of the contractual marriage took place in the day of the Khaybar campaign. Yet it had been established in Sahih of Muslim that Muhammad allowed them again to (sign) a contractual marriage in the Day of Mecca's conquest. Then he prohibited it. The Shafi'i said: 'I do not know any other thing which was made lawful, then prohibited, then made lawful again, then unlawful except the contractual marriage, which was prohibited in the year in which Mecca was conquered, then after that it became lawful'" (pp. 365,366).

Ibn Hisham recorded the same text in part 4, p.55.

Ibn Qayyim al-Jawziyya

In part 3, pp. 459, Ibn Qayyim al-Jawziyya repeated this same statement of al-Shafi'i. He also said on p.345:

> "After the death of Muhammad, Ibn'Abbas made it lawful when there was a need for it. He used to say that the apostle prohibited it when it was dispensable, but it was made lawful when it became a necessity."

He also says on p.46 1:

> "Ibn Mas'ud said: 'I made it lawful when it became indispensable for a man.'"

Imam al-Baydawi

He agrees with all the above in his famous book, "The Interpretation of the Baydawi". He says,

"The purpose of the contractual marriage is the mere
pleasure of intercourse with a woman, and her own
enjoyment in what she has given" (p. 108).

I believe that all those scholars were very lucid in their
statements and it is sufficient for us. They are Ibn'Abbas, Ibn
Mas'ud, Sahih al Bukhari, sahih Muslim, Ibn Hisham Ibn Kathir,
Ibn Qayyim al-Jawziyya and al-Imam al-Baydawi. Those
scholars are recognized by all. Muslims and all contemporary
scholars agree absolutely.

The Contemporary Scholars

1. The Saudi scholars: In the context of their interpretation of
the Sahih al Bukhari (Vol. 7, p.36), they indicate:

"Nikah-al-Muta (marriage of pleasure) means temporary
marriage for a limited period of time. This type of
marriage was allowed in the early days of Islam."

2. In his book, "Nur al-Yaqin" ("The Light of Certainty"), the
Sheikh al-Khudary says,

"The contractual marriage, which was a marriage for a
definite time, had been practiced since the inception of
Islam" (p. 207).

3. The scholar Musa al-Musawi

In his famous book, "The Shi'ites and the Reformation", he
lucidly tells us:

"All the legists believe that Muhammad made this matter
lawful at the inception of Islam" (p. 108).

4. The current Sheikh of Islam, Muhammad Mutawalli al-sharawi, indicates in his book, "al-Fatawi" ("The Legal Opinions"),

"The Imam Fakhr al-Din al-Razi, leading other scholars,
mentioned that contractual marriages were made lawful by
the prophet and they were not abolished nor rescinded, but
many scholars said that this matter was abolished later and
that Muhammad, after making it lawful for a particular
time during Islamic history, prohibited it" (p. 26).

We say to Dr. Musawi and to Sheikh al-Sha'rawi: Your statement that all the legists believe that Muhammad made it lawful at the inception of Islam is sufficient for us. This statement and this acknowledgment are what we want the reader to know. It is evident, however, that the scholars who said that this practice was not abolished or prohibited were among the most esteemed scholars such as Ibn'Abbas, Ibn Mas'ud, and the Imam Fakhr al-Razi. In his book, "The History of Islamic Law", Dr. Ahmad Shalabi states that Ibn'Abbas said that it is possible to allow contractual marriages when they are necessary (p. 190). Ibn Kathir also emphasizes in his book, "al-Bidaya Wa al-Nihaya" ("The Beginning and the End"), Vol. 8, p.300, that Ibn'Abbas was of the opinion that contractual marriage should be made lawful. In his Sahih, al-Bukhari records this dialogue,

> "I heard Ibn Abbas when he was asked about Muta (pleasure) with women, and he permitted this kind of marriage. Only a slave of his said to him, 'That is only when it is badly needed and women are scarce.' At that Ibn Abbas said, 'Yes'" (Vol. 7, p. 37).

Who is Ibn Abbas?

All the scholars acknowledge that he is of the opinion that the contractual marriage should be made lawful when it is needed, and he believes that its ordinance is still applicable and has not been abolished. If we open Vol. 8 of Ibn Kathir's book, "al-Bidaya We al-Nihaya" (pp. 295-307), we come across ample references pertaining to Ibn' Abbas' highly esteemed status among Muhammad's relatives and companions in regard to his knowledge and thought. We would like to allude briefly to some of what is said about him.

Ibn Kathir says:

> "Ibn 'Abbas is the most knowledgeable person among the people as to what God has revealed to Muhammad. Umar Ibn al-Khattab used to say that the interpreter of the Qur'an is Ibn'Abbas. He was accustomed to telling him:

'You have acquired a knowledge which we never
received. You are the most expert in the book of God'"
(pp. 299, 300).

Ibn'Abbas was the official legist of the Islamic law during the
era of 'Umar Ibn al-Khattab, and 'Uthman Ibn 'Affan. When he
died, Muhammad's friend said,

> "This nation has been afflicted with an incurable tragedy
> because Ibn'Abbas was the most knowledgeable among
> the people. We always needed him from sunrise to
> sunset."

These references to Ibn'Abbas, Muhammad's cousin, are
sufficient to convince the most skeptical of the importance of
Ibn'Abbas' status. It is well known that the argument of Ibn'
Abbas was strong and it was conclusive to the continuation of
the practice of temporary contractual marriage because
Muhammad made it lawful then unlawful, then he made it lawful
again when it was necessary.

Yet, even if we assume that Ibn'Abbas (who was the most
knowledgeable among people of what God had revealed to
Muhammad) was mistaken, as well as Ibn Mas'ud al-Razi and
many other scholars, and that Abu Bakr was also wrong since he
allowed people to practice this matter during his reign; even if
we assume that Muhammad made it unlawful permanently after
he made it permissible, and that all those people were wrong, we
still have this pressing, unanswerable question: Why did
Muhammad make this disgraceful matter lawful in the first
place; i.e., adultery and immorality? Why, even for a short
period of time, would he legalize prostitution and call it
contractual marriage? Why did Muhammad tell his followers,
"Make an agreement with any woman to make love to her for
three days, then give her compensation, such as a robe." His
companions did so. Later, Muhammad prohibited it, then made it
lawful again according to the need.

We would like to refer to Dr. Musa al Musawi's statement in his book, "The Shi'ites and The Reformation", in which he says:

"This contractual marriage contains a license for licentiousness and degradation of woman's dignity, the thing which we do not find even among permissive societies in ancient and modern history" (p. 109).

Then he adds (p. III), concerning the characteristics of this marriage:

"This marriage is carried out without a witness. The period of this marriage could be a quarter of an hour, or a day, or any period of time. In it, it is permissible for a man to have collectively an unaccountable number of women at the same time. The woman may not inherit her husband's possessions, and a man does not give alimony to the spouse. Divorce is also carried out without a witness. This marriage is nothing but a license to practice sex provided that the woman is not married to another man."

Dr. Musa has a Ph.D. in Islamic law from the University of Tehran He taught Islamic philosophy and was elected as President of the Supreme Counsel of West America. Of course, Dr. Musawi's criticism of the contractual marriage is appropriate. He indicates that this type of marriage has been abolished, yet he acknowledges (p.108 of his book) that all the scholars and legists without exception say that Muhammad made it lawful for his companions from the very beginning.

My friend, we had to discuss the issue of contractual marriage, or "legal prostitution" (as some would like to call it) in detail, but this prolongation is significant because this is an important matter for our practical life. It is also related to the dignity of women and reveals Muhammad's view of women as being nothing more than tools for pleasure.

Fire In Hell—Most Of Its Inhabitants Are Women

Muhammad, the prophet of Islam, expresses clearly that most of those who enter hell are women, not men. None of the scholars deny these statements. We will quote only contemporary Azhar scholars of Egypt.

In the "Liwa al-Islami" magazine which was issued on August 13, 1987, under the title, "Women In Tradition", we read the following:

> "The apostle of God said: 'Oh assembly of women, give charity, even from your jewelry, for you (comprise) the majority of the inhabitants of hell in the day of resurrection'" (p. 21).

Of course, the Azhar scholars are the people most acquainted with Muhammad's sayings.

Ancient Scholars

These scholars are quoted from Sahih of al-Bukhari (Vol. 7, p.96),

> "Muhammad said: 'I saw Paradise and I stretched my hand to pluck a bunch of grapes, then I saw Hell (fire), and I have never before seen such a horrible sight as that the majority of its dwellers were women.' The people asked, 'O Allah's apostle, what is the reason for that?' He replied, 'Because of their ungratefulness.' It was said, 'Do they disbelieve in Allah (God)?' He replied, 'They are not thankful to their husbands and they are ungrateful for the favors done to them. Even if you do some good to one of them all your life when she sees some harshness from you she will say, "I have never seen any good from you."'"

The same text is repeated in Vol. 1, p.83. In Vol. 7 of the same book (p.94), Muhammad says,

> "I stood at the gate of the fire and saw that the majority of those who entered it were women."

In the Mishkat al-Masabih (p. 14), we encounter the following exciting episode about Muhammad who, when met by some women, had the following conversation (Mishkat al Masabih p. 14),

> "Allah's messenger went out to the place of worship and he passed by the women and said to them, 'O women, give charity, for I have been shown that the majority of the inmates of Hell are amongst you.' They said: 'Allah's Apostle, wherefore?' He said, 'It is because of the fact that you curse one another very much and show ungratefulness to your husbands.'"

It seems that Muhammad, the prophet of Islam, utters meaningless statements because who can say that **only women** curse each other? Do not men behave the same way in their quarrels? Do not men kill each other in bitter wars? Who said that **only women**, if they suffer from their husband's abuses, forget all the good characteristics of their spouses? Do not men cheat on their wives, abandon them and divorce them for the most insignificant reasons or for no reason at all? Do not Muslim men marry two, three, even four wives at a time, causing deep psychological pain and material loss for their wives? It is nonsense to say that the majority of the people in the fires of hell are women because they curse each other and they do not acknowledge the merits of their of husbands.

It is nonsense to make these accusations or to label women in general. Even if Muhammad had painful experiences with his various wives so that he almost divorced them (as we will see), he still should not have issued verdicts against all women.

How miserable women are in Muhammad's view. He orders men **to scourge** them, forces young girls to **marry against their will**, and **exploits single women** as tools of pleasure. He also declares that **the majority of people in hell are women**.

"Women Are Short Of Faith And Intelligence"— Muhammad Said

The Egyptian contemporary scholar Sheikh al-Sha'rawi stresses the fact that Muhammad uttered this statement. This is recorded in Vol. 4, p.21 of his famous book, "You Ask And Islam Answers". Al-Sha'rawi, who is regarded as the Sheik of Islam, relies on the former recognized scholars. We encounter the following dialogue in the Sahih of al-Bukhari (Vol. l, p. 83) and in the Mishkat al-Masabih (p.15) which took place between Muhammad and some women:

> "Muhammad said: 'I have seen that you, in spite of being deficient in mind and religion, rob even a wise man of his senses.' They said: 'Allah's messenger, where lies our deficiency of reason and faith?' He said: 'Is not the evidence (testimony) of a woman equal to half the evidence of a man?' They said: 'Yes.' He said: 'This is because of the deficiency of your minds (mental status). Is it not a fact that when you enter the period of menses, you neither observe prayer nor observe fast?' They said, 'Yes.' Then he said: 'This is the deficiency in your faith.'"

"Women are short of faith and intelligence!" A strange statement uttered by Muhammad which is an obvious insult to the women who asked him. Why, Why, Muhammad? He responds with the above-mentioned, weird reasons. If God does not command women to fast or to pray during their menstrual period, why should He regard this matter as a lack of faith and religion? Is it because they obey God's orders? Or is prayer a mere physical exercise of standing up and prostrating? Or is it a matter of lifting the heart up to God at any time?

What about the woman's testimony in court? According to Islamic law, the testimony of a woman is equal to one half of a man's testimony. This is one of the incomprehensible, unjustifiable Qur'anic laws which is regarded as another insult to women. If Muhammad attempted to justify this on the basis of women's lack of faith and intelligence, it would be an excuse which is worse than an offense. Thus, when Muhammad tried to justify his attitude, he really rendered women another insult especially by claiming that a woman is equal to half a man.

A Female Inherits Only Half Of A Male's Portion

A female inherits only half of a male's portion and her testimony is regarded as half a man's testimony. Though the general public is not aware of this fact, the Qur'anic text is very blunt concerning this matter, and is also acknowledged by all the Muslim scholars without exception.

First, concerning an inheritance, The Qur'an clearly indicates:

> "Allah chargeth you concerning your children—to the male a portion equivalent to that of two females" (Chapter 4: 11).

This is in regard to a man's offspring, whether they are males or females. The same concept is applied to the brothers and sisters of a deceased person. The Qur'an says:

> "If there be brethren - men and women - unto the male, the equivalent of the portion of two females" (Surah 4: 176).

This matter is a well-known fact and practiced all over the Islamic world.

al-Bukhari, al-Jalalan and al-Baydawi

The Bukhari alluded to it (part 6, p.55), as well as the Jal-alan in their famous commentary (p.65). We read:

> "A male may have the portion of two females if they are related to each other. He takes half of the inheritance and the two females take the other half. If the male has one sister only, she takes one-third of it and he takes two-thirds" (p.65).

On page 66, the Jalalan says:

> "If he leaves his parents an inheritance, his mother takes one-third and the father two-thirds."

Al-Baydawi (page 104) and the rest of the scholars follow the same interpretation which is based on the indisputable Qur'anic verse.

The Contemporary Scholars

1) In his book, "Islam in the Face of Modern Challenges", Abu al-a'la al-Mawdudi states conclusively:

> "There is no room in Islam for the idea that a woman's portion of an inheritance be equivalent to the man's portion. The prohibitory reason is one of decisive Islamic laws" (p.264).

The Sheikh al-Sha'rawi

He also acknowledges this fact in part II of his book, "You Ask and Islam Answers":

> "The portion for a woman from an inheritance is half of the man's portion because a woman is not responsible for her livelihood but rather the man is the responsible one (p 39, part 2).

French Philosopher, Roge Jaroudi

Even the French philosopher, Roge Jaroudi, who was converted to Islam reiterates in the magazine, "The League of the Islamic World" (the issue of February/March, 1984), the same logic of al-Sha'rawi. Jaroudi says:

> "Concerning the inheritance, it is true that the female inherits half of the portion her brother inherits, but in view of that, the responsibility of taking care of her falls on her brother's shoulder" (p.39).

Dr. Ahmad Shalabi repeated the same meaning in his book, "The History of Islamic Legislation" (p. 137).

The statement of al-Sha'rawi and the French philosopher that a woman should inherit half of the portion because man is the one who bears responsibility for her livelihood is a meaningless and unacceptable justification because it is very possible that a woman may be much more in need of the money than her brother. Why should she receive only half of what her brother inherits from his parents? Is it not possible that the sister may be married to a poor man and have many children, while her brother may be a rich businessman or single without responsibilities?

Even if the sister is still single, why should her brother receive double her portion from the inheritance and have control over her expenditures? He may spend the money on his own pleasures while his sister could be wiser and more prudent than her brother, who may be younger than she. These situations happen daily in Arab and Islamic countries. Any man takes twice what his sister receives. The only reason for it is the inequality between females and males. Why does this happen? Al-Mawdudi tells us it is because this is one of the decisive Islamic laws based on an indisputable Qur'anic verse in the Chapter of Women. This is the inequality of unfair Islamic law.

Secondly, what about a woman's testimony before the court and in business contracts? In the Chapter of the Cow (282), we read:

> "From among your men, two witnesses, and if two men be not at hand then a man and two women of such as you approve as witnesses, so that if the one erreth (through forgetfulness) the other will remember (and we read about what Muhammad said about the testimony of a woman)."

The Ancient Scholars

Scholars have agreed upon the interpretation of this verse which is recorded in the chapter of the Cow concerning the testimony of women because it is very conspicuous and unquestionable. We would like to refer briefly here to the statements of al-Baydawi and the Jalalan. The Jalalan says (on page 41):

> "There must be two adult free Muslim witnesses. If they are not available then (let it be) a man and two women.

(The reason for having) numerous women is that if one of them forgot something because of lack of intelligence, the other one would remind her."

These are the same words of Muhammad and the Qur'an.

On page 64, the Baydawi says:

"The two men must be two free Muslims, or one man and two women. (The reason for having) numerous women is because of their lack of intelligence and to obtain accurate information."

But the statement of the Jalalan and Bawdawi that the witness should be "two free Muslims" is because Islam does not accept the testimony of non-Muslims or slaves, as we will see later.

Nobody denies this about Islam, including all the Azhar scholars as well as the Saudi and Pakistani scholars. Among them, the Grand Imam Dr. Mahmud Shaltut emphasizes this point in his book, "Islam: A Dogma And A Law" (p.237).

In its February/March, 1985 issue (p.17), the magazine, "The League of the Islamic World", records for us **an incident which took place in Pakistan** during the enactment of some of the Islamic laws. The magazine says:

"Three groups of women demonstrated against the new law which gives women only half of the men's rights when they sign business contracts. These groups which are located in Lahore in Pakistan, say that this law, derived from Islamic Law, intends to insult women and debase their dignity."

It is obvious that any intelligent, thinking man who enjoys a sensitive conscience would object to this unfair Islamic law, just as these female groups objected. How could a woman's testimony be regarded as half of a man's testimony in court and when signing business contracts? The same magazine also published on the same page, the response of Dr. Aly Farrukha, Director of Islamic Studies in Chicago, in which he says:

"The issue of a woman's testimony in court is a divine
order which necessitates that a woman who is a witness
should be accompanied by another woman in order to
remind her if she forgets (some details) and to correct her
if she makes an error. This verdict does not intend to insult
women but rather to help them."

This is the conclusion of Dr. Farruka, who senses that this law
really does insult women, but tries to defend Muhammad, the
Qur'an and Islamic law. However, the insult is inevitable and
there is no way to avoid it. The statement of Dr. Aly that there is
a need for two women in opposition to one man in the case of
testimony **in order to help the women** not to forget or to be
corrected if she makes an error, is a polite statement, though it
does not negate that in Islam, women are treated as second class
and cannot be trusted to be accurate when witnessing in court.

Actually Muhammad was more pointed than Dr. Aly
Farrukha. He expressed his opinion without any vagueness. He
says that the reason that a woman's testimony is regarded as
equal to one half of a man's testimony is not to help her but
because she is short of intelligence!

Men Belong To A Higher Level Than Women— They Are Better Than Women

While the Bible assures us in I Corinthians 11:11 that man is
not less than woman and woman is not less than man, the Qur'an
declares to us in Chapter 2:22 that men are a degree above
women. It also says in Chapter 4:34:

"Men are in charge of women because Allah has made the
one of them excel the other."

Of course, we do not believe that the God of "equality among
people" says that men surpass women. If the reader wonders
what these Qur'anic verses mean and why Islam says that men

are a degree above women and they are better than them, we would like to refer him to the answer of the Muslim scholars.

The Ancient Scholars

On page 79, the Jalalan says:

> "Men have been given authority over women to discipline and control them by the merits of knowledge, intelligence and custody, etc., which God bestowed on some over others."

In his commentary, page 111, the Baydawi says:

> "God preferred man over woman, and the reason for the bestowing of this verse (4:34) is a well-known episode which says that a man from the helpers beat his wife, whose name was Habiba, the daughter of Zayd. Her father took her to the apostle of God (to complain). Muhammad said: "Let us punish him." But God sent down this verse 4:34. The woman returned home without having her husband punished. Muhammad said: 'I intended to do something (that is, to punish the man), but God willed otherwise, and what God wills is better.'"

This famous incident was the reason God sent down this verse which prefers men to women and prohibits the retribution of men if they abuse their wives. This episode is mentioned also in the commentary of the Jalalan (page 69) as well as in the suyuti's book, "Reasons for Sending the Verses From God" (Asbab al-Nuzul, p.75). Suyuti tells us that the women said to Muhammad:

> "My husband beat me and left some marks on my face. In spite of that, the man was not punished though Muhammad wanted to do so but the just God, the God of equality, declined and did not allow Muhammad to punish the man for abusing his wife."

What a compassionate God who sympathizes with relentless men! Is this the God who honors women? This God revealed a verse which confirms that men are better than women and above them by one degree, and that they have the right to discipline them. However, what concerns us here is to stress the point that the **Qur'an says** that men are a degree above women and better than them.

The Contemporary Scholars

It is sufficient here to quote the Azher scholars: Mrs. Iman Kamil corresponded with the Azhar scholars and Sheikhs inquiring about this critical subject in order to comprehend the meaning of the verse under discussion (4:34). The following is her question and the answer she received as they were published in "Liwa al-Islamic"("The Islamic Banner") in its issue of July 4, 1985, page 6. The question was:

> "What is the interpretation of the Qur'anic verse: 'Men are the managers of the affairs of women for that God preferred in bounty one of them over another?'"

The answer of the Azhar scholars was:

> "Abu al-Hasan al-Basri said: 'A woman came to the prophet complaining against her husband, who slapped her face. The apostle of God said: "(He must be) punished." But God sent down this verse, and the woman returned home empty-handed.' The meaning of his saying: 'Manager' is that a man is the woman's lord and her disciplinarian whenever she disobeys him. God has explained that the reason for this lordship is that men excel women."

What more can be said after this issue has become so obvious? The reader can easily discern if God is the one who composed it to please the powerful men among his followers.

The Gospel in various places indicates that man is the head of the woman; that is, he sacrifices himself for her sake as Christ is the head of the church; that is, He gave himself for it. But it is obvious from the comment of the ancient scholars as well as the Azhar scholars that Islam does not penalize a man when he abuses his wife because men are superior to women! The story is well known, and it was cited by all the Muslim scholars without exception.

The Muhallil—Men Who Make Something Lawful

Who is a Muhallil? A person who marries a divorced woman even for one night in order to make it possible for her ex-husband to reinstate her.

The Qur'an, as well as Muhammad say clearly that if a man divorces his wife, he can reinstate her, but if he said to her: "You are divorced three times" or if he divorces her three times, he would not be able to get her back easily. In order to reinstate her, she has to get married to another man and have sex with him at least once before the second man divorces her, then she can go back to her first husband. This practice is in vogue all over the Islamic world and is practiced whenever there is a need for it because there is a well-known Qur'anic verse on this subject.

Was this the verdict of Muhammad and the Qur'an? Muhammad not only supported it, but even ordered a woman to practice it if she wished to go back to her first husband. It is recorded in an episode which all Muslim scholars acknowledge as authentic. But let us first scrutinize the Qur'anic verse. It is recorded in the Sura of Cow:

> "And if he divorced her, then she is not lawful unto him thereafter until she has wed another husband" (Surah 2:230).

This second husband is called by Islam "The Muhallil" because he makes the woman lawful to go back to her ex-husband by marrying her for only one night, then later divorcing her so that she can go back to her first husband. All the scholars agree on this interpretation of that verse. An example is found in the Zomokchory (Vol. 1, p.368, Alkashaf), Jalalan (page 32), and al-Baydawi (page 50). The Baydawi says plainly that a real marriage (not a marriage in name only) must take place between the Muhallil and the wife. Also, the Baydawi recounts for us the famous episode which occurred between Muhammad and the wife of Rafa'a. This incident is recorded in most of the Islamic books such as Asbab al-Nuzl by al-Suyuti (pages 45,46). Also Ibn Qayyim al-Jawziyya alluded to it several times in part 5 of his book, "Zad al-Ma'ad". In part seven (page 136) Sahih al-Bukhari quoted it several times. This is the story as it is recorded in the Shih and other books:

> "The wife of Rifa'a Al-Qurazi came to Allah's apostle and said, 'O Allah's Apostle, Rifa'a divorced me irrevocably. Afterward, I married Abdul-Rahman bin Az-Zubair, who proved to be impotent.' Allah's apostle said to her, 'Perhaps you want to return to Rifa'a? Nay, you cannot, until you and Abdul-Rahman consummate your marriage.'"

In his book, "Asbab al-Nuzul" (p.46), the Suyuti states that this woman came to Muhammad and told him:

> "'Abdul-Rahman (the Muhallil whom she wed after she was divorced) has divorced me without having any sexual intercourse with me. May I go back to my ex-husband?' Muhammad said to her: 'No, that is not permissible until Abdul-Rahman has sex with you first, then you may go back to Rafa'a.'"

This incident is confirmed and recorded in al-Baydawi, al-Suyuti, al-Bukhari and the rest of the sources. Al-Bukhari mentions another similar story in which the woman receives the same answer from Muhammad because the order of the Qur'anic verse is very plain: "... until she has wed another husband."

We wonder (and the free human conscience wonders with us) if there is more insult and more humiliation to the dignity and honor of a woman and her husband than this? Muhammad is supposed to either allow her to return to her husband, Rafa'a, or to stay away from him, but to impose such a condition on her is to humiliate her, her husband and children, for who is the man who would allow such things to happen to his divorced wife? Or is there a respectable woman who would be inclined to carry out such a practice?

The contemporary scholars who defend this verdict argue that Muhammad enacted this law to make it difficult for a husband to divorce his wife three times. A man, according to Islamic law, may divorce his wife by saying: "You are divorced... you are divorced... you are divorced" or "You are divorced by three" in a moment of anger which he later regrets and makes every effort to restore her for himself and her children. Of course, she would like to go back to her husband and her children who might be still very young or teenagers. Thus, is it comprehensible, according to all standards of mercy, chastity, purity and dignity of a woman, her husband and children, for Muhammad to state that it is not permissible for her to return to her husband and children unless she has sexual intercourse at least once before she is restored to her husband and children. Would the reader agree with this verdict imposed on a mother, wife or daughter? Oh God have mercy on these people and protect them from the laws of the Islamic religion.

You may say, "All the evidence which you have presented concerning the alleged claim that Islam honors women is sufficient to remove this deceptive veil. Muhammad's perspective towards women has become very apparent. Why do you want to present additional arguments?" True, the aforementioned issues are sufficient, but after you read the following discussions, the picture will become even clearer concerning this vital and basic issue in every religion, that is women.

Polygamy, Mistresses and Concubines

The Islamic religion is very lenient when it comes to the issue of marriage and divorce which causes serious emotional, psychological and economic disasters to women, in order to satisfy man's desires. The Qur'an allows a man to be married to four women at the same time. If he wishes to marry other women, all he has to do is to divorce one of them and to replace her with another. Several verses emphasize this point. However, the reader might not be aware that the Qur'an allows a man to own as many women as he wants in addition to the four legal wives; that is, he is permitted to have concubines, mistresses and maid-slaves. In this respect, Ibn Hazm indicates (Vol. 6, part 9, pp. 441 and 467) that,

> "No one is allowed to wed to more than four women, but he is permitted however, in addition to them, to buy (women), as many as he wants."

Thus, we are going to see that Muhammad, his successors and his relatives owned (in addition to their many wives) concubines and maid-servants who were taken as prisoners of war or purchased. They had sexual intercourse with them as they willed. This is, of course, in addition to the contractual marriages which Muhammad permitted when it was "necessary". A Muslim is not allowed lawfully to have more than four wives at the same time. Only Muhammad had the right to marry as many as he wanted because this was one of his distinctive privileges because he was a prophet and an apostle. There are various indisputable verses which the angel Gabriel supposedly revealed to Muhammad, allowing him to enjoy this status; however, we will confine our study to the general practice of polygamy and easy divorce.

The Qur'anic Verses And The Comments Of The Scholars

The Sura of the Parties: 50

The Qur'an stresses that it is lawful for a man to have several wives and to own concubines. The Qur'an says,

> "We are aware that we enjoined on them (the believers) concerning their wives and those whom their right hands possess."

We read the same text in Sura of Women: 3 and Sura of the Believers: 5 which indicates:

"The captive from war that your right hand possessed" (Sura 4:3).

War bounties, whether they were women or children or money, used to be distributed among Muslim fighters after Muhammad received one-fifth. Therefore, most Muslims (led by Muhammad the prophet) had many captive women who were regarded as owned slaves and concubines. It happened that in one of the invasions (Awtas Hunayn) that some Muslim warriors among Muhammad's companions captured some women whose husbands were still alive. Some Muslims refrained from having sex with them out of shame, but Muhammad told them that it was lawful for them to sleep with them because they were what "their right hand possessed". Then God sent a Qur'anic verse (chapter 4:24) making it lawful.

In regard to the concubines, the Baydawi, on page 102 says:

"A man is not forced to treat the concubines equally as he is obliged to do with the (legal) wives."

A little provision (food and clothes) were sufficient.

The Jalalan says on page 64:

"The maid-slaves do not have rights as the wives."

If we examine the volumes of Ibn Timiyya, we read in volume 32, p.7 I the following plain text:

"It is lawful for a Muslim to (have sex) **with as many as he wishes of those whom his right hand possesses**, but he is allowed to wed four women only. Yet, God has bestowed on the apostle of God (enough) strength to marry more than four women. Also God allowed him to marry without paying a dowry. Muslims are not prohibited from having more than four concubines provided that no two sisters are among them."

This is similar to the above mentioned quotation from Ibn Hazm. In the same volume (page 89), Ibn Timiyya says boastfully,

"Islam has made it lawful to its followers to have sex through marriage as well as with what the right hand possesses, while (for Jews and Christians) they may have sex through marriage only. They are not (allowed to have sex with) what their hand possesses. The beginning of slavery were the captives of war.

"The war bounty has not become lawful for any nation except the nation of Muhammad by the evidence of sound tradition. Muhammad said, 'God has preferred me over the prophets by making the bounties of war lawful to me. This was not made lawful to anyone before me.'"

In this respect, the Gospel is very clear and denotes that a man must have only one wife on whom he bestows all his love. Therefore, we read:

"Let every man have his own wife and let every woman have her own husband ... let the husband render unto the wife due benevolence and likewise also the wife unto the husband" (I Cor. 7:2-3).

To be wed to one woman is a natural thing because God created Adam then **one** Eve. He did not create four women for Adam plus a number of concubines. Some famous men of the Old Testament such as Solomon, wed many women, but that was against God's plan. God regarded that as a perversion from the right worship, and admonished him for his sins. God did not allow this practice in the Holy Scriptures, whether in the Old Testament or in the Gospel. If some biblical characters deviated from God's plan, they committed a sin, and they were subject to God's disciplinary action—they harvested problems. This took place before Christ, but after the coming of Christ we do not know about any of God's men who married more than one women or who had concubines or who was allowed to divorce his wife to replace her with whomever he wanted until the rise of Muhammad and the inception of Islam.

The Harmful Consequences of Polygamy

The consequences of polygamy such as jealousy, envy, quarrels, and conflict among the wives are evident. A woman has to wait for several days for her turn to enjoy the love and the care of her husband; that is, if he has preserved some of his love for her and for the children. A man who has four wives and numerous concubines begets, of course, many children. So what can he do to please all of them?

Muhammad himself was the first to know the nature of the quarrels which take place among the various wives as the result of his personal experiences with his wives, who used to join forces against him (Bukhari part 3, p. 204). Later, we will discuss Muhammad's wives' conspiracies, especially those of A'isha. This particular problem made Muhammad express his displeasure to his son-in-law, Ali Ibn Abi Talib, who was married to Fatima, Muhammad's daughter, when he wished to marry a second wife besides Fatima. This incident is recorded by all the chroniclers such as Ibn Qayyim al-Jawziyya (part S, p. 117); Ibn Hisham (part 4, p. 114); as well as al-Bukhari, who mentioned it twice (part 7, pp. 115 and 152). Let us read together what is recorded in the Bukhari:

> "I heard Allah's apostle who was in the pulpit saying 'Bano-hisham bin Al-Mughira have requested me to allow them to marry their daughter to Ali bin Abi Taleb, but I do not give them permission and will not give permission unless Ali divorces my daughter because Fatima is a part of my body, and I hate what she hates to see and what hurts her."

So Muhammad knew well that marrying more than one woman hurts the first wife. Then, why did he wed so many women causing so much harm to each one of them? Why did he permit Muslims to practice polygamy? Ali's incident is rather strange, but it also reveals Muhammad's consuming selfishness. According to the account of Ibn Hisham, the girl's name whom Ali intended to marry was Juwayriyya. Muhammad used to encourage people to practice polygamy. Bukhari tells us (Vol. 7, p. 124) that Muhammad, while talking to a man, discovered that he had just married a divorced woman. He told him to find himself another virgin girl.

It is obvious that polygamy was the rule practiced by Muhammad's successors and companions. For example, Umar Ibn al-Khattab married seven women in the course of his life (including those whom he divorced), in addition to two maid-slaves who were called Fakhiyya and Lahiyya. Uthman Ibn Affan was wed to eight women. After the death of Fatima, Ali Ibn Abi Talib (to whom Muhammad denied permission to marry a second wife beside Fatima) married ten women and housed nineteen concubines and maid-slaves for a total of 29 women. This is Ali, the cousin of Muhammad and the fourth Caliph who assumed power after the death of Uthman.

When we indicate the number of wives as seven, ten, etc., we do not mean that those men housed them at the same time because it was not admissible for any Moslem to have more than four wives at any given time, but these men would "taste" the beauty of a woman and then plan to enjoy the "taste" of another woman without any regard to the feelings of the first wife. If it was necessary, he would divorce her for no reason but to be able to get married to another woman without exceeding a total number of four wives.

This situation accurately applies to al-Hasan Ibn Ali, of whom Muhammad said that he is the master of the youth of paradise. This Hasan (Muhammad's grandson) during the course of his life, married seventy women and begot thirty-one children. Sometimes he used to divorce two women in a day. Even his father urged the residents of Iraq not to marry their daughters to him because he was a man who constantly divorced his wives, but the Kufa's people continued to marry their daughters to him hoping that their daughters would bear children who would be descendants of the prophet Muhammad.

All these episodes are recorded in the biographies, such as the Bidaya and the Nihaya, by Ibn Kathir, V. VII and VIII; also, the Chronicles of the Caliphs, by Suyuti, who indicated that the Hasan was accustomed to divorcing four women and marrying another four instead. He also mentioned that the number of maid-slaves during the era of Yazid Ibn Abd-ul-Malik was in the hundreds, and grew into the thousands during the time of the Abbasid Caliphs. Al-Mutawakki, one of the Abbasid Caliphs, housed about four thousand maid-slaves.

The reader can refer to the "Book of Al-Aghani" ("The Book of Songs") by al-Isfahani; the "Akhbar al-Msa" ("The Necklace of the Dove") by Ibn Hazm, and "al-Imta wa al-Mu'anasa" ("Entertainment and Friendly Sociability") by Abu Hayyan al-Tawhidi to obtain more information. In Vol. VIII of his book, Ibn Kathir reports that al-Mughira Ibn Shu'ba (who was one of Muhammad's greatest friends and the ruler over some Islamic districts) had been wed to three hundred women.

The Qur'an states clearly that a woman is like a piece of property which a husband can replace easily. The Qur'an says in Sura of Women (20):

> "If you wish to exchange one wife for another and you
> have given unto one of them a sum of money take nothing
> from it."

What a glorious Qur'an and what a merciful God is Allah! This is the only condition for the replacement: If a man intends to replace a woman with another, he is not allowed to take from the first woman an object or money he has already given her at the time of the marriage. No other conditions are stated. A man is free to divorce his wife for a reason or for no reason, and at any time he wishes And he has the right (if he divorces his wife) to reinstate her without her permission during a certain period of time (several months) as long as there are no other conditions pronounced in the marriage contract. In volume 32, p. 238, Ibn Timiyya taught that **men can divorce their wives**, but that women are not allowed to divorce their husbands.

Ibn Qayyim al-Jawziyya emphasizes in his book, "Zad al-Ma ad" (part 5, page 278) that the knot of marriage is in the hand of the man and only he has the right to divorce.

The Easiness of Divorce

Divorce in Islam is made very easy. By uttering the phrase, "You are divorced," the divorce takes place. In part 7, page 145 of al-Bukhari we read, " A man can suddenly tell his wife, 'I am not in need of you.' Then the verdict is to be given according to his intention."

Most often, that wife would need his support and help, but that is no concern of Islamic law as long as the man does not need that wife. Thus, the Qur'an says: "It is no sin for you if you divorce women" (Sura 2:236).

Most probably the man felt bored with that wife or he lusted after another woman who was younger and more beautiful. Since he was not able to support two women at the same time, he divorced one to marry the other. If the great men of Islam, the famous companions of the prophet and the Caliphs did so, what remained for the public but to follow the example of those great men of their religion in dealing with the matters of marriage and divorce?

The Qur'an allows this easy divorce. It does not impose certain conditions or limits on this painful action which causes a great deal of suffering among women, treating her as if she were a piece of furniture. Let us listen to the al-Bukhari as he explains to us (Part VII, pages 145-146) how this easy divorce takes place:

> "If a man says to his wife, 'Go to your family,' then his intention is to be taken into consideration. Or if someone says to his wife, 'If you become pregnant, then you are

divorced thrice'; then, if her pregnancy becomes apparent,
she will be regarded as divorced irrevocably! If he wants
her back she must marry another man first."

It is that easy for a man to divorce his wife if he wishes, even
if she does not commit any wrongdoing. This often happens in
Arab and Islamic countries without any regard to the woman's
dignity. The husband says: "If this thing does not happen, my
wife is divorced by three". These things actually happen, as the
Bukhari said, and the wife finds herself divorced for reasons
entirely unknown to her, because every divorce is lawful (except
the divorce made in drunkenness) according to the Muslim
scholars. As long as the husband was not drunk when he made
the divorce, even if it was in a moment of anger, that divorce
becomes lawful (refer to Bukhari, part VII, p. 145).

The Azhar scholars, when they were asked about that, gave
the same answer: Every divorce is admissible except the divorce
made by a drunkard. What a joke! Or what a tragedy. Daily
Arabic newspapers are filled with such tragic news and the
courts are overloaded with thousands of divorce suits which
causes the eviction of children and wives who are helpless and
dependent mainly on their husbands. This tragic situation made
an Egyptian Muslim lady, Dr. Nawal Sa'dawi (the great
Egyptian writer and thinker), voice her objection loudly during a
dialogue between her and the Azhar scholars by saying:

"I want to say that a Christian wife enjoys a secure
married life compared to the Muslim woman because she
is not afraid of a surprise divorce made by her husband in
a day and a night" (Refer to al-Liwa al- Islami newspaper,
issued on July 9,1987, page 6).

You are right Dr. Sadawi. You are acknowledging the truth as
you describe the status of women in Islam. Your words have
powerful effect because you are a Muslim and a woman also.
But what could the Sheiks of Azhar tell you if this is the law of
Islam and if Muhammad himself was allowed to divorce all his

wives in one day and claimed that he received (through Gabriel) a verse inspired by God in which he threatened them. The verse:

> "It may happen that His Lord—if he (the prophet) divorced you—will give him in your stead wives better than you" (Chapter 66:5).

What could the Azhar Sheikhs tell you if Muhammad himself had actually divorced one of his wives by telling her, "Go to your people?" She was the daughter of June, as the Bukhari remarked (page 131 of Vol. VII). He also divorced Hafasa, daughter of Umar Ibn al-Khattab, then brought her back, as well as his wife Sawda (daughter of Zam'a), then restored her to his household after she asked for his mercy, telling him: "I will give up my day (that is the day he allocated to Sawda) to A'isha," as we read in the "Book of Women of the Prophet "("Nisa' al-Nabi") by Bint al-Shati (p. 125 and p.66 regarding Hafsa and Sawda).

This same author, who is a contemporary Muslim scholar and writer, said:

> "When Muhammad intended to divorce Sawda or when he actually divorced her, she received the news with utmost bewilderment, and she almost fainted. She wept in the presence of Muhammad and said: 'Keep me and I assign the right of my night and day to your young wife A'isha' (p.66); he agreed. It is well known that this Sawda had served Muhammad very well and was very good to him and no one had accused her of any wrongdoing. But **because of lack of beauty**, he intended to divorce her."

Divorce in Christianity

In spite of escalating problems, and regardless of the nature of numerous causes (such as sickness or barrenness), it is not permissible for a divorce to take place among true Christians who learn from the Lord the meaning of love and humility. A conflict may exist, and the husband may lose his temper for all of us are human beings subject to making mistakes. We may scream or show anger or encounter conflicts, yet a true Christian will never think of divorce. Divorce does not exist in the dictionary of relationships between Christian couples.

The Christian wife can rest at peace concerning her future because the church will not allow her husband to divorce her except in one case; namely, adultery. In this case, Christ himself gives the man or the woman the right to divorce the guilty party and remarry another person. Yet even this circumstance is almost non existent among true Christians. In case of genuine repentance, the innocent party is encouraged to show forgiveness and shun a divorce. However, the innocent party has the right to divorce and to remarry whether this innocent party is a man or a woman.

In the Gospel, we read the following dialogue between Christ and some of the Pharisees from among the Jewish religious leaders:

> "The Pharisees also came to Him, testing Him, and saying to Him, 'Is it lawful for a man to divorce his wife for just any reason?' And He answered and said to them, 'Have you not read that He who made them at the beginning "made them male and female," and said, "For this reason a man shall leave his father and mother and shall be joined to his wife, and the two shall become one flesh"? So then, they are no longer two but one flesh. Therefore what God has joined together, let not man separate'" (Matt. 19:4-6).

Christianity does not say that "divorce is lawful but unfavorable," but rather that it is unlawful and is not allowable except for adultery. That is because the interests of the spouse, the children and society are above all other considerations and greater than any marital conflict. It is supposed that problems, struggles (whatever they are) can be solved by prayer, humility, and a deeper relationship with the Lord. God is able to sow love in human hearts, give the ability for forbearance and He is capable of changing the most wicked man or woman because

Christianity believes in the experience of spiritual new birth and the work of the Spirit of God.

Divorce in the West...In the East

It is obvious that the percentages of divorce in Europe and America is very high, but it is also obvious that most of those who divorce their spouses are (at best) nominal Christians who have not committed their lives to Christ. Christ and the Gospel are very clear in this regard. The Gospel is not guilty because of some practices of westerners, such as sexual corruption and the increasing number of divorces.

We **do not blame Islam** or the Qur'an for things committed by Muslims which are against their religion. We are examining Islam as it is manifested in the Qur'an and practiced by Muhammad and Muslim scholars. When we discuss Christianity, we quote Gospel references and Christ's life. Certainly, there is sexual corruption in the East, though it is practiced in secrecy. Westerners, in this case, relinquish hypocrisy. They don't seem to care what other people may say against them, contrary to Easterners.

If we take a quick glimpse at the Christian East, we will realize the rarity of divorce cases. I have lived dozens of years in Arab countries, especially in Egypt which has a population of thirteen million Christians, and yet I have heard about only one divorce in the Christian community. Westerners must recognize this fact in order to learn from the Eastern Christians this Christian biblical principle. Of course, premarital sexual relationships (which are in vogue in the West) are not practiced among Christian Easterners. It is possible to say that in the Christian East there is one divorce for every one hundred thousand marriages.

Yet even if a divorce takes place (whether in the East or in the West), the door of repentance is open to anyone who is ready to repent because every sin is forgivable if it is accompanied by repentance.

I would like to urge the leaders of Islamic and Arabic countries to enact laws and restrictions to solve marital problems, similar to those laws practiced by Tunisia, which do not allow polygamy or easy divorce—in order to protect the wife and the children from eviction and agony. If Muhammad and the Qur'an have failed to do so, the leaders of Arab and Islamic states are able to pass laws to protect women and children (and thus, the entire society) from tragedies and fragmentation. If these states would allow opportunity for the Gospel to be preached through radio and television, most of the problems of society would diminish because many Muslims would become Christians.

A Woman is the Husband's Slave, His Captive!

Readers may wonder if this is true. Is it possible that Islam and Muhammad say that a woman is a man's slave—his captive? Yes, my dear reader, this is a fact which no Muslim scholar denies. Let us scrutinize this matter which is really amazing when we read Muhammad's unquestionable statements.

Ibn Qayyim al-Jawziyya

In Zad al-Ma'ad (part V, p. 189), we read:

> "In sound tradition, Muhammad called woman an 'aniya'. The 'ani' is a prisoner of war (or captive). The duty of the captive is to serve his master. There is no doubt that marriage is a sort of slavery as some of the former scholars indicated: **Marriage is slavery**, thus let each one of you be sure of the man to whom you would like to **enslave** your daughter."

This text tells us that according to sound Hadith (approved by all scholars), Muhammad said so. Therefore, scholars emphasize that a father must choose a good man for his daughter because marriage is slavery.

Ibn Qayyim states also (part V, page 188), "A woman must serve her husband because he has already paid the dowry, and if a man served his wife at home he would commit a grave sin."

Ibn Timiyya (Sheikh al-Islam)

He was very plain when he discussed this issue. In Vol. 32, p.262, Ibn Timiyya unquestionably agrees with the statement of the former scholars that marriage is slavery. He states that Umar Ibn al- Khattab himself is the one who uttered those words. Also, on pages 305-307, he remarks,

> "If a woman said to her husband, 'Divorce me' and he responded by saying, 'I divorce you,' then this divorce is final and irrevocable for the husband because it is regarded a ransom by which a woman redeems herself from her husband, as a captive redeems herself from captivity. It is also permissible for any person to redeem the wife, as in the case of the redemption of the captive. As it is admissible for anyone to pay a ransom to the master of a slave to set him free, it is also allowable for a woman to set herself free from the slavery of the husband. The purpose of that is to disclaim the ownership and slavery of the woman in order to be free from his slavery, as in the case of freeing the slave and redeeming the captive."

Ibn Timiyya has repeated several times the phrase that the relationship of a wife to her husband is like a slave to his master—or like a prisoner of war.

Imam al-Nawawi

In his book, "Ryad al-Salihin" ("The Orchards of the Righteous Men", p 107), he repeats Muhammad's statement that "women are captives in your hands." He also adds:

> "The apostle of God here likens the woman as she comes under the authority of her husband to a captive; and Muhammad uttered these words in his address to men in the farewell year."

These are **the words of Muhammad himself** concerning women, and these are the declarations of three of the greatest Muslim scholars: Ibn Qayyim al-Jawziyya, Ibn Timiyya and the Imam al-Nawawi. These three confirm, according to tradition, that Muhammad is the one who said that a woman is like a prisoner and a slave to a man. Thus a woman is not only less than a man by a degree, and enjoys only half of his rights, but she is less than him by dozens of degrees. She holds the status of a slave or a captive.

A Donkey and a Dog

This is exactly what A'isha said to the great Caliphs and companions when she remarked:

> "You have put us on the same level with a donkey and a dog."

The question is why did A'isha make this statement to those great companions and scholars of the time of Muhammad. A'isha said that to Ali Ibn Abi Talib, Abdalla Ibn Abbas, Abuzarr, Abu Hurayra, Anas Ibn Malik and others on whose authority most of Muhammad's Hadith and interpretations of the Qur'an were handed down. Why did you say that A'isha?

She said it because those pillars of Islam assured people that Muhammad said that if a man is praying and a donkey, a dog, or a woman passes in front of him, his prayer will not be acceptable, and he has to perform ablution (washing) again and repeat his prayer. None of the scholars question this matter which is repeated daily—whenever a woman passes in front of a man while he is praying or if a dog or a donkey walks in front of him. In this case, he has to wash himself again and repeat his prayer; otherwise his prayer will not be counted.

Ibn Hazm Confirms and Quotes

In his book, "al-Muhalla", "The Sweetened" (part 4, p. 8), Ibn Hazm says:

"A prayer is rescinded by a dog, whether it is passing by
or not, and by a woman and a donkey!"

At the beginning of page 9, Ibn Hazm emphasizes that all the
great companions of the prophet without exception attested to
that. Then he records for us (page 11) that A'isha told them:
"You have put us on the same level with a donkey and a dog."
Why is it that if a man passes in front of a praying man his
prayer is not repealed, while if a woman walks in front of him,
the prayer must be repeated? Why is the presence of a woman
regarded as similar to the presence of a donkey or a dog? The
above-mentioned discussion does not need more comment.

Women are the Cause of Evil Omen

It is obvious that Sahih of al-Bukhari is a source upon which
all of the Islamicists depend whenever they want to learn
Muhammad's Hadith (sayings), and consequently, to know
Islamic laws and ordinances which the Qur'an doesn't mention.
If we open part VII of Sahih of al-Bukhari which is translated
into English (page 21), we read:

"Allah's apostle said: 'Evil omen is in the woman, the
house and the horse.'"

On the same page (21), we encounter the interpretation of the
above statement as follows: "The evil omen of a woman is her
bad character". The reader may wonder (if there is such a thing
as an "evil omen") why it is said then that a woman who has bad
character is the cause. Why it is not said that a **bad person** (in
general, whether a male or female) may cause an evil omen; that
is if there **is such a thing** as an evil omen since we do not
believe in the existence of evil omen among true believers. Why
is it always a woman? If a woman walks in front of a man while
he prays, he has to repeat his prayer because it does not count.
Since a woman has bad character, she causes an evil omen. In
the first case, Muhammad equates her with a donkey and a dog.
In the second case, he reduces her to the level of a horse and a

house. The woman. Always the woman. She is always persecuted in Islam. Even Muhammad believed that the majority of the people in hell are women, as it was revealed to him.

Women have Crooked Characters

All the scholars confirm that Muhammad said that women have crooked characters. He also said that a husband should not attempt to straighten his wife of the perversity. He must enjoy her though she is still subject to this waywardness. In Sahih of al-Bukhari (part 7, p. 80) the following is recorded,

> "Allah's Apostle said: 'The woman is like a rib: if you try to straighten her, she will break; so if you want to get benefit from her, do so while she still has some crookedness.'"

Also in "Riyadh al-Salihim" by Imam al-Nawawi (p. 106), we find a quote by Sahih of Muslim,

> "Muhammad said, 'A woman was created from a crooked rib; thus she would never be straightened by any means. If you enjoy her, you do that along with her crookedness and if you endeavor to straighten her, you will break her, and breaking her is divorcing her.'"

We have here two questions: First, why is the woman the one who is crooked? Muhammad answers: "Because she is created from a crooked rib!" Is it possible that man is free from any crookedness? Can we not find one thousand women who would say, "My husband has many detestable characteristics. He is always drunk, gambling, or violent and abusive." Why is it always the woman who is crooked?

Then there is the other question which we cannot avoid: If there is a crookedness in a woman, why does the husband not attempt to straighten her in humility, love, prayer and understanding? Why does he have to leave her on her own without rendering any help lest the crooked rib breaks; namely, to be divorced? Why all this ill-advice by Muhammad? Do prophets tell the husband to scourge his wife or forsake her on the one hand and urge him to leave her alone with her crookedness on the other? Muhammad himself told his wives upon occasion that he would divorce them and replace them with other women.

The Sheikh al-Sharawi, the contemporary Sheikh of Islam in Egypt, acknowledges in his book, "You Ask and Islam Answers" (part II, p. 5) that Muhammad said this, but the Sharawi tries intelligently to justify Muhammad's statement by saying that Muhammad meant that the woman usually shows compassion and is bent over her child like a crooked rib! If this is what Muhammad meant, then how are we to interpret his saying she will never be straightened by any means, it is impossible to change her, and men should not attempt to do so because that will be conducive to divorce, but they should rather enjoy women along with their crookedness? Is this crookedness a virtue, like showing tenderness towards a child? Crookedness is something bad and difficult to change or straighten.

The Sharawi also interprets Muhammad's testimony that women lack intelligence and faith as being not required to perform all the duties and ordinances of the religion; they lack faith by way of commission! We tell him: Do they lack intelligence by way of commission also? What about their testimony being regarded equal to a half man's testimony? Is that by way of commission also or lack of intelligence so that if one of them forgot something the other one would remind her?

Women are Harmful to Men

This is another statement which all the scholars agree that Muhammad uttered against women. In part 7, p.22 of Sahih al-Bukhari, we read,

"The prophet said: 'I have not left any affliction more harmful to men than women.'"

The Imam al-Nawawi in his book, "Riyadh al-Salihin" (p. 110), reiterates that these words were spoken by Muhammad. Of course, Christianity rejects such statements and disapproves of all these accusations against women.

Lastly, we have to ask: If this was Muhammad's view of women, why then, did he possess so many wives, concubines and prisoners of war?

Conclusion

This is the true status of women according to Muhammad and to Islam. We have presented this discussion so that no one will say that Islam honors females, whether they are daughters, single or married.

- We have seen that the father has the right to force a daughter to marry without her permission. She does not have any choice.

- Muhammad made it lawful for a man to have sexual relationships with a single woman in lieu of some presents, then leave her without any rights. This is what is called in Islam "contractual marriage".

- As for married women, the mother of children, Muhammad, in the Qur'an, commanded men to scourge them (if they show any sign of disobedience) if instruction, admonishing, and abandoning their beds fail to bring forth any results. Scholars say that scourging should not lead to breaking bones, but to be a deterring element. A man scourged his wife and left some marks on her face. When she complained to Muhammad, he refrained from punishing him and claimed to have received a verse in which he declared that men are above women and better than them. Men are their custodians, entitled to discipline them and to deter them by punishment and beating.

- We also see that a married woman is a slave to her husband; she is his captive, his prisoner because marriage is a type of slavery.

Muhammad himself, the prophet of freedom, equality and honoring of women said so, as well as Umar Ibn al-Khattab.

- We also discussed polygamy and how a man is allowed to marry as many as many as four women at the same time, in addition to what he owns of maid-slaves.

- We have examined also the issue of easy divorce and replacement of wives as it is manifested clearly in the Qur'anic verses and exemplified by the behavior of Muhammad, the Caliphs and the companions. This divorce drives away the woman and her children and propagates corruption in society. Islam does not enforce any restriction or limitation against it (as Christianity does) to protect women, children and society. If a man divorced his wife by uttering three times, "You are divorced," then he wished to restore her and she agrees to do so, Muhammad insists that she should get married to somebody else first and actually have sexual intercourse; then she could go back to her first husband and her children as Rafa'a's wife did when she wanted to return to her ex-husband. Muhammad told her that she had to have an actual marriage and full sexual intercourse with her new husband, Abdul Rahman, before she could return to her first husband. Muhammad relied on a clear text "revealed" to him through Gabriel the angel for this judgment. He said it was revealed that the divorced wife is not lawful for the first husband until she marries another man (Chapter 2:230).

- Women in general (as Muhammad declared) are the majority of the people in hell on the day of judgment.

- They are the cause of evil omens.

- They lack intelligence and faith.

- In regard to inheritance, they are entitled only to one-half of the man's rightful inheritance.

- Her testimony in courts and business contracts is equal to one-half of the man's testimony and value.

- Muhammad also said that women possess sinister characters.

- Lastly, if a woman walks in front of a man while he is praying, she will invalidate his prayer and he has to repeat it. Muhammad said that a prayer would be nullified if a donkey, a dog or a woman pass in front of the praying man.

The greatest among the companions, such as Ibn Abbas, Abu Zarr, Abu Hurayra, as well as the Caliphs (like Ali Ibn Abi Talib) have confirmed these statements. All Muslims know who these famous personalities are and what position they occupy in transmitting the Hadiths. Such abuses made A'isha scream in their faces, "You have put us on the same level with a donkey and a dog!"

Chapter Four
Discrimination Between a Muslim and a Non–Muslim

In this short life, love is the most significant element. It is the most important thing to God. Christianity in its essence reveals to us God's love as well as the thoughts of His heart; a heart which is aflame with love for mankind. For this reason, Christ came to our earth.

However, we must take note that love has varying degrees, levels, and phases. The most excellent degree and the highest level of love is the life of unconditional giving and sacrifice which we observe in Christianity from Christ Himself, who gave Himself for our sake. He also called upon us to give ourselves for the sake of others. The Gospel says:

> "By this we know love, because He laid down His life for us. And we also ought to lay down our lives for the brethren" (I John 3: 16).

This is the highest degree—the highest expression of love. The lowest degree of love is nondiscrimination, justice and equality among people. This is the simplest fact of love. Its primary principle is to respect the other person in his capacity as a person, not to persecute or humiliate him, and not to harm him. If any one of these occurs, then love is non-existent and the person who commits such wickedness walks in darkness and

125

does not know God, the only living God. God, in essence, is love. The Gospel indicates with finality:

> "He who does not love does not know God, for **God is love**" (I John 4:8).

When we discussed human rights in chapter one, we said that Islam and Muhammad do not have even one drop of love for others. Anyone who denies his faith, whether he is an old man or a weak woman, is subject to death, even a person such as Um Marawan, whom Muhammad ordered to re-embrace Islam or be killed. If the non-Muslim is an atheist, he will be offered two options—Islam or death. If he is a Jew or a Christian, he will be presented with three options—Islam, death, or paying the head tax and humiliation We will talk more about the ill treatment of non-Muslims In the previous pages, we have seen how women were persecuted, humiliated and inhumanely treated. We will also discuss the poor treatment of slaves. Frankly, Islam is devoid of the simplest facet of love.

Non-Muslims in Islamic Society

Muslim propagandists use an attractive motto which says that Islam is the religion of justice and equality. It is the religion of freedom and women's dignity, they say, but this cannot be proved by mere talk and a loud voice, especially among Occidentalists who do not know the reality of Islam. It is also true that even most Arabs don't know the truth about Islam. However, a case is proved by presenting facts and empirical evidence.

When we discussed the issue of women and removed the beautiful (but deceptive) veil of Social Equality, we revealed the ugly face of Islam. Muslim propagandists claim that Islam is the religion of equality and justice. Where do you get that idea? Show us. How could that be if Islam says that Christians whose lands are invaded by Muslims and conquered by force are not allowed to build new churches or even to renovate the destroyed ones? This was what Islam said, and this was the verdict of Umar Ibn al-Khattab who was known as the Just Caliph, as he was called by Muslims.

Tell us where equality is if a non-Muslim's testimony is not acceptable or even allowed in court against Muslims or even against other non-Muslims, as the most famous Muslim scholars indicate? And of course, non-Muslims do not have the right to assume leading jobs in the state.

Tell us where the justice and equality is in Islam when a Muslim's life is spared even if he kills a Christian intentionally while a Muslim may only be required to die if he assassinates another Muslim. The reason, as Muhammad said is that "only Muslims' blood is regarded equal." Thus, no Muslim should be killed for murdering a non-Muslim. If Muhammad says–according to all scholars–that "only Muslims' blood is equal" (have the same value), we have the right to ask, "Where, then, is equality?" Muhammad says to us, "I meant the equality between a Muslim and another Muslim and not between a Muslim and a non-Muslim."

On the other hand, we will see that if a non-Muslim merely curses a Muslim, he must either be sentenced to death or be converted to Islam. However, if a Muslim murders a non-Muslim, he will only pay a fine.

Abu Al-Ala Al-Mawdudi's View - Discrimination is Necessary!

In his book, "Rights of Non-Muslims in Islamic States" which has been translated into many languages, this great scholar asserts that we should distinguish between the rights of non-Muslims and the rights of Muslims. On pp. 2-3, Abu Ala al-Mawdudi says:

> "An Islamic state ... is by its very nature bound to distinguish between Muslims and non-Muslims, and, in an honest and upright manner, not only publicly declares this

state of affairs but also precisely states what rights will be conferred upon its non-Muslim citizens and which of them will not be enjoyed by them."

Now let us analyze the rights which are not supposed to be conferred on non-Muslims We will witness the worst practices of racial discrimination and religious segregation.

A Muslim Must Not Be Sentenced To Death For Murdering A Non-Believer

Muhammad himself gives justification for this. He says only Muslims' have blood that is alike; thus a Muslim should not be put to death for murdering a non-Muslim but must pay for the blood feud to the family of the murdered man. As expected, the great Muslim legists and scholars such as Ibn Timiyya, Ibn Hazm, Al-Shafii, Ibn Qayyim al-Jawziyya, Al-Jalalan, Al-Bukhari and Muslim agree on this important point.

Ibn Timiyya

Ibn Timiyya emphasizes forcefully in Volume 14,

> "Nothing in the law of Muhammad states that the blood of the disbeliever is equal to the blood of the Muslim because faith is necessary for equality. The people of the Covenant (Jews or Christians) do not believe in Muhammad and Islam, thus their blood and the Muslim's blood cannot be equal. These are distinctive texts which indicate that a Muslim is not to be put to death for (murdering) one of the people of the covenant or an unbeliever, but a free Muslim must be killed for a free Muslim, regardless of the race" (Vol. 14, p. 85).

He reiterates the same statement (Vol. 20, p. 282) that a Muslim must not be killed for one of the people of the covenant; that is, a Christian or a Jew

The Imam al-Shafii

In section one of "Ahkam al-Qur'an" ("The Ordinances of the Qur'an", page 275), he says: "A Muslim is not to be killed for an unbeliever". Then he says (page 284),

> "If a believer murders an unbeliever, he has to pay blood feud to the Jew or Christian which is one-third of the blood feud of the believer, though Malik says it must be one half."

Ibn Timiyya inclines towards Malik's opinion and indicates (Vol. 20, p. 385) that:

> "The blood feud should be one half because this is what was transmitted by tradition about the prophet Muhammad and as the Sunnis said also."

Whether the blood feud is one third or one half is not important. What really matters is that a Muslim is not to be put to death for a non-Muslim. Despite the disagreement among the Muslim scholars about the actual amount of the blood feud to be paid, the important thing is that the blood feud of the unbeliever is less than the blood feud of the believer, and that a Muslim is not to be put to death for a non-Muslim.

Of course, if a Muslim murders another Muslim, the murderer must be sentenced to death because he assasinated another Muslim. According to al-Shafii, in this case the victim's relatives have the option either to accept a blood feud or to kill the criminal. However, if the murdered is non-Muslim, his relatives have no choice but to accept the blood feud ("The Ordinances of the Qur'an", Sect. I, pp. 180, 279).

Ibn Qayyim al-Jawziyya

In his book, "Zad-al-Maad" (Sec. III, p.124), he says:

> "Muslim blood is alike (has the same value). A Muslim is not to be put to death for killing an unbeliever."

"Sahih" of al-Bukhan and" Sahih of Muslim"

These are two authorized books acknowledged by all Islam scholars pertaining to Muhammad's sayings. We read in Part 9 of al-Bukhari's book (p. 16,) "A Muslim is not to be sentenced to death for an unbeliever." He stresses that this is also the opinion of Ali Ibn Abi Talib.

In "Sahih of Muslim" interpreted by Nawawi (Part 4, p. 244), we read,

> "A Muslim is not to be sentenced to death for one of the people of the covenant nor for a free man or a slave."

The Jalalan

In their famous commentary, in the context of their interpretation of Sura the Women, the Jalalan clearly and distinctly states the following (p. 178),

> "On the topic of punishment, whether or not a man embraces the same religion will be considered. Thus a Muslim is not to be sentenced to death, even if he is a slave and the victim was a free man—not a Muslim.

It is obvious from these words that there is discrimination between a slave and a freeman. What matters to us is that if a Muslim slave murdered a non-Muslim freeman, he is not to be sentenced to death because he is a Muslim and the murdered man is a non-Muslim.

These are the scholars who have quoted the words of Muhammad himself in this regard: Ibn Timiyya, Shafii, al-Jalalan, Ibn-Qayyim al-Jawziyya, Sahih of Muslim and Sahih of al-Bukhari. They are more acquainted with his sayings and traditions than anyone else.

Ibn Hazm

In part Twelve of Vol. 8 (page 39), he asserts and demonstrates by practical and empirical examples the same opinion we have already observed. He indicates,

"If one of the people of the covenant murdered another one of the people of the covenant, and then the murderer was converted to Islam, he would not be subject to punishment based on the prophet Muhammad's saying, "A Muslim is not to be sentenced to death for an unbeliever." But if the injured was converted to Islam, and died as a Muslim, the murderer must be sentenced to death because believers' blood is alike. If a Muslim injures a non-Muslim intentionally, he is not to be punished because the injured is a non-Muslim, based on the Qur'anic verse. But if the injured confessed Islam and then died, the Muslim must be punished."

It is obvious here that Ibn Hazm relies on Muhammad's sayings and does not present his own personal opinion. He explains how a murderer can spare himself punishment, even if he is not a Muslim. He offers him an easy way to escape by embracing Islam after he murders his non-Muslim friend ! In other words, Islam tells a murderer frankly, "Confess: 'There is no God, but God and Muhammad is the apostle of God' and you spare yourself the sentence of death because you became a Muslim, and in this case you will only pay a fine."

Places Of Worship Are Not Allowed To Be Built Or To Be Renovated Or To Be Rebuilt If They Are Destroyed

Can the reader believe this unjust verdict? This is **practiced** in countries which were originally Christian such as Syria and Egypt. These countries had been invaded and occupied by Muslims and torn by war. Because of the attitude of Islam against the Christian places of worship, we discover obvious persecution and inequality.

Umar Ibn al-Khattab

Muslims claim that Umar was the most just Caliph. The title, "just", is his famous attribute. He was the second Caliph and the father of Hafasa, Muhammad's wife. He was also one of the greatest companions of Muhammad who was responsible for enacting legislation because he received it directly from Muhammad. Muhammad himself used to say, "Take as examples those who come after me—Abu Bakr and Umar" (Ibn Timiyya Vol. 28, p. 651 as well as other sources).

Now what did Umar Ibn al-Khattab say? Ibn Hazm, Ibn Timiyya and all the Chroniclers assert that when Umar signed the peace treaty with the Christians of Syria, he dictated some conditions to be carried out by the Muslim governors throughout the conquered Christian countries. One of these conditions was that Christians were prohibited from building a monastery or a church, and from rebuilding those that were destroyed even the cell of a monk (Ibn Hazm, Vol. 4, part 7, p.346).

This same words (uttered by Umar) are quoted also by Ibn Timiyya (Vol. 28, p.652).

In his above-mentioned book, Abu al-ala al-Mawdudi, the contemporary scholar, says (page 28),

> "In lands owned by Muslims, the non-Muslims are not entitled to build new places of worship."

That refers to the countries which Muslims possessed by war. Christians are not permitted to build new churches in them. It happened that a ruined church was actually renovated, but what was the punishment? Ahmad Ibn Timiyya, the Sheikh of Islam and the Mufti of Muslims in his time, was asked about this matter (Vol. 28, p. 648).

> "Question: A Christian priest lives in a house next to a site on which there is a ruined church without a roof. The priest bought the site and renovated it and made the church part of the building in which he gathered people (to pray). Is he allowed to do so?
>
> "Answer: He does not have the right to do so even if there were the ruins of an old church because Muslims had conquered these places by force and possessed the churches, and it is permissible for them to destroy them according to Muslim scholars. Therefore, all those who

helped him must be punished, and the Christian priest's blood must be shed and his properties must be confiscated according to some legists because he violated the terms imposed on them by Muslims."

Ibn Timiyya's words are very clear. He says that it is not permissible to renovate a ruined church. Notice also Ibn Timiyya's statement that all the scholars agree on the permissibility of Muslims destroying churches in countries which they conquer by war. Pertaining to the death sentence inflicted upon anyone who builds a church, this verdict is voiced by Umar Ibn al-Khattab after he imposed his terms on the Christians. Umar told them,

"Anyone who violates such terms will be unprotected. And it will be permissible for the Muslims to treat them as rebels or dissenters namely, it is permissible to kill them" (Ibn Timiyya Vol. 28:652).

Concerning demolishing the churches or confiscating them, Abu Ala al-Mawdudi in his above-mentioned book (p. 11), indicates,

"Muslims have the right to confiscate places of worship in such towns as have been taken by storm."

Another important question reveals strange historical and eccentric events which took place in Cairo, Egypt. In the same volume of Ibn Timiyya (Vol. 28, p. 632), we find the answer to the following question:

"If Christians claim that the churches which had been closed by the rulers were unjustly closed and they have the right to re-open them, and if they made their request to the rulers, should the rulers approve their case? Re-opening those churches may incur a change in the hearts of Muslims in all the earth because Christians will rejoice and will be pleased to go to churches. This will cause annoyance to the righteous Muslims and others so that they invoke God against whoever allowed that and assisted it.

Answer: Ibn Timiyya, the Mufti of the Muslims responded to this question at the beginning of page 634. He said,

> "Praise be to God: The allegation of Christians that Muslims were unjust to them by closing their churches is contrary to the consensus of Muslims because Muslim scholars who belong to the four schools of Abu Hanifa, Malik Al-Shafii and Ahmaad as well as others of the Imam, such as Sufyan al-Thawri, al-Uzai, al-Laith Ibn sad and others, and before them some of the companions (of the prophet) and their successors, have consented that the Muslim Imam, even if he destroyed every church in the conquered land by war (such as Egypt, Iraq, and Syria) **that would not be regarded as injustice done by him**, but rather he must be obeyed in that. If Christians refuse to accept the verdict of the governor, they would be violating the covenant, **and their blood and their properties** become lawful (to the Muslims).
>
> "It is well known that Umar Ibn al-Khattab made it a condition that Christians are not to build a church even in a land that was conquered through a peace treaty. If they had a church and the Muslims erected a city, the Muslims have the right to confiscate the church. Even if there were churches on the lands of Cairo before it was built, the Muslims would have the right to seize them after the erection of the city, because the city which is inhabited by Muslims who own mosques in it should be free of tokens of ungodliness, churches or anything similar.
>
> "Because of the same principle, the prophet said: 'Expel the Jews and Christians from the Arab peninsula.' So no Jews were left in Khaybar. The prophet (until then) had agreed to keep them there after he invaded Khaybar and conquered it. Later, he gave his order to expel the Jews and Christians from all the Arab peninsula. That happened after the Muslims began to inhabit it. Thus, some rulers such as Umar Ibn Abdul-Aziz and Harun al-Rashid and others used to demolish the Christian churches to support God's cause. May (God's) support and victory be upon them !"

We have quoted the text of Ibn Timiyya word for word, as we usually do. Do these words need any comment? The matter is very clear and the reader can re-read these words. Sheikh al-Islam here clearly states all the historical facts, and the consensus of all the scholars, and the companions (Muhammad's friends) who call for the abolishment of the churches and prohibition of building a new church. Only during a weakened Islam when the rulers did not apply the Islamic law were some churches built, but in case of a strong ruler, such as Umar Ibn Abdul-Aziz and Harun al-Rashid and others, God's order was carried out and churches were demolished!

Whenever Christians refused to obey the order, their blood and properties became lawful to Muslims. What an insult and injustice. Yet in spite of that they talk boastfully about justice and equality. Even during the time of the Caliph Umar Ibn al-Khattab, the Muslims confiscated the largest church in Damascus and converted it into a mosque which is now called the "Amawi Mosque" (Ibn Kathir, Part 7, p. 21).

The Inadmissibility of the Testimony of the People of the Covenant

This simply means that a non-Muslim (whether they are Jews or Christians) is not allowed to give his testimony in any matter in a court. Basically, their testimony is not acceptable because they are not Muslims. Is it possible that an entire society does not accept the testimony of its citizens because they are not Muslims? How then, can court cases be justly conducted, and where is equality?

My dear reader, this is Islamic law which does not comprehend the meaning of equality. Equality in Islam is delusion and deception. Islam is nothing but the religion of inequality.

The Sayings of Muslim Scholars and Legists

All Muslim scholars agree on this matter. I have chosen to show you the greatest and the most famous from among them, such as al-Bukhari, al-Shafii, Ibn Hazm, Ibn Timiyya and Malik Ibn Ons.

Malik Ibn Ons

In Vol. 5, Section 13, p. 156, we read the following plain statement,

> "Non-Muslims' testimony is not permissible at all, even against each other! Of course, their testimony is not allowable against Muslims but Muslim testimony against them is acceptable."

Concerning non-Muslim women he says also,

> "The testimony of the women of the people of the covenant is not permissible even in birth! But the testimony of the women of Muslims is acceptable provided two women testify. One woman's testimony is not acceptable" (p. 157).

The statement is very clear. Christian or Jewish testimonies are not acceptable, even against each other. Their women's testimony is not acceptable even in matters of birth.

The Imam Al-Shafii

In his famous book, "The Ordinances of the Qur'an" ("Ahkam Al-Qur'an", Part 2, p.142), the Shafii says,

> "The testimony of the people of the covenant is not permissible . The witness must be one who belongs to our religion and he must be a freeman not a slave. Testimony is acceptable only from our freeman who belongs to our religion."

This is an unquestionable statement—The witness must be a Muslim, a freeman not a slave.

The Bukhari

In Part 3, p.237 of the Sahih, the Bukhari indicates,

"Polytheists are not to be asked for a testimony or anything else. The testimony of the people of other religions against each other is not allowable, based on the Qur'anic saying: 'We caused enmity among them,' and because the prophet Muhammad said: 'Do not believe the people of the Book.'"

That is, a Christian cannot testify against another Christian, according to al-Bukhari, one of the most famous scholars of Islam. He quotes a verse from the Qur'an which says that God has caused enmity to prevail among Christians, thus their testimony is not acceptable against each other—as if there is no hostility, homicide, war and destruction among Muslims! Then the Bukhari cites Muhammad's saying: "Do not believe the people of the Book." The non-Muslim's testimony is not acceptable.

Ibn Hazm

In Vol. 6, Part 9, pp. 405-408, Ibn Hazm remarks,

"The testimony of a Christian or a Jew is not permissible unless a Muslim man dies in a foreign land void of Muslims! Apart from this, the testimony of a Jew or a Christian is not acceptable against another Muslim or even against a Jew or a Christian like him."

In order to authenticate his statement Ibn Hazm quotes the most famous among the companions of Muhammad, such as Ibn Abbas and Abu Musa, as well as some of Muhammad's wives.

Ibn Timiyya

In Vol. 14, p. 87, Ibn Timiyya indicates plainly and decisively: "The testimony of the people of the covenant is not admissible."

I believe the texts quoted from the works of these prestigious Muslim authorities are sufficient to clarify this point. Otherwise, tell us, my dear Muslim friend, who are more famous than al-Bukhari, Malik, Ibn Timiyya? If you want to know the opinion of the Imam Abu Hanifa, he also declared that the testimony of a non-Muslim is not allowed against a Muslim. **He agrees with all other scholars in this matter**, but he adds that the testimony of a **non-Muslim against another non-Muslim** like him may be admissible because all of them are ungodly men. The rest of the scholars (without exception) disagree with him in this matter.

The Prohibition Against Employing non-Muslims

There exists a prohibition against employing non-Muslims in certain jobs, such as management positions. All scholars and legists of Islamic law agree on this view.

Umar Ibn Al-Khattab, (the "Just" Caliph)

In Vol. 28, pp. 643, 644 Ibn Timiyya narrates the following significant events:

> "Khalid Ibn Al-Walid wrote to Umar Ibn Al-Khattab saying: 'In Syria there is a Christian secretary who is in full charge of accounting the taxes.' Umar wrote to him: 'Do not use him.' Khalid answered: 'He is indispensable and if we do not put him in charge of it, the treasury will be lost.' Umar responded again: 'Do not use him.'"

It was quoted in Sahih Al-Bukhari that Muhammad said,

> "'I will not ask the assistance of a polytheist.'

> "One day, Abu Musa Al-Ashari came to Umar while he was in the mosque to lay before him the income of Iraq. Umar was pleased with the outcome and said: 'Summon your secretary to read it for me.' Abu Musa told him: 'He would not enter the mosque because he is a Christian.' Umar attempted to scourge Abu Musa with a whip. Had it touched him, it would have hurt him and Umar said: 'Do not honor them after God has humiliated them. Do not believe them after God has disbelieved them'" (Ibn Timiyya, Vol. 28).

Based on Ibn Timiyya's volumes, it is well known that Umar Ibn al-Khattab used to command the Muslims and their governors saying, "Humiliate the Christians." This is the second Caliph who succeeded Abu Bakr. He refused to let Khalid appoint a Christian to take care of the taxes in spite of Khalid's evaluation that no one knew better than he. When he also discovered that Abu Musa had employed a Christian to oversee the accounts of Iraq, he scourged him with a whip. Then Ibn Timiyya adds in the same volume (p. 646),

> "Some who were less qualified than the Christians were appointed; that would be more useful to Muslims for their religion and earthly welfare. A little of what is lawful will be abundantly blessed, and abundance of what is unlawful will be wasted."

Ibn Timiyya meant here that regardless of how little the qualification of a Muslim, God will bless it because employing a Muslim is lawful; and no matter how great the qualification of a Christian, employing him is an unlawful matter which God has forbidden.

Of course, it is not allowed that any Christian be appointed to a position of leadership. All scholars agree on that. Ibn Hazm says, "No one but a mature, sane Muslim should assume the office of judge" (Vol. 6, part 9, p.363). Umar Ibn al-Khattab said; "No one of them should hold a position in which he can have power over a Muslim."

Contemporary Scholars—The Azhar Scholars of Egypt

It is sufficient to quote the Azhar Scholars of Egypt and the Mawdudi of Pakistan. Dr. Abdul Moumin says,

> "All Muslims Jurists agree that a judge should be a Muslim and it is forbidden for a non-Muslim to be a judge according to the Qur'anic verse, 'There is no authority of the infidels over the Muslims.' Judgment is considered authority and judgment requires that the judge be a mature and wise Muslim. In addition, a non-Muslim **should be humiliated as an infidel, whereas the position of judge**

requires respect, and he is ineligible even to be a
witness."

This article is from the "Journal of the Administration of
Governmental Judicial Cases" (1979 July-September)
concerning the general rules prohibiting non-Muslims from
being judges in court according to Qur'anic verses and Islamic
teachings. This article was written by Dr. Badr El Deen Abdel
Moumin, teacher at the international university of Al-Azhar. The
Journal is published by the Egyptian Government. This Islamic
law **is not applied now** in Egypt, but it is an Islamic law
according to the Qur'an and Muhammad's teaching.

The Mawdudi

In his previous book, "Rights of Non-Muslims in Islamic
State", the Mawdudi says, "They cannot become members of the
Council and they do not have the right to participate in electing
members to these positions" (Arabic version, p.31).

Also, in his book, "Islam and Encountering the Challenges",
the Mawdudi also says,

> "Non-Muslim sects must not be made equal to Muslims in
> political rights; even the right of election is prohibited for
> non- Muslims" (p. 268).

On the same page, the Mawdudi asserts that non-Muslims do
not have the right to propagate their religion in Muslim lands.

It is apparent to everyone, therefore, that the position of a
judge is prohibited for a non-Muslim or a woman because
Muhammad said plainly,

> "May God curse the people who appoint a woman to
> govern them" (Bukhari, Volume 6, p. 10, and Volume 9, p.
> 70).

What a significant saying of Muhammad! This is a tradition
upon which scholars rely. It is even known to the ordinary man.
This is why some Kuwaiti and Saudi newspapers warned the
people of Pakistan against electing Mrs. Buto to be Prime

Minister of Pakistan. Pakistani officials said that there is nothing in their constitution which prohibits it.

The People of the Covenant are Subject to the Qur'an

In Vol. 6, part 9, p. 425, Ibn Hazm reiterates these auspicious words,

> "The Jew and the Christian and the Magian are to be judged by the laws of the people of Islam in everything, whether they like it or not, whether they come to us or not. It is unlawful to refer them to the law of their faith. There is a verse in the Qur'an which says to Muhammad, 'If they come to you, pass arbitrary judgment among them or turn away from them.' Another verse was inspired which abrogated this verse. It says, 'Pass your judgment on them according to what God revealed to you.' This is what Ibn Abbas has said."

In his book, "The Islamic State" (p. 105), Taqiy al-Din al-Nabahani of Jerusalem attests to Ibn Hazms's statement:

> "The Islamic state was carrying out the laws of Islam in the Countries which were subject to its authority. It used to implement the ordinances, and apply the punishments as well as the business deals and to administer the people's matters according to Islamic principles. Scholars of the foundation of jurisprudence believed that the one who was addressed by legal ordinances must comprehend the message, whether he is a Muslim or non-Muslim—all who embrace Islam and those who do not yield to its ordinances."

The important thing here is that Muslims attacked Christian lands and occupied them, then they imposed Islamic law on Christian inhabitants.

The Remainder of Umar's Terms

We have already mentioned that Umar Ibn Al-Khattab made it mandatory that Christians not build a new church or renovate any of the ruined churches. Now let us complete the study of the restrictions which Umar imposed on Christians as they are recorded in the same reference (Ibn Timiyya, Vol. 28, and Ibn Hazm, Vol. 4). Umar says,

"Christians should not hinder any Muslim from staying in their churches for three days during which they offer them food and serve the Muslims. They ought to give them their seats if the Muslims wish to sit down. Christians should not resemble Muslims in anything, such as their dress, tiaras, turbans or shoes or parting of the hair. They should not ride a donkey with a saddle. They must shave their foreheads. They should not display any of their (religious) books on the streets of the Muslims. They should not bury their dead next to Muslims and must not read loudly in their churches. They should not mourn loudly over their dead. They should not buy slaves who fall under the portion of Muslims Not one of them should assume any position by which he has any authority over a Muslim. If they infringe any of these terms, they lose the right of protection and it is admissible for the Muslims to treat them as people of rebellion and quarrel; that is, it is permissible to kill them. Head tax must be imposed on them, free men as well as the slaves, male or female, poor and rich and on the monks" (cited from Ibn Hazm).

Ibn Timiyya asserts that these are the conditions which Umar Ibn al-Khattab actually made. He completely agrees with Ibn Hazm because this is the history of Islam. When Umar made a peace treaty with the Christians of Syria, he offered them these terms in a clear document. Sufyan al-Thawri, who is one of the ancient Muslim scholars and chroniclers acknowledged by all Muslims, attests to this. Ibn Timiyya adds in the same volume (page 654):

"These terms are constantly renewed and imposed on the Christians by any one of the Muslim rulers who, God may be exalted, has bestowed on him success, as Umar Ibn Abdul-Aziz did during his reign, who strictly followed the path of Umar Ibn al-Khattab. Harun Al-Rashid. Jafar al-Mutawakkil and others renewed them and ordered the demolishing of the churches which ought to be demolished, like the churches of the entire Egyptian lands."

Ibn Timiyya recorded the above after he praised the rulers who carried out these terms which Umar Ibn al-Khattab, father of Hafasa, wife of Muhammad and the second Caliph who succeeded Aby Bakr a imposed on Christians. Ibn Timiyya declares to us (Vol. 28, p.654):

"These terms are mentioned by the chief scholars who belong to the acknowledged schools. They alluded to the fact that the Imam ought to oblige the people of the Book to subjugate them to these terms [because Muhammad said many times, 'Follow Abu Bakr and Omar!']."

Ibn Timiyya also indicated that Umar Ibn al-Khattab said about the people of the covenant, "Humiliate them," because the Qur'an said distinctly that they should pay the head tax with humiliation (9:29).

1. These unjust humiliating terms imposed on Christians are acknowledged not only by Ibn Timiyya and Ibn Hazm but also by the chief scholars (who belong to the four schools which are followed by the majority of the Muslims) among them Sufyan al-Thawri, who is one of the great companions and chroniclers. These terms were not only carried out during the era of Umar Ibn al-Khattab but were implemented by many Arab Muslim rulers during their occupation of the lands of Christian people.

2. After Umar Ibn Al-Khattab presented these terms to the inhabitants of Syria and Damascus, he told them plainly:

"If any Christian violates any of these terms, it will be permissible to kill him."

Imagine the extent of the relentlessness and injustice of this verdict. This means that if a Christian dressed like a Muslim, it would be permissible to kill him. If he refused to host the Muslims in the church for three days, or if he did not move from his seat to let the Muslim sit in his place, he could be killed.

Also, if **Christians pray loudly in the churches or mourn loudly over their dead**, or if one of them renovated a ruined church he would be killed. What a just man, Umar Ibn Khattab! As all Muslims say about him, "The Just Caliph!"

A Christian Is Condemned To Death If He Curses A Muslim!

Who can believe this matter? No one, unless he reads it clearly in Ibn Hazm's book (Vol. 8, part 11, p. 274). He said:

> "It is **mandatory** to kill anyone of the people of the Covenant who **curses** a Muslim, whether he is a Jew or a Christian because God says, 'Pay the tribute readily, being brought low [humiliated]'" (9:29).

> "That is humiliation. If anyone violates this principle by cursing a Muslim, he must be killed or taken into captivity. His properties become lawful for Muslims nor does it matter whether the person who did it was a man or a woman. If any one of them cursed a Muslim, he would have no choice but either to embrace Islam or be killed" (p. 274).

Ibn Hazm (page 275) added, "Of course, if a Muslim curses another Muslim like him, he would only be whipped."

Ibn Timiyya states that in general, any Christian who curses a Muslim must be killed **immediately** (Vol. 28:668).

It is easy for the reader to imagine all the situations in which a Christian who is humiliated in his own land might get angry, react impulsively, and curse a Muslim. However, if he does, there is nothing left for him but to accept Islam or to be killed, as Ibn Hazm indicated. What a merciful religion! A religion of equality and love and understanding—and justice!

Before we conclude this discussion, we would like to mention briefly three specific things out of dozens of other issues. What we have already discussed is sufficient for anyone who is interested in knowing the facts about equality and justice as they arc practiced by Muhammad and Islam. It is enough to remove this veil, yet there are three more things:

1. If a Christian father executed or arranged a marriage for his Muslim daughter (even with her approval) that marriage is not permissible and is void because the rather is a Christian and she is a Muslim - **even if the daughter approved of it** (Malik Ibn Anas, Vol. 2, part 4, p. 176). That is, the father cannot be the legal guardian of his Muslim daughter even if she herself wants it. A Muslim who is a stranger to her will become her legal guardian.

2. Muhammad said, "Do not meet Jews or Christians with **greetings**. If you ever meet them in the street, **force them to the narrowest part of it**" (refer to Sahih of Muslim, "Interpretation of Nawawi", Vol. 5, p. 7; also Ibn Qayyim al-Jawziyya: Zad al-Ma'ad, Part 2, pp. 424, 425). This is a well-known statement of Muhammad.

3. Last, we would like to state here a remark made by one of the contemporary Muslim scholars, Dr. Ahmad 'Umar Hashim, in which he reveals the real face of Islam. He says,

> "Islam does not prohibit [Muslims] from conducting business with non-Muslims, but Islam prohibits hearty friendships because hearty friendship should only be between a Muslim and his brother Muslim" (Al-Liwa al-lslami, issue no. 153 - Al Azhar).

What a sad statement. Yet, this is not foreign to Islam and, of course, Al Azhar knows exactly what Islam does and does not prohibit.

You may have a Muslim friend who tells you that Muhammad said of the people of the Book, "They enjoy the privileges we enjoy and they arc subject to the duties to which we arc subject." What does this statement mean? How does it agree with what we have already cad which reveals clearly that there is a striking discrimination between the Muslim and the non-Muslim?

Besides, we have seen that the people of the Book are subject to ill-treatment and contempt.

The answer is very simple. Muhammad spelled out this statement about the people of the Book provided that they became Muslims like them. In this case, they would be treated as Muslims without any discrimination and they would be subject to the same privileges and duties as other Muslims because they have become Muslims. If they do not embrace Islam, they will be subject to the head tax and all the terms which 'Umar Ibn al-Khattab mentioned in his document. It is relevant here, my friend, to know the situation concerning to which the above statement refers because many Muslims wrongly believe that it means equality between Muslims and non-Muslims.

They Have the Rights and Duties We Have

If we open the "Biography of the Prophet" ("Al-Road Al Anf", Ibn Hisham and Al-Sohaly, part 4, p. 216), we read that Muhammad sent a letter to some of the Byzantines who accepted Islam saying,

> "From Muhammad, the Apostle of God: I received what you have sent and I became aware of your acceptance of Islam and your fight against the infidels. You have to practice praying, pay the alms and give one-fifth of the bounty to God and to His apostle. Any one of the Jews or Christians who accepts Islam will enjoy the same rights we enjoy and will be subject to the same duties to which we are subject. But anyone who holds fast to his faith must pay the head tax."

What is important to us in this quotation is not Muhammad's request that they send him one fifth of the bounty which was captured during their raids, but rather his plain statement that anyone who embraces Islam will have the same rights and will be subject to the same duties imposed on the Muslims. Those who hold fast to their own religion must pay the head tax (the tribute). This is what is recorded in Ibn Hisham's biography which has become the most authoritative source about Muhammad's life.

If we examine the "Chronicle of al-Tabari" (Part 2, pp. 145-196), we see the same principle. Muhammad himself says,

> "Whoever prays our prayer is a Muslim, and will enjoy the same rights as Muslims and be subject to the same duties. But those who reject (Islam) must pay the head tax."

In Part One, we discussed the wars which Muslims waged in order to spread Islam and indicated that 'Amru Ibn al-'As, when he invaded Egypt, said to Maquqas who was the ruler at that time,

> "**If you accept Islam** you will become our brothers, enjoying the same rights as we do and subject to the same duties to which we are subject" ("al-Khulafa al-Rashidun" by Dr. Abu Zayd Shalabi, p. 145).

Chapter Five
Slavery in Islam

All the ancient as well as the contemporary scholars acknowledge the fact of slavery in Islam and clarify the status of slaves. I have chosen the opinions of the most famous scholars to shed light on their position.

The Scholars of al-Azhar in Egypt

In his book, "You Ask and Islam Answers", Dr. 'Abdul-Latif Mushtahari, the general supervisor and director of homiletics and guidance at the Azhar University, says (pp. 51,52),

> "Islam does not prohibit slavery but retains it for two reasons. The first reason is war (whether it is a civil war or a foreign war in which the captive is **either killed or enslaved**) provided that the war is not with Muslims against each other—it is not acceptable to enslave the violators, or the offenders, if they are Muslims. Only non-Muslim captives may be enslaved or killed. The second reason is the sexual propagation of slaves, which would generate more slaves for their owner."

The text is plain that all prisoners of war must either be killed or become slaves. The ancient scholars are in full agreement over this issue, such as Ibn Timiyya, Ibn Hisham, Malik etc. Ibn Timiyya says (Vol. 32, p. 89),

149

"The root of the beginning of slavery is prisoners of war; the bounties have become lawful to the nation of Muhammad."

Then (Vol. 31, p. 380), he indicates clearly and without shame,

"Slavery is justified because of the war itself; however, it is not permissible to enslave a free Muslim. It is lawful to kill the infidel or to enslave him; and it also makes it lawful to take his offspring into captivity.

In Part 4, p. 177 of the "Prophet Biography" ("Al Road Al-Anf'), Ibn Hisham says,

"According to Islamic law concerning prisoners of war, the decision is left to the Muslim Imam. He has the choice either to kill them or to exchange them for Muslim captives, or to enslave them. This is in regard to men; however women and children are not permitted to be killed, but must be exchanged (to redeem Muslim captives) or enslaved—take them as slaves and maids."

This is the statement of Ibn Hisham, on whom all Muslims and students of Muhammad's biography rely. Of course, these matters which Ibn Hisham recorded used to take place continuously in all of Muhammad's wars and invasions. All of Muhammad's people (his wives, and Muhammad himself) owned many slaves—males and females. In his campaign against the children of Qurayza (the Jewish tribe), Muhammad killed all the males (700-900) in one day. Then, he divided the women and the children among his people.

The Caliphs across the ages followed Muhammad's footsteps and enslaved (by hundreds and thousands) men and women who were captured in wars. Many of them were Persians and Byzantines. All the Islamic Chroniclers, without exception, have recorded these facts. The way Arab Muslims invaded Africa and killed and enslaved Africans is a well-known, historical fact.

In Vol. 2, Part 3, p. 13, Malik Ibn Anas repeated the same text as did Ibn Hisham who is also quoted by Ibn Timiyya, and Ibn Qayyim al-Jawziyya in his book, "Zad al-Ma'ad" (part 3, p. 486). All of them taught the same principle and said the same words.

This question was delivered to Ibn Timiyya, who was Mufti of Islam (Vol. 31, pp. 376, 377),

> "A man married a maid-slave who bore him a child. Would that child be free or would he be an owned slave?"

Ibn Timiyya says emphatically,

> "Her child whom she bore from him would be the property of her master, according to all the Imams (heads of the four Islamic schools of law) because the child follows the (status) of his mother in freedom or slavery. If the child is not of the race of Arabs, then he is definitely an owned slave according to the scholars, but the scholars disputed (his status) among themselves if he was from the Arabs—whether he must be enslaved or not, because when A'isha (Muhammad's wife) had a maid-slave who was an Arab, Muhammad said to A'isha, 'Set this maid free because she is from the children of Ishmael.'"

Then Ibn Timiyya states (Vol. 31, p. 380) that the legist Abu Hanifa says, "Muhammad is an Arab; thus it is not admissible to enslave Arabs because of the nobility of this race, since Muhammad is from them." Yet other scholars disagree with him, emphasizing that Muhammad (in one of his campaign's) enslaved Arabs, too. However, it is evident from Muhammad's traditions that he regarded Arabs to be the most noble race, especially the Quraysh, his tribe. His famous saying (that the caliphs must be elected from the Quraysh tribe) is acknowledged by all translators of the tradition, without exception.

He should have told A'isha, "Set her free because she is a human being like you. It is not important whether she is a descendant of Ishmael or of Isaac!"

Islam Encourages Muslims to Keep Slaves—No Liberation

All Muslim scholars acknowledge that Islam has retained the principle of slavery, though some of them claim that Islam encourages the liberation of slaves. Maybe some of Muhammad's sayings and a few Qur'anic verses indicate so, yet from a practical point of view, we realize that the liberation of slaves was a rare occurrence. The reason is well known. Neither Muhammad nor his wives or companions were a good example in this regard. Sometimes, Muhammad used to talk about the merits of liberating a slave, yet he himself owned dozens of slaves and maid-slaves. However, we encounter a strange opinion spelled out by Muhammad's wives and his friends in which he encourages them to retain their slaves. In Vol. 33, p. 61 Ibn Timiyya says,

> "Anyone who says, 'If I do so (such a thing), every slave I own will become free' **is not obligated** by his oath and he can redeem his oath by any means and retain his slaves. (He can do that) by fasting a few days or by feeding some hungry people."

On the same page, Ibn Timiyya stresses that this is what all Muhammad's friends said (such as Ibn 'Abbas and Ibn 'Umar) as well as his wives (such as Zaynab, A'isha, and Um Salama).

Is the liberation of slaves a bad thing so that it is possible for a man who swears he will liberate his slaves to renounce his oath and retain them? It should be said that whoever takes an oath to free his slaves if so-and-so happens, is obliged to fulfill his oath and liberate his slaves, but we see that Muhammad's wives, his great companions and his relatives say something different, according to the testimony of Ibn Timiyya.

The Qur'an itself (in several places) approves of slavery and assures the Muslim the right to own dozens of male and female slaves, either by purchasing them or as bounty of war. The

Qur'an talks about the possession of slaves as "the possession of their necks" (Chapter 58:3, Surah Al-Mujadilah).

Slaves of Muhammad—Prophet of Freedom and Equality!

Muhammad himself owned numerous slaves after he proclaimed himself to be a prophet. I would like here to quote Ibn Qayyim al-Jawziyya who is one of the greatest scholars and chroniclers of Islam. In his book, "Zad al-Ma'ad" (Part I, p. 160), he says,

> "Muhammad had many male and female slaves. He used to buy and sell them, but he purchased (more slaves) than he sold, **especially after God empowered him** by His message, as well as after his immigration from Mecca. He (once) sold one black slave for two. His name was Jacob al-Mudbir. His purchases of slaves were more (than he sold). He was used to renting out and hiring many slaves, but he hired more slaves than he rented out.

This trading used to take place in the slave market in the Arab Peninsula and in Mecca. Muhammad was accustomed to sell, purchase, hire, rent, and to exchange one slave for two. Thus, he had an increasing number of slaves, **especially after he claimed to be a prophet**, and after his immigration from Mecca to escape death at the hand of his tribe Quraysh. Also, the slaves of Muhammad and his followers were constantly increasing as the result of those who were captured in wars and not only by purchase. This should alert those who have accepted Islam—the Muslims of New York, Chicago, Georgia, Detroit, Los Angeles as well as all the Africans and all Muslims of the world. Even among the Arabs are Muslims who are not aware of these facts concerning Muhammad. Sadly, this is only a small part of the facts of which they are unaware concerning Muhammad.

The Names of Muhammad's Slaves

A) Male Slaves:

Ibn Qayyim al-Jawziyya relies always on the prophet's biographies written by great ancient scholars. Therefore, he is regarded by Muslims as an authority, a primary source and a leader among the students of the Islamic religion. This scholar tells us in his book, "Zad al-Ma'ad" (part 1, pp. 114, 115, and 116), the following,

> "These are the names of Muhammad's male slaves: Yakan Abu Sharh, Aflah, 'Ubayd, Dhakwan, Tahman, Mirwan, Hunayn, Sanad, Fadala Yamamin, Anjasha al-Hadi, Mad'am, Karkara, Abu Rafi', Thawban, Ab Kabsha, Salih, Rabah, Yara Nubyan, Fadila, Waqid, Mabur, Abu Waqid, Kasam, Abu 'Ayb, Abu Muwayhiba, Zayd Ibn Haritha, and also **a black slave called Mahran, who was re-named (by Muhammad) Safina ('ship'). He himself relates his own story**; he says:

> "The apostle of God and his companions went on a trip. (When) their belongings became too heavy for them to carry, Muhammad told me, 'Spread your garment.' They filled it with their belongings, then they put it on me. The apostle of God told me, 'Carry (it), for you are a ship.' Even if I was carrying the load of six or seven donkeys while we were on a journey, anyone who felt weak would throw his clothes or his shield or his sword on me, so I would carry that, a heavy load. The prophet told me, 'You arc a ship'" (refer to Ibn Qayyim, pp. 115-116; al-Hulya, Vol. 1, p. 369, quoted from Ahmad 5:222).

The story shows their ruthlessness and does not need explanation or clarification. The ill treatment Muhammad and his companions made of Mahran is very repulsive. Ibn Qayyim al-Jawziyya is not the only one who recorded this episode and the list of names of Muhammad's slaves. The Tabari also (in his Chronicles, Volume 2 p. 216, 217, 218) presents us with these accounts. No one among the contemporary Muslim leaders denies these matters, especially if he is faced with the Tabari's and Ibn Qayyim al-Jawziyya's records.

Still, in regard to Muhammad's slave, Zayd Ibn Haritha, Muhammad set him free and adopted him, then he married him to his (Muhammad's) cousin Zaynab. Later Zayd divorced her after he realized that Muhammad was captivated by her. The scandalous story is documented by verses in the Qur'an, and Muslim scholars admit it.

B) Maid Slaves:

In this same Section (One, p. 116), Ibn Qayyim al-Jawziyya, as well as other Muslim authors of chronicles, recorded the list of names of Muhammad's maid-slaves. They are Salma Um Rafi', Maymuna, daughter of Abu Asib, Maymuna, daughter of Sa'd, Khadra, Radwa, Razina, Um Damira, Rayhana, Mary the Coptic, in addition to two other maid-slaves, one of them given to him as a present by his cousin, Zaynab, and the other one captured in a war.

The Status of the Slave Under Islam's Unjust Laws

Let us survey together some strange things embraced by Muhammad and Islam pertaining to slaves. Then let us shed some light on the attitude of Christianity towards this issue.

The Freeman Should Not Be Killed For A Slave

The Qur'an, as well as Muslim scholars, are explicit in this regard. The Qur'an (the Chapter of the Cow:178) shamelessly says,

> "O ye who believe! Retaliation is prescribed for you in the matter of the murdered—the free man for the free man, and the slave for the slave, and the female for the female."

The reader does not need the interpretations of the scholars to understand these explicit words which indicate that the free man should be killed only for another free man, a slave for a slave, and a female for a female. Still, I promised to stick to the interpretations of the great expositors of these Qur'anic verses from among the Muslim scholars because they are more knowledgeable of their Book and its verses. We rely on their interpretations and not on our own. In the commentary of the Jalalan (p. 24), we read the following regarding the above mentioned verse,

> "The same punishment was imposed on believers, and what is similar to the act of the crime in the case of a homicide, by virtue of description or actuality. A free man should be killed for another free man but not for a slave, a female for a female, but a Muslim (even if he is a slave) must not be killed for an infidel, even if that infidel is a freeman."

What kind of equality is this between human beings!

To explain the aforementioned verse (2:178), the Baydawi relates what really happened with the prophet Muhammad, Abu Bakr and 'Umar. This is recorded in his book entitled, "The Commentary of al-Baydawi". On p. 36, we read,

> "The Shafi'i and Malik prohibit the killing of a free man if he slays his slave or other men's slaves. This is because 'Ali Ibn Abi-Talib mentioned that a man had killed his slave and Muhammad scourged him only; he did not kill him. It was related on the authority of Muhammad that he said a Muslim should not be killed for a non-Muslim, nor a freeman for a slave; also because Abu Bakr and 'Umar Ibn al-Khattab did not kill a free man for a slave. (This was said) in the presence of all Muhammad's companions, and no one disapproved or objected to it."

These are the verses of the Qur'an and this is the attitude of Muhammad himself as well as Abu Bakr and 'Umar after him.

The Muslim legists

The Shafi'i, Malik and Ibn Timiyya, pronounce the same principle as in the Qur'an (2:187).

The Imam Shafi'i tells us plainly and decisively in Part I of his book, "Ahkam al-Qur'an" ("The Ordinances of the Qur'an", p. 275),

> "A man is not to be killed for his slave nor the free man for a slave."

On the same page he adds,

> "A believer is not to be killed for a non-believer, nor a man for his son, or a man for his slave or for a woman."

What justice! What equality! Then he adds,

> "The freeman is not to be killed for a slave according to the scholars."

Malik Ibn Anas was asked: "What is the punishment of a master who beats his slave to death?" He answered: "Nothing!" (Vol. 6, Part 15, p 164).

In Vol. 28, p. 378, Ibn Timiyya also says:

> "What we mentioned in regard to the believer's whose blood is treated equally is restricted to the free Muslim against another free Muslim."

I do not have better witnesses in this regard than these scholars: Abu Bakr, 'Umar, 'Ali and Muhammad's deeds, and all great, popular Muslim scholars.

A Slave Is Not Entitled To Property Or Money

Ibn Hazm says in Vol. 6, Part 9,

> "The slave is not permitted to write a will when he dies, nor can he bequeath (anything), because his entire possessions belong to his master."

In part I, p. 180 of his book, "The Ordinances of the Qur'an", the Shafi'i also says,

> "The Qur'anic verse; 'Marry of the women who seem good to you, two or three or four are meant for the free man only and not for the slaves, because he says in it that the one who acts fairly is the person who owns money, and slaves do not own money.'"

He also indicates in Part II, p. 21, "The owned one does not have money." Besides, according to the Islamic law, all Muslims receive portions of war bounty, except slaves and women. Malik Ibn Anas says (Vol. 2, Part 3, pp. 33,34),

> "Slaves and women do not have any portion in the bounty."

This is true even if they have been fighting with the rest of the Muslims. In Part III of the "Prophetic Biography" (p. 386), Ibn Kathir says,

> "The slave does not get anything from the bounty, whether the bounty is money or women."

The Testimony Of The Slave Is Not Admissible

In Vol. 35, p. 409 Ibn Timiyya remarks,

> "The Shafi'i, Malik, and Abu Hanifa, who are the legists of Islam, assert that the testimony of the slave is not acceptable."

If we also turn the pages of the "Ordinances of the Qur'an" by the Shafi'i (part II, p. 142), he determines,

> "The witnesses must be from among our free man, not from our slaves, but from free man who belong to our religion! "

The testimony of a Jew or a Christian is not acceptable, as we have mentioned before, even if justice would be hindered for lack of their witness. This is not important. In his "Sahih" (Part III, p. 223), the Bukhari remarks,

> "The testimony of a slave is not acceptable in marriages."

What is the meaning of the Shafi'i's statement,

"A witness should not be from our possessed slaves."

Does not Mr. Shafi'i know that God only is the One who owns people? How dare he utter the phrase, "our possessed slaves."

There Is No Punishment For One Who Makes False Accusation Against Slaves

It is well known that if a Muslim falsely accuses another free Muslim and slanders his honor, he will be punished by being flogged with eighty lashes. This is what happened when some of Muhammad's companions and relatives accused A'isha, his wife, of adultery with one of the young men because they stayed behind after the departure of the caravan, then later in the morning they arrived together. Muhammad ordered each one of them flogged with eighty lashes. But if a Muslim calumniates a slave, he would not be punished. This is the opinion of all the scholars.

For instance (Vol. 8, Part II, p. 27 1), Ibn Hazm asserts that this is the opinion of Abu Hanifa, Shafi'i, Malik, and Sufyan al-Thawri and not only his own opinion. This is what the Sharawi shamelessly remarks,

"Female slaves are deprived of dignity and subject to abuse because they are not 'an honor' to anyone (that is, they are not free, respectable women who belong to a free man). These arc the same words reiterated by the Shafi'i (Part I, p. 307) in his book, 'Ahkam of the Qur'an'; thus a female slave must not be veiled. Whenever Muhammad took a woman as a captive, if he imposed the veil on her, Muslims would say he took her as a wife, but if he left her unveiled they would say, 'He owned her as a slave'; that is, she became a property of his right hand."

A good example is the incident of Safiyya, daughter of Hay, who was taken as a bounty in the war of Khaybar. All the chronicles (as well as the biographies without exception) have recorded, "We wonder why it is said about women and girls that they are of 'shed dignity'." The Shafi'i and the Sharawi state this word for word. Is it necessary for us to repeat that Islam sheds the dignity of man under the pretense that he is a slave, that she is a woman, or that he is a non-Muslim?

On Matters Of Sex And Marriage—and About Black Slaves

1. The Slave cannot choose for himself.

This was confirmed by all the Muslim scholars on the authority of Muhammad. In Vol. 6, Part 9, p. 467, Ibn Hazm said,

> "If a slave gets married without the permission of his master, his marriage will be invalid and he must be whipped because he has committed adultery. He must be separated from his wife. She is also regarded as an adulteress, because Muhammad said, 'Any slave who gets married without the approval of his master is a prostitute.'"

The same text is quoted by Ibn Qayyim al-Jawziyya (Part 5, p. 117 of "Zad al-Maad"), as well as Ibn Timiyya (Vol. 32, p. 201). Malik Ibn Anas relates (Vol. 2, Part 4) more than that. He says (pp. 199, 201, 206),

> "The slave does not get married without the approval of his master. If he is a slave to two masters, he has to obtain the approval of both men."

2. The male slave and the female slave are forced to get married.

Malik Ibn Anas says explicitly,

> "The master has the right to force his male or female slave to marry without obtaining their approval" (Vol. 2, p. 155).

Ibn Hazm says that Sufyan al-Thawri, too, has said that the master has the right to force his male or female slave to marry without securing their approval (Vol. 6, Part 9, p. 469). Ibn Timiyya is of the same opinion.

I must not fail in this regard to mention that Malik Ibn Ons, who (after agreeing with the other scholars that the master has the right to force his male or female slave to get married) added,

> "The master does not have the right to force the female slave to wed to an ugly black slave if she is beautiful and agile, unless in case of utmost necessity" (refer to Ibn Hazm, Vol. 6, Part 9, p. 469).

We wonder here, what did Malik Ibn Anas mean when he said, "**An ugly black slave**"? Is a man valued on the basis of the color of his skin? Do you say that, O Malik Ibn Anas, and you are one of the great four legists? Or is a man valued on the basis of his personality, reasoning, and heart? We also have the right to wonder why **Mihran, the black slave**, suffered the humiliation afflicted on him by Muhammad and his companions when they made him carry their belongings in the burning desert while Muhammad was saying to him, "Carry them, for you are a ship." Thus he became known by that surname. Did they not have dozens of other slaves?

Muhammad even discriminated (in Islam) between a black dog and a white dog. Yet, what concerns us here is what I pointed out about slaves in general, their masters treat them as if they are not human beings who have feelings, desires and self-will.

Let us continue our discussion in order to have a more complete picture about how the Islamic religion abuses the dignity of men and women under the pretense that they are slaves and not free human beings.

3. The Arab freeman does not marry a slave unless it is inevitable:

In Vol. 31, p. 383, Ibn Timiyya says,

"It is not permissible for the Arab freeman to marry an owned slave unless it is inevitable, such as being unable to get married to a free woman. If it happened, and he were wed to a slave, her children would be slaves, too, because they follow (the status) of the mother in slavery."

Malik Ibn Anas notes,

"It is not allowable for a man to wed a slave besides his free woman wife. In this case, his wife has the right to divorce him. Likewise, if he marries a free woman while he is already married to a slave, and he fails to tell her so, the free woman has the right to leave him" (Malik, Vol. 2, p. 204).

I do not have any comment on these strange principles, yet I wonder why an Arab freeman cannot marry a slave. Is not he a man and she a woman? And why (if it is inevitable that he should marry her) should all her descendants be slaves? These are iniquitous and ruthless ordinances. It is obvious that Muhammad **failed to change the traditions of the tribal society** of the pre-Islamic period. Most Arab Muslims had slaves. His companions, wives, and he himself, owned and retained dozens of them. He bought more after he claimed his prophethood and declared his message—the message of equality, and freedom, and human rights.

What Would Happen If A Free woman Married Her Slave?

She might be an open-minded woman who did not discriminate between one man and another. Thus she might have fallen in love with her slave, who also loved her, and they intended, officially, to get married. What is the attitude of Islam in this case? If something like that took place in Islamic society, it would be a disaster. Let us see the reaction of Umar Ibn Khattab in these situations. In Vol. 8, Part 11, pp. 248, 249, Ibn Hazm remarks,

"A woman was wed to her male slave. Umar intended **to stone her**, but instead he made them separate and sent the slave to exile. He told the woman, 'It is unlawful for you to get married to your owned slave!' Another woman got married to her slave. Umar **scourged her** with a whip and **forbade any man to marry her**. Another time, a free woman came to Umar and told him, 'I am not a pretty woman and I have a slave to whom I would like to get married.' Umar refused to do so. He **whipped the slave** and ordered him to be sold in a foreign country. He told the woman, 'It is unlawful for you to get married to what your right hand owns. Only men have the right to get wed to what their right hand owns. Even if you set him free in order to marry him, and he becomes a free man, the manumission will be invalid and the marriage is not valid.'"

Is there any comment on the ruthlessness of this second caliph, who was Muhammad's father-in-law, and one of the ten to whom Muhammad promised paradise? He is one of the two whom Muhammad requested the people to follow as a model when he declared, "Emulate Abu Bakr and Umar." Yet Umar was a tyrant, a ruthless man without a heart, who attempted to stone a woman for no reason except she married a man who was her slave. He also scourged another woman, forbidding any other man to marry her, and beat and exiled a slave. And when a third woman wanted to free her slave in order to marry him and live happily together, especially after she lost hope in getting married to a freeman, Islam and Umar intervened and said, "No, this is not permissible." He scourged the slave and sold him into a foreign country. By that, he became an example of relentlessness, a hard heart, and detestable oppression.

In matters of sex and marriage, Ibn Timiyya states:

"The one who owns the mother also owns her children. Being the master of the mother makes him the owner of her children whether they were born to a husband or they were illegitimate children. Therefore, **the master has the**

right to have sexual intercourse with the daughters of his maid-slave because they are his property, provided he does not sleep with the mother at the same time" (Vol. 35, p. 54).

The Value Of The Slave—What Is His Price In Dinars?

"If an owned slave assaults somebody and damages his property, his crime will be tied to his neck. It will be said to his master, 'If you wish, you can pay the fine for the damages done by your slave or deliver him to be sentenced to death.' His master has to choose one of the two options—either the value of the slave and his price, or the damage the slave has caused" (Vol. 32, p. 202, Ibn Timiyya).

Is this how the value of a man is calculated? If the loss amounted, for example, to 600 dinars and the value of the slave, in the estimation of the master, did not exceed more than 400 dinars because he was sick or weak, his master would, in this case, deliver him to be killed.

We have looked at six points concerning the status of slaves in the Islamic religion. Actually, any one point, if we ponder it, is sufficient to clarify the truth. It reveals to us how human dignity is crushed in the practice of slavery. From the very beginning, we referred to the principle of slavery as it is manifested in this religion, and we have listed the names of Muhammad's slaves, the master and the "apostle of God!"

The Position of Christianity—the Teaching of the Gospel

Christianity is very decisive in this matter. The words and the spirit of the Gospel are very clear. From the very beginning, we have used a fundamental principle in this study and research; namely, the comparison must always be between the Gospel and the Qur'an—Christianity as religion and teachings, and Islam as religion, in order to see which one of the two reveals the thoughts of the true, living God. Also, the comparison should be between Muhammad, his life and his sayings on the one hand, and Christ, His life and teachings on the other.

If we were to find (for example) some Europeans or Americans who allowed themselves to acquire slaves, we should not blame Christianity for that because we must realize that the Gospel teaches something different. We see that Jesus and His disciples did not possess slaves.

We do blame Islam in this regard because Muhammad himself acquired male and female slaves by dozens. All his friends, his wives and most Muslims of his time and after, owned slaves. The Qur'an encourages that, and the scholars do not negate it. We blame Islamic thought and the behavior of Muhammad in regard to this matter and other issues recorded in the most authentic Islamic sources.

We should not, in any subject, dwell on the behavior of **some** Christians or **some** Muslims but rather try to examine the attitude of Islamic thought (or Christian thought) toward the issues under discussion. Some people, for instance, believe that a man like Khomeini is an extremist because of Islam, the religion of tolerance, love, and reason. We, for our part, feel surprised to hear that, because who says that this statement is true? Islam is not the religion of tolerance, love, or reason. Not at all! Islam is the exact opposite of this claim.

Did we not see that this religion humiliates and persecutes women and non-Muslims, as well as waging offensive wars and encouraging Muslims to kill apostates? Is Muhammad, who ordered the killing of a woman who insulted him, the prophet of tolerance? Why should we blame Khomeini when he issued an order to kill Rushdie? Does not Rushdie (according to the law of Islam and Muhammad, not the law of the United Nations) deserve death for attacking the Qur'an, Muhammad and his wives? Khomeini was never **radical**; he was always **a true student of Muhammad**. He intended to enforce the Islamic laws and to fight nations which do not comply with them—such as Iraq (even though Islam is its official religion).

When Muslims kill one another, it is because Muhammad's friends and disciples did so immediately after his death, each one of them trying to force his friend to go in the right way. Khomemi is a true Muslim who follows Muhammad and his friends. Thus, we hear about "exporting the Islamic revolution" to other countries. All these things are **compatible** with the views of Muhammad and the rightly guided Caliphs who succeeded him, such as Abu Bakr, Umar and Ali. When Khomeini slaughtered his opponents, he was following the footsteps of Ali, who killed the dissenters, like Talha, Al Zubair and Al Khwareg, even though they were faithful Muslims.

Now, what does the New Testament say about slaves? If we turn in the pages of the New Testament we read these verses:

> "There is neither Jew nor Greek, there is neither slave nor free, there is neither male nor female; for you are all one in Christ Jesus" (Gal. 3:28).

Christ was always warning his disciples, and all believers, from calling themselves masters. He said to them:

> "But you, do not be called 'Rabbi' [master]; for One is your Teacher [master], the Christ, and you are all brethren" (Matt. 23:8).

> "But he who is greatest among you shall be your servant. And whoever exalts himself will be abased (humbled); and he who humbles himself will be exalted" (Matt. 23:12).

By these last words, Christ has over turned all the feeble human standards—The "... greatest among you shall be your servant." How profound and deep are these wonderful words!

This truth is clearly taught in the New Testament by the guidance of the Holy Spirit. It happened that there was a slave called Onesimus who ran away from his master, Philemon.

Onesimus met the apostle Paul in Rome, and was converted to Christianity. Paul sent him back to Philemon with a very impressive letter which is included in the New Testament, and in which we read these shining words,

> "I am sending him back. You therefore receive him, that is, my own heart. Receive him ... no longer as a slave but ... as a beloved brother, ..., both in the flesh and in the Lord" (Chapter 1).

Paul, Peter and the rest of the disciples did not have the authority to abolish slavery within the Roman Empire. Paul was not one of the Roman governors, but a fugitive and a persecuted man. Later, he and most of the disciples were killed at the hands of the Romans, along with thousands of their Christian brothers. Muhammad and his successors were rulers and could have outlawed slavery. Instead, they retained it and kept their slaves.

In another letter, Paul urged the Christians to "give your servants what is just and fair" (Col. 4:1). The text emphasizes these two words—**brotherhood and justice**—because there is neither slave nor freeman, but all are one in Christ.

Egyptian history relates a story about a courageous man, who stood in front of his tyrannical rulers who mistreated people, and wondered in agony, "Why have you enslaved people whose mothers gave birth to them as free persons?" This brave man did not know that he was addressing multitudes of people across the ages, whether ruthless Westerners in Europe and America, or the prophet of Islam himself who failed to liberate the slaves because he himself had acquired dozens of them.

Christian religious leaders such as John Wesley, boldly condemned slavery in Europe, and sent strong messages to the rulers of Europe and America. They led the movement of slaves' liberation during the day of Abraham Lincoln. Now there are multiplied black men who hold various positions of honor and respect in America. They teach in colleges and universities. They sit on the bench of the courts of the land, even the Supreme

Court. They are freely elected to local, county, state and federal positions. They hold high military offices. They build their own fortunes with which they do as they wish. They freely marry and raise their families, **without fear.**

This is what Jesus taught—"There is no difference ...."

Section Three

The Veil of Divine Inspiration of the Qur'an

Our Muslim brothers believe that the Qur'an is the book of God and that it pre-existed with God from eternity. They believe God then revealed it to Muhammad by the arch-angel Gabriel on different occasions through the course of several years. This was Muhammad's claim, which he related to them. At first, Muhammad was not sure of this process; he was unsure and afraid to make such claims. Later, however, he became very sure.

For now, however, we would like to shed some light on the Qur'an and its contents, in order to reveal the amazing truth to our brethren, the Muslims, few of whom have read what the great authors of Islam have said about the Qur'an. They would also be very surprised to discover that Muhammad's companions, as well as the rightly guided Caliphs, said that some parts of the Qur'an were lost. Moreover, the Qur'an was subjected to perversion and alteration, and Muhammad's companions disagreed over some chapters of the Qur'an, some verses and their meanings. It is almost impossible for Muslims to imagine such things about their book which they dearly regard and respect. The sacred halo which encompasses the Qur'an must be dispelled and the veil which covers its face must be removed. If this disturbs and annoys Muslims, it will also help them to wake up from the slumber of their delusion, which does not benefit them at all, but rather hurts them instead Those who love the truth and would like to worship the only true God faithfully and truthfully, will be filled with real joy.

Chapter Six
Scientific Errors of the Qur'an

We will start by pointing out the Qur'an's scientific, historical, and grammatical errors, namely those which deviate from the well-known rules of Arabic grammar. Muslims believe that the distinctiveness of the Qur'an is found in the eloquence and excellence of the Arabic language in which it is written; thus, it is impossible for them to imagine that the language of the Qur'an is full of errors. First, however, we will be content to allude to three scientific errors pertaining to the sun, earth and the two phenomenon of thunder and lighting.

The Sun

In plain words, the Qur'an says that one of the righteous men of God's servants saw the sun set in a certain place of the earth—in particular a well full of water and mud. There, this man found some people. Let us read what is recorded in the Qur'an (chapter "the Cave", verse 86),

> "When he reached the setting place of the sun, he found it setting in a muddy spring and found a people thereabout. We said: 'O Dhul-Qarneyn! Either punish or show them kindness'" (Surah 18:86).

Lest I failed to understand what the Qur'an meant by these strange words, I referred to the famous students of the Qur'an as

171

well as to the ancient scholars. I discovered that all of them concurred with this rendering and said that Muhammad's friends inquired about the sunset and that he gave them that answer. All the scholars, such as the Baydawi, Jalalan, and Zamakhshari, confirm it. The Zamakhshari remarks in his book, "the Kashshaf",

> "Abu Dharr (one of Muhammad's close companions) was with Muhammad during the sunset. Muhammad asked him: 'Do you know, O Abu Dharr, where this sets?' He answered: 'God and His apostle know better.' Muhammad said: 'It sets in a spring of slimy water'" (3rd Edition, Volume 2 p. 743,1987).

In his book, "The Lights of Revelation" (p. 399), the Baydawi indicates,

> "The sun sets in a slimy spring; that is, a well which contains mud. Some of the readers of the Qur'an read it, '...a hot spring', thus the spring combines the two descriptions. It was said that Ibn 'Abbas found Mu'awiya reading it (as) hot. He told him, 'It is muddy.' Mu'awiya sent to Ka'b al-Ahbar and asked him, 'Where does the sun set?' He said in water and mud, and there were some people. So he agreed with the statement of ibn al-'Abbas. And there was a man who composed a few verses of poetry about the setting of the sun in the slimy spring."

The Jalalan (p. 251) says that the setting of the sun is in a well which contains a murky mud. We found the same interpretation and text in the Tabari's commentaries (p. 339), as well as in "Concise Interpretation of the Tabari" (p. 19 of part 2), in which he remarks that the well in which the sun sets "contains lime and murky mud".

These are the comments of the pillars of Islam and the intimate companions of Muhammad, such as ibn Abbas and Aba Dharr. Also it is obvious from the Qur'an (chapter 36:38) that the sun ran, then settled down. The verse says:

> "And the sun runs on into a resting place."

On page 585, the Baydawi says,

> "The sun runs in its course to a certain extent; then it stops. It is similar to the passenger's repose after he completes his journey" (refer also the book of al-Itqan by the Suyuti, p. 242).

This is the story of the setting of the sun in the well and its course as a passenger.

The Phenomena of Thunder and Lightning

It is common knowledge, as scientists teach, that thunder is a sound caused by the impact between electrical charges found in the clouds. Yet Muhammad, the prophet of Muslims, has a different opinion in this matter. He claims that the thunder and the lightning are two of God's angels—exactly like Gabriel.

In the Qur'an, there is a chapter under the title of "Thunder", in which it is recorded that the thunder praises God. We might think that it does not mean that literally, because thunder is not a living being—although, spiritually speaking, all of nature glorifies God. The expounders of the Qur'an and its chief scholars, however, insist that Muhammad said that the thunder is an angel exactly like the angel Gabriel. In his commentary (p. 329), the Baydawi comments on verse 13 of chapter of the Thunder,

> "Ibn 'Abbas asked the apostle of God about the thunder. He told him, 'It is an angel who is in charge of the cloud, who (carries) with him swindles of fire by which he drives the clouds.'"

In the commentary of the Jalalan (p. 206), we read about this verse:

> "The thunder is an angel in charge of the clouds, to drive them."

Not only ibn 'Abbas asked Muhammad about the essence of the thunder, but the Jews did, too. In the book, "al-Itqan", by Suyuti (part 4, p. 230), we read the following dialogue:

> "On the authority of Ibn 'Abbas, he said the Jews came to the prophet (peace be upon him) and said, 'Tell us about the thunder. What is it?' He told them: 'It is one of God's angels in charge of the clouds. He carries in his hand a swindle of fire by which he pricks the clouds to drive them to where God has ordered them.' They said to him, 'What is this sound that we hear?' He said: '(It is) his voice (The angel's voice).'"

The same incident—the question of the Jews and Muhammad's answer are mentioned by most scholars. Refer, for instance, to al-Sahih al-Musnad Min Asbab Nuzul al-Ayat (stories related to the verses of Qur'an, p. 11) and al-Kash-shaf by the Imam al-Kamakhshari (part 2, pp. 518, 519). He reiterates the same story and the same words of Muhammad. Thus, the incident is in vogue among all Muslim scholars, and the story and the dialogue between Muhammad and the Jews is well-known.

We have mentioned what the Baydawi, Jalalan, Zamakhshari, Suyuti, and ibn 'Abbas have said. We do not know (among the ancient scholars) any who are more famous than these. Concerning lighting, Muhammad affirms that it is an angel like the thunder and like Gabriel and Michael. On page 230 of the above references, Suyuti alludes to it. Also on page 68 of part 4 of the "Itqan", the Suyuti records for us the names of the angels, which are: "Gabriel, Michael, Harut, Marut, the Thunder and the Lightning, (He said) that the lightning has four faces."

The Suyuti listed all these under the sub-title, "The names of God's Angels". He also indicated that Muhammad said that the lightning is the tail end of an angel whose name is Rafael (refer to part 4, p. 230 of the Itqan).

The Earth

Several thousand years ago, the Holy Bible clearly recorded that the earth is round and that it is hung on nothing.

"It is He who sits above the circle of the earth" (Isa. 40:22).

"He stretches out the north over empty space; He hangs the earth on nothing" (Job 26:7).

Yet, the Qur'an challenges these established scientific facts. In many places, it alludes to the fact that the earth is flat and its mountains are like poles which create a balance so that the Earth does not tilt. Let us consider what the Qur'an says about the Earth:

In chapter 88:17,20, it is recorded,

"Will they not regard the camels how they are created...and the Earth how it is spread?"

In page 509, the Jalalan says,

"In his phrase, 'how it is spread', he denotes that the earth is flat. **All the scholars of Islamic law agree upon this. It is not round as the physicists claim.**"

The Qur'anic teaching is obvious from the comment of Jalalan that "the earth is flat and not round as the scientists claim". What made Jalal al-Din say so is that the Qur'an hints in many chapters that the earth is flat(refer to 19:6, 79:30, 18:7, and 21:30). Also the Qur'an indicates that:

"We have placed in the earth firm hills lest it quake so as not to sway and hurt people" (21:31).

Scholars who agree upon the meaning of this verse believe as the Jalalan states (pp. 270-271),

"God has founded firm mountains on earth lest it shake people."

On page 429, al-Baydawi says,

"God has made firm mountains on earth lest it sway
people and quake. He also made heaven as a ceiling and
kept it from falling down!"

The Zamakhshari agrees with the above authors and reiterates
the same words (refer to Zamakhshari part 3, p. 114).

In the Qur'an (chapter 50:7), we find another verse which
carries the same meaning,

"And the earth have we spread out, and have flung firm
hills therein" (Surah Qaf: 7).

This is accompanied by the same comment by the above
Muslim scholars (refer to Jalalan, p. 437; Baydawi, p. 686,
Tabari, p. 589, and Zamakhshari, part 4, p. 381). All of them
assure us that "if it were not for these unshakable mountains, the
earth would slip away."

Zamakhshari, the Baydawi and the Jalalan say: "God has built
heaven without pillars, but He placed unshakable mountains on
Earth, lest it tilt with people." Concerning chapter 50:7, the
Suyuti says that scholars indicate that "Qaf is a mountain which
encompasses the entire earth" (refer to Itqan, part 3, p. 29). Qaf
is an Arabic L like K.

These are the comments of the ancient Muslim scholars, word
for word. Even some Saudi scholars wrote a book a few years
ago to disprove the spherical aspect of the earth, and they
claimed that it is a myth, agreed with the above mentioned
scholars, and said we must believe the Qur'an and reject the
spherical aspect of the earth.

It is also well-known that the Qur'an proclaims that there are
seven earths—not just one (refer to the commentary of the
Jalalan, p. 476, al-Baydawi, p. 745 as they interpret chapter
61:12, Surah Divorce: 1 2).

It is very clear that the sun does not traverse the heaven and
set down in a murky, muddy well, or slimy water, or a place

which contains both of them, as the Baydawi, Zamakhshari, and the Qur'an remark.

Nor is the earth flat, and the mountains the pillars, and the towerings which prevent the earth from moving, as the Qur'an and the scholars said. Nor is there a mountain which encompasses the whole earth—nor are there seven earths.

Neither is the lightning an angel whose name is Rafael, nor is the thunder an angel. It never happened that the angel Gabriel inspired Muhammad to write a complete chapter about his friend, the angel thunder. The thunder and lightning are natural phenomena and not God's angels, like Michael and Gabriel, as the prophet of Islam claims.

Chapter Seven
Historical Errors of the Qur'an

Historical errors are so many in the Qur'an that we cannot cover them all, but we will be content to point out some very obvious examples:

The Crucifixion of Christ

The Qur'an explicitly denies that Jesus was crucified. It claims that the Jews became so confused that they crucified somebody else instead who had the likeness of Christ. It is recorded in the Qur'an 4:15,

> "They slew him not, nor crucified, but it appeared so unto them."

In his commentary on this verse the Baydawi said (p. 135),

> "A group of Jews cursed Christ and his mother. He invoked evil on them and, may He be exalted, turned them into monkeys and swine. The Jews gathered together to kill him, but God, may He be exalted, informed him (Jesus) that He was going to lift him up to heaven. Thus, (Jesus) said to his companions, 'Who would like to have my likeness cast on him, and be killed and crucified, then enter the paradise?' One of them volunteered (to do so), and God cast on him Christ's likeness. He was then arrested, crucified and killed. It is also said that (the

crucified one) was a traitor who went with the mob to
guide them to Christ (he meant Judas), thus God cast on
him the likeness of Jesus, and he was arrested, crucified
and killed."

The Baydawi is not the only one who records these mystical
stories, but all Muslim scholars who attempt to interpret the
above verse, plainly state that Jesus was not crucified. The
Qur'an has ignored not only the records of Matthew, Mark,
Luke, and John, and the rest of the New Testament, but also all
the chroniclers from every race. It ignores the history of the
Roman Empire, which documented that a Jewish man by the
name of Jesus was crucified during the time of Pilate the
Pontius, the Roman Governor who gave way to the demands of
the chief priests of the Jews.

It is well known that Christ's trial took place in front of the
chief priests and the Roman Governor. It is also common
knowledge that the arrested man did not remonstrate and say, "I
am not Christ, I am Judas who wanted to betray Him and give
Him away to you." All Jesus' words on the cross denote that He
was Christ, especially His statement, "Father, forgive them, for
they do not know what they do" (Luke 23:34).

Jesus Himself told His disciples that He must be delivered to
the chief priests and be crucified; then He would rise from the
dead on the third day. Christ Himself foretold that, and the
crucifixion was fulfilled according to the many prophecies
recorded in the Old Testament, which predicted His crucifixion
centuries before. Christ came to accomplish God's plan for
man's salvation.

Therefore, it is not reasonable that six hundred years after
Christ's crucifixion, a man should appear and declare to the
world (ignoring all the historical evidence) that the one who was
crucified was not Christ. This is similar to a man who comes
hundreds of years from now to tell us that the one who was
assassinated in the twentieth century was not Martin Luther King
(or John F. Kennedy or Zia al-Haqq) but rather someone else

who looked like him. Of course, nobody would believe him, even if he claimed that the angel Gabriel (or the thunder angel) revealed it to him.

The Virgin Mary

In many places, the Qur'an mentions Mary as the sister of Moses and Aaron, and the daughter of Imran. The Qur'an has confused Jesus' mother with Aaron's sister because both of them carry the same name, though there are several centuries between them. The Qur'an indicates that Mary (Christ's mother) had a brother whose name was Aaron (chapter 19:28), and a father whose name is Imran (chapter 66:12). Their mother was called "the wife of Imran" (chapter 3:35), which eliminates any doubt that it confuses Mary, mother of Jesus, with Mary, sister of Aaron.

Muslim scholars acknowledge what happened, and they are confused and fail in their desperate attempts to justify this grave error. Their contradictory interpretations fail to help them to find a solution to this dilemma. Let us examine these interpretations to see these conflicting views.

In the context of his comment on the Qur'anic statement that Mary is Aaron's sister (which is recorded in chapter 19:28), the Baydawi (p. 405)said,

> "Oh, sister of Aaron (the prophet). And she was an offspring of some of those who were with him who belonged to the same class of brotherhood. It was also said that she was one of Aaron's descendants though there were a thousand years between them. It was said too, that he (Aaron) was a righteous or a wicked man who lived during their time (time of Mary). They likened her to him , to ridicule her or to insult her."

Yet Baydawi's statement is repealed by the Qur'an because the Qur'an did not refer to a moral relationship but stressed the literal meaning. If the Qur'an had meant to elevate Mary to the same level of Aaron, the prophet, or to the status of a daughter of Imran, why then did it mention that her mother was the wife of Imran, as it is recorded in chapter 3:35? It is very obvious that the matter was either confused in the mind of Muhammad or of Gabriel, the angel. It is not acceptable that the Qur'an intended to say that Mary enjoys the same status as a sister of Aaron and a daughter of Imran. Therefore, it is impossible to treat Mary (the mother of Jesus) as if she were the sister of Aaron and Moses.

The contemporary scholar who translated the Qur'an, which was authorized by the Saudi authorities, said (in the introduction of page 47 of chapter of the Family of Imran),

"Al Imran takes its title from v. 32, where 'the family of Imran' (the father of Moses) occurs as a generic name for all the Hebrew prophets from Moses to John the Baptist and Jesus Christ. This with the mention of the mother of Mary as 'the wife of Imran' (v. 34) and the words 'sister of Aaron' addressed to Mary (XIX.28) have given rise to a charge of anachronism. **Some say that the prophet confused Mary, the mother of Jesus, with Mary, the sister of Moses.** Most Muslims believe (on the authority of the Qur'an) that the grandfather of Jesus Christ was named 'Imran' which may also have been the name of the father of Moses. In Surah XIX 28, where Mary is addressed as 'sister of Aaron', they hold the ancestral sense to be the more probable, **while denying that there is any reason to suppose that the virgin Mary had not a brother named Aaron."**

Thus, they fail to explain to us why the Qur'an said that the mother of Mary was the wife of Imran, especially if the Qur'an intended (as they say) to show the moral relationship only. It is an obvious historical mistake, my dear reader, because Mary had no brother named Aaron.

Alexander the Great

It is amazing to see the Qur'an talking about Alexander the Great as if he were a righteous man and a teacher, though it is well-known that the Greek, Alexander, was idolatrous and claimed to be the son of Amun, the God of Egypt. If the reader wonders where it is recorded in the Qur'an that Alexander was a righteous man, we would refer him to the chapter of the Cave 18:83-98 where we encounter sixteen verses which talk about this military general. These verses explicitly say that God assisted him, guided him, and removed all obstacles from his way, in order that he could accomplish his plans and fulfill his desires. They indicate that Alexander was the one who reached the place of the sunset and found it set down in a well of water and mud. They claim that he encountered some people and God gave him the option to torment them, to kill them or to take them captive, call them to the faith and to lead them in a straight path.

These comments are expressed by all the scholars without any exception (refer to Baydawi, p. 399, al-Jalalan, p. 25 1, al-Tabari, p. 339, al-Zamakhshari, part 2 of al-Kash-shaf, p. 743). If we do not refer to these great expounders of the Qur'an, to whom, then, shall we refer? The Greek Alexander was not a righteous servant of God as the Qur'an said, but he was a licentious, belligerent, idolatrous man. He did not have any relationship with God, and God never asked him to guide people and to teach them the faith.

Other Historical Errors

Does the reader believe that Abraham did not offer Isaac, but **Ishmael**, as a sacrifice? This is what all Muslim scholars say. Do you know that the Qur'an claims that Haman was **pharaoh's prime minister,** even though Haman lived in Babylon one thousand years later? Yet the Qur'an says so. The Qur'an says that the one who picked Moses from the river was not his sister, but **his mother** (28:6-8), and that a **Samaritan** was the one who molded the golden calf for the children of Israel and misguided them, and the **golden calf was lowing** (refer to chapter 20:85-88), though it is well-known that Samaria was not in existence at that time. The Samaritans came after the Babylonian exile. How could one of them have made the golden calf for the people of Israel?

Concerning the birth of Christ, the Qur'an teaches that the Virgin Mary gave birth to him under the shade of a **palm tree** and not in a manger of sheep (refer to Mary 19:23). The Qur'an **ignores all the documented historical evidence,** available to all people across the ages, and brings us new discoveries.

The Qur'an claims (Chapter 2:125-127) that Abraham and Ishmael, his son, are the ones who built The Ka'ba in Mecca, in Saudi Arabia. This claim made the late Dr. Taha Husayn (the most famous professor of Arabic literature in Egypt)acknowledge that the information recorded in the Qur'an pertaining to the construction of Ka'ba at the hand of Abraham and Ishmael is not historically documented. He said:

> "The case of this episode is very obvious because it is of recent date and came into vogue just before the rise of Islam. Islam exploited it for religious reasons" (quoted in Mizan al-Islam by Anwar al-Jundi, p. 170).

This declaration invoked the rage of the Muslim scholars against him. The former president of Tunisia did the same thing when he stated that the Qur'an contains mythical stories. Muslim scholars revolted against him and threatened to kill him because these are Muhammad's orders—kill anybody who insults the Qur'an. So what could Taha Husayn or Abu Raqiba (or we) do if the Qur'an rejects the most scientifically documented historical stories? Are we supposed to shut up our mouth and close our minds lest we be killed?

Chapter Eight
Qur'anic Language and Grammatical Mistakes

Our Muslim brethren say that the eloquence of the Qur'an, the supremacy of its language and the beauty of its expression, are conclusive evidence that the Qur'an is the Word of God, because the distinctiveness of the Qur'an lies in its beautiful style of the Arabic language. We acknowledge that the Qur'an (in some of its parts and chapters) has been written in an eloquent style and impressive words. This fact is beyond any doubt and anyone who denies that does not have any taste for the Arabic language. Yet, on the other hand, we say that there are many clear language errors in other parts of the Qur'an pertaining to the simplest principles of style, literary expression, and the well-known grammatical rules of the Arabic language and its expression.

We even find in the Qur'an many words which do not have any meaning and are not found in any language. There is also a great deal of vocabulary which no one can understand. Muhammad's companions themselves have acknowledged that, as we will see; but before we examine all these issues, I would like to clarify two important points.

First, from a linguistic point of view, the eloquence of any book cannot be an evidence of the greatness of the book and proof that it was revealed by God, because what is important to

185

God is not to manifest His power in the eloquence of style and the expressive forcefulness of the classical Arabic language, but rather, to embody His power in the sublime spiritual meaning contained in that book which will lead the people to a high spiritual level which enables them to live together in peace and love. It helps them to enjoy an internal, profound joy and spiritual, psychological fullness—abundant life. God does not care to teach the people of the Earth the rules and the principles of the Arabic language. God is not a teacher of a fading classical Arabic language; but the true living God is our spiritual leader in life of love and joy.

Is the content of the Qur'an properly fit to be ascribed to God? All that we intend to do here is to determine that eloquence of style is not always an evidence that the words uttered come from heaven or that the one who has spoken them is a prophet. The German poet Schiller is not a prophet, and the Iliad and the Odessa are not composed by a prophet, but rather by a Greek poet. The masterpieces of Shakespeare's poems and plays in English literature, which are translated and published more than the Qur'an by ten fold, have not compelled the British to say that the angel Gabriel is the one who revealed them to Shakespeare.

The **second** very significant point is that the eloquence of the Qur'an and the supremacy of the classical Arabic language in which the Qur'an is written have created difficulty in reading and understanding, even for the Arabs themselves. So what would we say about the non-Arabs even if they learn the Arabic language? The Qur'an will continue to be a problem for them, because it is not sufficient for a person to learn the Arabic language to be able to read the Qur'an. He also has to study the literature of the Arabic language thoroughly. Thus, we find that the majority of Arabs themselves do not understand the classical language of the Qur'an, which contains hundreds of words which confused Muhammad's companions who mastered the language but failed to explain their meanings, along with many other words which even Muhammad's companions could not comprehend.

Jalal al-Din al-Suyuti composed at least **one hundred pages** in part II of his famous book, "The Itqan", to explain the difficult words included in the chapters of the Qur'an, under the title "The Foreign words of the Qur'an". The vocabulary of the classical Arabic language and some of its expressions are not in use anymore among the Arabs. The language itself was so diversified that the Shafi'i was led to say, "No one can have a comprehensive knowledge of the language except a prophet" (Itqan II: p 106).

The question which imposes itself on us is: What advantage do the people of the world get out of the Book of God if it is written in a difficult language which makes it impossible for Arabs (even Muhammad's companions and his relatives) to comprehend it? Does God write a book in which people do not comprehend the meaning of many words included in the text, especially when the scholars insist that the Qur'an must be read only in Arabic? In his book al-Itqan, Al Suyuti says,

> "It is utterly inadmissible for the Qur'an to be read in languages other than Arabic, whether the reader masters the language or not, during the prayer time or at other times, lest the inimitability of the Qur'an is lost. On the authority of the Qaffal (one of the most famous scholars of jurisprudence, fundamentals and exposition), reading the Qur'an in Persian cannot be imagined. But it was said to him, 'Then no one will be able to interpret the Qur'an.' He said, 'It is not so, because he will bring forth some of God's purposes and will fail to reveal others, but if somebody wants to read it in Persian, he will never bring forth (any) of God's purposes.'"

This is why non-Arabs repeat the Qur'anic text without understanding it, because they utter it in Arabic. The same words have been repeated in Dr. Shalabi's book (p. 97), "The History of Islamic Law". He also adds,

"If the Qur'an is translated into a non-Arabic language, it will lose its eloquent distinctiveness. **The distinctiveness is intended for itself.** It is permissible to translate the meaning without being literal."

The same principle is followed by those who worked on the English authorized translation. They said (page iii),

"The Qur'an cannot be translated—that is the belief of traditional Sheikhs (religious leaders). The Arabic Qur'an is an distinctiveness symphony, the very sounds of which move men to tears and ecstasy."

This is true. If the Qur'an were translated literally into English, for example, it would lose its linguistic beauty, and could not then be compared to any other book in English, French, or German literature. In addition, a person might wonder how the many incomprehensible Arabic words could be translated.

The other question which confronts us is this, Does God belong to the Arabs only? If His book can only be in Arabic, then it is written only to the Arabs, and it should not be read except in Arabic as the scholars claim, as if God were an Arabic God. Thus, the scholars prohibit praying to God in any other language than Arabic in all mosques. It is also required that the call for prayers and the confession of faith, which attests that the man is a Muslim, must be uttered in Arabic, because Muhammad (the prophet of Islam) said that Arabic is the language of paradise and the Arabs are the best nation created among peoples.

Among the famous prophetic traditions which Muhammad said to the Muslims is, "Love the Arabs for three (things): Because I am an Arab, the Qur'an is in Arabic and the language of the people of the paradise is Arabic" (refer to al-Mustadrak by the Hakim, and Fayd al-Ghadir).

Let us now examine the failure of the Arabic language in which the Qur'an is written, and limit ourselves to the following points:

The Original Qur'anic Text Was Without Diacritical Points, Vocalization, And Some Of Its Letters Are Omitted.

We will attempt to explain this problem to the English reader as plainly as possible. We hope he will find it exciting and interesting. The Arabic reader knows fairly well that the meanings of the words require the use of diacritical points above or below the letters, otherwise it becomes very difficult (if not impossible) to comprehend their meanings. Vocalization also is very significant in the field of desinential inflection, along with writing all the letters of the word without omitting any of them. Thus, the reader of the Arabic language cannot believe or imagine that the Qur'an was written originally without these significant requirements; but let us assure you that this is a historical fact, well-known and acknowledged by all Muslim scholars, without any exception.

We will also see that there is a large number of words about which the scholars could not agree as to their meanings. One simple example helps us to visualize the nature of the problem. Let us take the Arabic letter "ba". By changing the diacritical points, we get three different letters—"ta", "ba", and "tha". So when these letters are written without the diacritical points, it becomes difficult for the reader to know the word that is intended.

Examine the following words. Look thoroughly at the diacritical points (I repent), (plant), (house), (girl) (abided). Another example (rich), (stupid), and so on. Without these diacritical points it is very hard to distinguish the words from each other. Thus, the meaning differs from one word to another depending on the place of these diacritical points. Many of the

Arabic alphabets require the presence of the diacritical point to differentiate between one alphabet and another, and hence, between one word and another.

Now let us quote the Muslim scholars who have the final word in these matters.

1) In his famous book, "The History of Islamic Law" (p.43), Dr. Ahmad Shalabi, professor of Islamic history and civilization remarks,

> "The Qur'an was written in the **Kufi script without diacritical points**, vocalization or literary productions. No distinction was made between such words as 'slaves', 'a slave', and 'at' or 'to have', or between 'to trick' and 'to deceive each other', or between 'to investigate' or 'to make sure'. Because of the Arab skill in Arabic language, their reading was precise. Later, when non-Arabs embraced Islam, errors began to appear in the reading of the Qur'an when those non-Arabs and other Arabs whose language was corrupted, read it. The incorrect reading changed the meaning sometimes."

The same statement is made by Taha Husayn in "Taha Husayn" (p. 143), by Anwar al-Jundi.

Then, Dr. Ahmad alluded to those who invented the vocalization and diacritical points and applied them to the Qur'anic text many years after Muhammad's death, such as Abu al-Aswad al Du'ali, Nasr ibn 'Asim and al-Khalil ibn Ahmad. He also added (on the same page) that "without these diacritical points, a man would believe that verse 3 of the chapter, 'The Repentance', would mean that **God is done with the idolaters and His apostle**— free from obligation to the idolaters and His apostle—while the real meaning of the verse is that **God and His apostle are done with the idolaters**—free from further obligation to the idolaters.

Now the question we would like to ask Dr. Ahmad and all those wise men: Why was not the Qur'an revealed to

Muhammad in a perfect Arabic language, complete with the literary indicators and the diacritical points, lest a difference or change of meaning occur? If a student of Arabic writes an essay in Arabic without the diacritical points, would the teacher give him more than zero? The answer is known to two hundred million Arabs.

The second question is: Did God inspire those who added the diacritical points and the vocalization through an angel, for example, to eliminate the different meanings on which the scholars disagree? Who instructed Nasr ibn 'Asim, Abu al-Aswad al Du'ali and Khalil ibn Ahmad to undertake this serious task and create the diacritical points and the vocalization for the Qur'anic text? Was it not more appropriate that Muhammad himself or some of his successors or companions like ibn 'Abbas and ibn Mas'ud should accomplish this work? Yet al-Suyuti himself tells us that ibn Mas'ud was not pleased with that (refer to "Itqan", part 2, p. 160), nor were other leading companions and scholars such as ibn Sirin and the Nakha'i.

2) Ibn Timiyya, Sheik of the Muslims (vol. XII, p. 101), tells us,

> "The companions of Muhammad had never used the diacritical points or the vocalization for the Qur'an. For each word, there were two readings—either to use (for instance) 'ya' or 'tah' in such words as 'they do' or 'you do'. The companion did not forbid one of the readings in favor of the other; then some successor of the companions began to use the diacritical points and vocalization for the Qur'an."

On pp. 576 and 586, he adds,

> "The companions (Muhammad's friends) did not vocalize or provide diacritical points for the letters of the Qur'anic copies which they wrote; but later during the last part of the companions' era, when reading errors came into being, they began to provide diacritical points for the copies of the Qur'an, and to vocalize them. This was admissible by

the authority of the majority of the scholars, though some of them disliked it. The truth is, it should not be disliked because the situation necessitated it, and the diacritical points distinguish the letters from each other, while vocalization explains the grammatical inflection."

There is a candid acknowledgment from ibn Timiyya that diacritical points are required; but did not God and His angel Gabriel along with Muhammad and his successors know about this problem? The simplest principles of sound Arabic language demand that words should have diacritical points and their letters should be written in complete form. Didn't they know that disagreements among Muslim scholars would take place and that they would fight among themselves, and that even death would result from the differences in reading the Qur'anic text? Didn't they know also that the differences in meaning of the Qur'anic vocabulary would be decisive in the interpretation and judgments of Islamic law?

It is surprising that such things had not occurred to the mind of God, Gabriel, Muhammad, and the companions and the caliphs; then, three persons come later and insert these changes into the Qur'anic text. Yet, what is really more surprising is that when the companions discovered the differences in the readings of the Qur'anic text (as Ibn Timiyya says), they did not have any objection against any of the **different readings,** and they did not prohibit either one. The justification for that was that Muhammad himself had acknowledged the presence of seven different readings, not just two readings, as was clearly stated in the Sahih al-Bukhari, (vol. 6, p. 227). This fact is common knowledge among all the scholars.

3) Jalal-al-Din al-Suyuti

In his famous book, "al-Itqan Fi Ulum al-Qur'an" ("Adjusted Qur'anic Science"), al-Suyuti reiterates (part four, p. 160) the same words of ibn Timiyya which had been quoted by Dr. Ahmad Shalabi about those who invented the diacritical points and the vocalization of the words. He also said that some of the scholars detested that, as we mentioned before. There the Suyuti presents (part four, pp. 156,157) a list of words which could be read differently. One of them is the reading by which the Qur'an was written, though Muhammad himself had accepted and acknowledged both readings.

In part one, p. 226 of "The Itqan", the Suyuti makes an important declaration in which he says that the **difference in reading has led to differences in Islamic law.** He illustrated that by the following example: He indicated that some scholars demanded of the worshipper that he wash himself again (the ablution) before he prays, if he shook hands with a woman. Yet other scholars require him to do so only in case of sexual intercourse and not just because he shook hands with her or touched her hand.

The reason for this disagreement is ascribed to **one word** found in the Chapter of Women (verse 43) and whether it has a long vowel a or not. The Jalalan (p. 70) and the Baydawi (p. 113) record for us that both ibn 'Umar and al-Shafi'i seriously disagree with ibn 'Abbas in the way they interpret this verse, because ibn 'Abbas insisted that the meaning intended here is actual intercourse while the former said no, it is enough for a man to touch the skin of a woman or her hand to require having his ablution (washing) repeated.

In four full pages (226-229), the Suyuti stated that the many arguments and various interpretations pertaining to the above word have brought about different ordinances. When we read the commentary of the Jalalan or the Baydawi, we realize that whenever they come across certain words which could be read in more than one form, they say: This word is read in two different forms.

Before concluding this part, let me call attention to the following everyday story: A man was asking about the place of two verses in the Qur'an. He was told that he could locate them in the Chapters of Resurrection and the Hypocrites. He made every effort to find these two chapters, but in vain. Then he was told that the Chapter of Resurrection is number 75 and the chapter of the Hypocrites is number 63. He told them that chapter 75 is named "The Value" and chapter 63 is named or called "The Spenders". They told him you say so because you read them without the letter A (long vowel A). His logical answer was: "I have read them in exactly the form in which they were written, without the long vowel A. Why should I add the long vowel A to the words of the Qur'an which would change the meaning?"

My dear English reader, have you recognized the purpose of the above paragraph? Is the word "reply" the same as "replay"? There are dozens of words like that in the Qur'an; even some of the titles of the Qur'anic chapters have been written without the long vowel A. For example, the word "masajid" (mosques) is written "masjid" (a mosque), and "sadaqat" (charities) as "sadaqta" (you said the truth). The meaning (as you see) has been completely changed, as Dr. Ahmad Shalabi and Suyuti remarked.

Meaningless Qur'anic words

All Muslim scholars acknowledge that the Qur'an contains words which even Muhammad's relatives and companions have failed to understand. In his book, "The Itqan" (part 2, p. 4), the Suyuti states clearly,

> "Muhammad's companions, who are genuine Arabs, eloquent in language, in whose dialect the Qur'an was given to them, have stopped short in front of some words and failed to know their meanings; thus they said nothing about them. When Abu Bakr was asked about the Qur'anic statement 'and fruits and fodder' (8:31), he said, 'What sky would cover me or what land would carry me if I say what I do not know about the book of God?' 'Umar ibn al-Khattab read the same text from the rostrum, then he said, 'This fruit we know, but what is fodder?' Sa'id

ibn Jubair was asked about the Qur'anic text in chapter 13 of Mary. He said, 'I asked ibn 'Abbas about it, but he kept silent.'"

Then the Suyuti indicated that ibn 'Abbas said that he does not know the meanings of some of the Qur'anic verses (like these in Chapter 69:36, 9:114 and 18:9).

I have quoted the Suyuti's text word for word, and stated the confession of ibn 'Abbas, who is interpreter of the Qur'an and legal jurist of the caliphs, for whom Muhammad pleaded with God to enlighten his mind to comprehend the meaning of the Qur'an. Also, who was closer to Muhammad, my dear Muslim, than Abu Bakr and Umar, the first two caliphs, along with ibn 'Abbas? All of them failed to comprehend many of the Qur'anic verses. Therefore, the Suyuti warns that anyone who attempts to conceive the meanings of these words will suffer complete failure. Then he mentions that the caliphs and ibn 'Abbas, themselves, did not know their meanings.

Of course, he was right, because if those great leaders had failed to know their meanings, who would? Certainly, those intimate companions of Muhammad asked him about the meanings of those obscure words; but it is clear enough that Muhammad himself failed to know their meanings. Otherwise he would have explained them to his companions, as he did on several other occasions.

In addition to these ambiguous words, there are at least 14 other words or symbols which are recorded at the introductory part of 29 Qur'anic chapter. These codes are entirely ambiguous. Also four of these codes are titles for four chapters; therefore, four Qur'anic chapters have meaningless titles. These chapters are chapter Taha, ya sin, Sad, and Qaf. When the Jalalan attempted to expound the meanings of these 14 obscure words and the titles of these chapters, they said, "God alone knows His own intention."

I am stating these words for the benefit of the reader as they are recorded in the authorized English translation of the Qur'an. "Aim-Alr-Almus-Hm" **means nothing in any language.** Is it a characteristic of Arabic eloquence to have meaningless words and titles of complete chapters which no body can comprehend?

The Qur'an says woe to anyone who asks for the meaning!

The Qur'an acknowledges that there are meaningless words. In chapter of Family of 'Umran: 7, it indicates that there are allegorical verses which "no one knoweth how to explain save God." The Qur'an does not tell us why these words have been recorded in the Qur'an if no one knows their meaning. In his book, "The Itqan" (part 3, p. 3), the Suyuti refers to the above verse, then he remarks,

> "The Qur'an is divided into sound, intelligible (verses) and obscure, unintelligible (verses). The obscure (verses) are only known to God, such as the detached alphabets at the beginning of the chapters."

On pp. 5 and 6, the Suyuti asserts that the majority of the companions and the successors of the companions, especially the Sunnis (among them ibn 'Abbas himself) affirm that there are words of which no one knows the interpretation save God only.

It is worthwhile mentioning here that anyone who attempted to comprehend the meaning of those words, or any of the obscured verses, was severely punished. On pp. 7 and 8 (part 3 of "The Itqan"), the Suyuti records for us a moving episode about a person called Sabigh who wanted to inquire about these same Qur'anic interpretations. 'Umar Ibn al-Khattab severely punished him on successive days until he was almost killed due to head injuries. This is "the just 'Umar", as they call him.

The Qur'an Gives The Antonym (opposite) Meaning Of Words And Phrases

This fact is well-known to all scholars. It clearly reveals that the Arabic language of the Qur'an is not always sound, as some believe. In the second part of "The Itqan", the Suyuti speaks explicitly about things which no one expected to find in the Qur'an. Actually, these defects are not supposed to occur in any standard Arabic book which complies with the rules and characteristics of the Arabic language. On page 135, the Suyuti says,

> "The word **'after'** has been mentioned twice in the Qur'an so as to mean **'before'**, as in this saying, 'We have written in the psalms (the scripture) "after the reminder" (21:105) while He meant "before."' Also in this saying, 'The earth "after" that He has extended (79:30) while he meant "before" and not "after", because the earth was created first "before" and not "after" He created the heavens,' as Abu Musa indicated."

These are the actual words of Suyuti. The question now is: Does this linguistic defect conform to any language in the world? Does this comply with the characteristics of writing and the artistic, eloquent style of Arabic language? Is it proper, in the Qur'anic style to write "after" when you mean "before"? How can the reader know the correct meaning since it is common knowledge that "after" and "before" are opposite words? Is it sensible that the angel Gabriel meant to say "before" but he instructed Muhammad to write "after"? It is difficult for us to believe that.

This problem is not confined to one word, because the Suyuti provides us with eight pages (Itqan, part 2, pp. 132-139) full of similar examples found in the Qur'an in which, according to the interpreters of the texts, the Qur'an meant the opposite meaning than the literal meaning of the expression. There is no connection between the literal meaning and the meaning intended by the Qur'an.

Let us examine together some of the examples the Suyuti presented to us in his book, the Itqan, part 2,

(A) "The Qur'an means, 'Do not those who believe **know** that had Allah willed, He could have guided all mankind', but he said, 'Do not those who believe **despair**!' instead of writing 'know' as he meant" (see Thunder: 31). Is "despair" the same as "know"?

B) "The Qur'an says in chapter 2:23, '... your martyrs', but it means here, ' ... your partners' (p. 133). After the Suyuti made this remark, he commented,

> "The martyr is supposed to be the person who is killed, or
> the one who testifies concerning people's matters, but here
> it means 'your partners.'"

C) "In chapter Joseph: 20 the word 'Bakhs' (too little) is meant to be 'haram' (forbidden, sacred), contrary to the usual meaning" (p. 132).

D) "In chapter Mariam (Mary):46 the phrase, 'I certainly will stone you', is interpreted to mean, 'I certainly will curse you', and not, 'I certainly will kill you,' as its literal meaning suggests" (p. 133).

Let the reader decide for himself as he examines these illustrations.

Why the Qur'an did not say: "Do not know those who believe.. " instead of "do not the believers give up all hope..." Is "despair" the same as knowledge? And if the Qur'an intended to say, "Did not ... know" would it be recorded as to mean "to give up all hope?" The same thing could be said about "too little" and "martyrs " Does not each word have a different meaning than the meaning indicated by the Qur'an? Is it one of the prerogatives of the language to use a word which has a different connotation than the intended meaning?

Let us state another illustration from "The Itqan" (part 3, p. 251) where the Suyuti says,

"In chapter the (Rahman):6, The Qur'an says: 'The "Nagm" stars and the trees bow themselves.' Here the Qur'an does not mean by 'the stars' the heavenly stars but the plants which do not have trunk. This is the far-fetched intended meaning."

We would like to state here that there is **no one** who would imagine or expect this meaning. Even the Saudi scholars who translated the Qur'an into English (p. 590) understood the word 'Nagm' ("star") to mean a heavenly star—and stated it as such. Thus, even the Saudi translators of the Qur'an could not imagine that the Qur'an has meant by the word "Nagm" ("star"), the plants which do not have trunks.

I, myself had some doubts about the Suyuti's explanation and thought maybe it was the Suyuti's fault and not the Qur'an's, or the Saudi scholars. Why should we attack the Qur'an and blame it for the Suyuti's error? Therefore, as a candid researcher, I decided to examine the interpretations of the former Muslim scholars to be sure of the proper interpretation. I referred to the Baydawi's commentary (p. 705) and found him in full harmony with the Suyuti's interpretation who, stressed that this word alludes to the plants which sprang from the earth without a trunk. The same interpretation, is found in the Jalalan (p. 450). In Al-Kash-shaf (part 4, p. 443), the Zamakh-Shari agreed with the mentioned scholars and remarks,

"And the 'star' which is a plant which springs from the earth without a trunk such as the herbs, for the trees do have trunks."

Thus, let the Saudi scholars correct the translation errors of the Qur'an, along with another error (as the Suyuti comprehended it), though they are right in their interpretation of it: The word "amid most" (chapter 2:143) means - according to Suyuti - righteous or just people (p. 251 also refer to the Baydawi p. 29 and Tabari 24). Thus Suyuti says,

"The conspicuous meaning of the word suggests the (idea) of intermediary, while **the intended meaning** is 'righteous' and this is the far-fetched meaning."

Another example in which the English translator was proper.

The Qur'an says in chapter 57:29: "Lest the people of the book may know." This is the literal translation of the phrase. The word means (in both Arabic and English) "lest" while the intended meaning is that they may know (refer to the commentary of Jalalan p. 459). The translators of the Qur'an correctly translated it as "**that** they may know," which is opposite to the literal meaning of the word in Arabic.

Yet, before we conclude the discussion of this point, I would like to share with the readers another strange phrase which illustrates the above mentioned point even more clearly.

In chapters 75: 1,2 and 90:1, the Qur'an repeats the phrase: "I do not swear..." This is the literal translation of the phrase, but the interpreters and the translators of the Qur'an insist that the meaning is: "I do call...," or "No, I swear" indicating that the word "do not" is redundant, and when He said, "I do not swear", he meant, "I swear" (refer to the Jalalan, p. 493, 511; Al-Kash-shaf, part 4, p. 658, 753; and Baydawi, pp. 772, 799). The Qur'an says,

"I do not swear by the Day of Resurrection"

"I do not swear by the reproachful soul"

"I do not swear by this city"

While he meant (according to all Muslim scholars) that He does swear by the above three things. The Zamakhshari noted that some had objected to that, and they have the right to object to this confusion, but others said that the pre-Islamic, great poet Emro Al-Qays used to do so.

In the Qur'an There Are Omitted Words, Incomplete Phrases, and Errors In The Structure Of Sentences

This is strange and unjustifiable. Why should many words or even completed phrases be omitted, confusing the meaning? In his book, "The Itqan", the Suyuti has discussed this matter and pointed to many omitted letters or words and sentences. He devoted ten pages of part 3, (pp. 181-192) to listing ample examples of which I quote but a few of them.

A) "We read in chapter (Surah) 22:32:

'It is from the piety of hearts.'

The Suyuti says it should have been written this way,

'Its glorification comes from the deeds of those of piety of hearts.'"

B) "Also, in chapter 20:96, the Qur'an says,

'So I took a handful (of dust) from the footprint of the apostle.'

The Suyuti says: It is supposed to be written as such:

'...from the footprint of the hoof of the apostle's mare'" (refer to p. 191)

C) Among the many striking examples of the omission of various sentences is what we read in chapter 8:45,46. The Suyuti comments in p. 192,

"The verse: 'Send ye me oh righteous Joseph...' **means,** 'Send ye me to Joseph to ask him for the interpretation of the dream.' So he did. He came to him and said, 'O, righteous Joseph....'"

In the Qur'an just two words at the beginning are written and two words at the end, and all the words in-between are omitted.

Let the reader decide for himself if it is possible to comprehend the intended meaning, having all these words omitted from the verse until it becomes entirely meaningless.

Other Language Errors In Sentence Structure

It is appropriate to refer to Muslim scholars when a person wants to study and comprehend the Qur'an. They are well acquainted with the principles of the Arabic language and the Qur'an. There is none better than the Suyuti, Baydawi, Tabari, Jalalan, and Zamakh-Shari, who are great, recognized scholars and linguists quoted by the Azhar scholars in Egypt, as well as the Saudi scholars. The American, European and Orientalist, with all due respect, do not understand the Qur'anic language like those great Muslim scholars. The Suyuti (part 3, p. 33), quoting several great Muslim scholars, says,

> "The Qur'anic verse: 'Let not their wealth nor their children astonish thee! Allah purposeth only to punish them in the world' (chapter 9:85). It actually means: 'Let not their properties and children astonish you on this Earth because God purposes to torment them in eternity.'"

Let the reader notice that there is no mention of eternity in the verse. In pp. 34 and 35, the Suyuti remarks:

> "The intended original word order of (the Qur'anic) text: 'Have you seen the one who made his God (the object of) his compassion?' (25:34) is to be read, '... who made his compassion his God' and not, '... his God (the object of) his compassion', because 'who made his God (the object) of his compassion' is not blameworthy."

In page 328, the Suyuti says that,

> "There are many verses in the Qur'an which were revealed without any connection to the verses which proceeded or preceded them, such as what we read in chapter 75:13-19, because the entire chapter talks about the states of resurrection. But these verses were revealed

because Muhammad used to hastily move his tongue when dictating the Qur'anic revelation. Some Muslims said that part of the chapter has been dropped, because these verses are not relevant to this chapter at all."

We conclude our discussion of this part by pointing to the boring repetition of certain phrases by which the Qur'an is characterized. The phrase, "O which of your Lord's bounties will you deny?" is repeated thirty-one times in a chapter in which there are no more than 78 verses (chapter 75). The story of Noah is repeated in 12 chapters. Abraham's story is repeated in 8 chapters, along with the episode of Lot. Moses' story is repeated in 7 chapters, Adam's in 4 chapters, and John's in 4 chapters. Moses' conversation with pharaoh is repeated in 12 chapters. Certainly these stories differ drastically from the stories recorded in the Old Testament.

There are approximately 15-20 grammatical errors found in the Qur'an, which cannot be denied by those who master Arabic grammar. This has created a heated argument because these grammatical errors are not expected in a book which Muslims claim is dictated by God and its distinctness lies in its perfect Arabic language. Thus, how can the Qur'an include grammatical mistakes which a junior high school student who has a basic background in Arabic would not make? If anyone of the Arab readers wishes to expand his knowledge of these errors, we would like to refer him to the following Qur'anic verses: Chapters 2:177; 3:39; 4:162; 5:69; 7:16; 20:63; 21:3; 22:19; 49:9 and 63:10. As an illustration, we refer to one example which is found in chapter 20:63. The Qur'an says,

> "These two are certainly magicians"—Inna Hazan Sahiran. The correct grammar must say, Inna **Hazyn** Sahiran.

According to Arabic grammar, these two **must be** in the accusative case after "Inna", but they are stated in the nominative case which is completely wrong.

Chapter Nine
Capricious Revelation of the Qur'an

The Qur'anic verses were revealed according to the caprices of Muhammad, his companions and his wives.

Muslim scholars believe that knowing the reasons for the revelation of the Qur'anic verses is very important and indispensable in comprehending the verses. The Suyuti wrote a full book concerning this fact. He called it, "The Core of Transmitted Traditions for the Reasons for the Revelations". In the book, "the Itqan" (part I, p. 82), he explains the significance of this matter to the greatest Muslim scholars, as it is the basis for understanding various verses which have been revealed after a certain incident or after a question was directed to Muhammad.

The Suyuti recorded for us several examples to prove that it was impossible to understand some verses unless the reasons for their revelation were known. This fact is confirmed not only by the former scholars but also by the Azhar and contemporary scholars (refer, for example, to Ahmad Shalabi's book, "The History of Islamic Law" (p. 36) and the "Legal Opinion" of Sheikh Kishk).

In the next few pages, we are going to discuss only two issues. First, we look at how the angel Gabriel used to comply immediately with the wishes of Muhammad's companions and his wives who used to instruct God and His Angel in what verses

205

He must reveal to Muhammad. 'Umar ibn al-Khattab played an outstanding role in this area.

Secondly, a throng of verses have been revealed for worthless reasons which do not interest anybody.

There is a third issue which we will study in another chapter, in which we will see how the angel Gabriel used to comply with Muhammad's personal desires and fulfill all his wishes, even if these wishes did not conform to the simplest principle of chastity, purity, and mercy. Even his wife 'Aisha told him: " I see that your Lord hastes to comply with your passion, O Muhammad," as the Bukhari record in his Sahih, part 6, p. 147.

The Angel Gabriel Complies With The Wishes Of Muhammad's Companions

We have already mentioned that 'Umar ibn al-Khattab played a major role in the revelation which descended upon Muhammad This is the claim of 'Umar and the scholars and not the claim of the author of this book. Whenever 'Umar wanted something, Muhammad answered, "Yes, God has already sent Gabriel who revealed to me this matter which 'Umar had requested" Even the inspiration, sometimes, was revealed using the same words and vocabulary of 'Umar. Thus, ibn 'Umar said, as the Suyuti mentioned, "God has placed the truth on Umar's tongue and on his heart" (The Itqan, part I, p. 99). On the same page, we find a statement which affirms ibn 'Umar's claim about his father. The Suyuti tells us:

> "The Bukhari and others have recorded that 'Umar ibn al-Khattab said, 'I have concurred with my Lord, or My Lord has concurred with me, in three (things): I said, O, apostle of God, I wish we would take the site of Abraham as a place of prayer! The verse came down: And take ye the site of Abraham as a place of prayer (2:125). Then I said, O, apostle of God: Your women are visited by the righteous and the debauchee. I wish you would command

them to stay behind a veil! So the verse of the veil came down. (When) the apostle's wives joined forces against him, I told them: It may be if he divorced you (all) that Allah will give him in exchange consorts better than you.' These exact words were bestowed in chapter 66:5."

It is common knowledge among all Muslims that the above verses which Muslims claim are inspired by God were really uttered by 'Umar. In addition to the Bukhari (Sahih, p. 6, p. 24), other scholars (without exception) confirm that (refer to Baydawi, p. 26; Jalalan, p. 18; Zamakh-shari in the Kash-shaf, part I, p. 310; Sahih al-Musnad, p. 13; and Asbabal-Nuzul by Suyuti, p.24). The Baydawi, for instance, tells us on p. 26:

> "Musnad took 'Umar's hand and told him, 'This is the site of Abraham.' 'Umar said, 'Shouldn't we take it as a place of prayer?' Muhammad said to him, 'God has not commanded me to do so.' But hardly the sun set when the inspired verse was given, 'And take the site of Abraham as a place of worship.'"

That is, the wish of 'Umar was immediately fulfilled within a few hours. Muhammad had already commanded his followers to worship toward Jerusalem for the sixteen months before this verse.

Another incident in which 'Umar was involved is an anecdote mentioned by most Muslim scholars and recorded for us by Suyuti in his book, "The Reasons For Verses Of Qur'an" (Asbab al-Nuzul, p. 31). The Suyuti says:

> "During Ramadan, (the fasting month), Muslim's were accustomed to eat, drink and have intercourse with women if they are not sleeping. After they sleep and wake up, they abstain. 'Umar had an intercourse with (one of his women) after he woke up from his sleep. He went to the prophet and told him what happened to him. God sent down this verse, 'It is made lawful for you to go unto your wives on the night of the fast'" (2:187).

This story is recorded not only by the Suyuti but by all the scholars also (refer, for instance, to the Bukhari, part 6, p. 31; Zamakh-shari in his book al-Kash-Shaf part I, p. 337; the Baydawi, p. 39; the Jalalan p. 26, and the Sahih al-Muswad p. 17).

In this episode, we find 'Umar ibn al-Khattab does not like to refrain from sexual intercourse with his wife during the fasting month and after sleeping. Therefore, after he and other Muslim men violated the commandment, Muhammad found that he did not have a choice but either to punish and to reprove them or to rescind the order by claiming that Gabriel had come down to him with the above mentioned verse. Muhammad chose the latter to appease 'Umar and his friends.

The Suyuti also relates to us another incident about 'Umar. In page 100, part 2 of his book, the Itqan, he says:

> "A Jew encountered 'Umar ibn al-Khattab and told him, 'Gabriel, whom your (prophet) mentions, is our foe.' 'Umar said, 'Who is an enemy to Allah and His angels and His messengers, to Gabriel and Michael, too, Allah is an enemy to disbelievers.'"

This statement was later revealed, word for word, to Muhammad (chapter 2:98), and became a verse in the Qur'an (refer to the Suyuti). Yet these incidents did not involve 'Umar only. Ibn Maktum (for instance), who was a blind man and one of Muhammad's companions, was another person to whom the Bukhari referred. In part 6, p. 227, the Bukhari conveys the following episode:

> "When this verse came: 'Not equal are those believers who sit (at home) and are not wounded, and those who strive and fight in the cause of Allah' (4:95). Muhammad said: 'Summon Zayd and let him sit down.' Then he told him: 'Write', and he dictated the above verse to him. 'Umru ibn Maktum who was blind, was sitting behind the prophet. (Ibn Maktum) said: 'O, apostle of God, I am a blind man! How can I go to fight? I have a handicap.'

Then, the following (phrase) was added to the above mentioned verse: 'Other than those who have a handicap'" (Part 6, p. 227).

It is as if God only realized the illegitimacy of His request after 'Umru ibn Maktum, Muhammad's friend, pointed it out. Then God revealed the additional phrase. Muhammad asked Zayd to rewrite the verse and to include the addition. This episode has been recorded not only by the Bukhari but by other scholars such as Baydawi (p. 123), Zamakh-shari in the Kash-Shaf (part I, p. 555); Suyuti in the Itqan (p. 98); Asbab al-Nuzul (p. 88); and the Sahih al-Muswad (p. 53). The Baydawi remarks clearly on p. 123:

"Zayd ibn Thabit said: 'This verse was sent down without the phrase "other than those who have a handicap". Ibn Maktum said: 'How could that be and I am blind?' The inspiration came upon the apostle of God in the assembly. His thigh fell on my thigh in such a way that I feared that it would break it. Then, the (inspiration) departed and he said: 'Zayd, write—other than those who have a handicap.'"

In my opinion, dear reader, Muhammad did not have to pretend that God had revealed this additional phrase to him, because it is not necessary and it is implicitly understood. God, indeed, would not obligate a blind man to go to war, but it seems that Muhammad believed it important to add these words in order to please ibn Maktum. If God had intended these words to be part of the verse, He would have mentioned them from the beginning. God does not need to learn from Muhammad's friend in order to change His opinion or to alter the verse.

Of Abdullah ibn Sa'd, too, in "Asbab al-Nuzul" (pp. 120-121), the Suyuti writes:

"'Abdul ibn Sa'd used to write for the prophet (like Zayd). When the prophet dictated, 'God is oft-mighty and oft-wise', he would write instead, 'God is oft-forgiving and compassionate.' Then he would read it to the prophet who

would approve it by saying, 'Yes... they are the same.' Ibn
Sa'd relinquished Islam and returned to Quraysh. He said,
'If God has inspired Muhammad, He has also inspired me.
If God sends down His revelation to him, He also sends it
down to me. Muhammad said, "...oft-mighty, oft-wise"
and I said, "...oft-forgiving, compassionate".'"

The Baydawi and the Imam Tabari agree with the Suyuti, and
both of them record the same episode (refer to the Tabari, p. 152,
and his comment on chapter 6:93).

It is very important to state here that this verse (6:93) which
was given to Muhammad without any justification proves that
Abdulla was right in his claim. This verse reveals the truth about
Muhammad and his claim concerning revelations from God.

Don't you see that 'Abdulla was right? If Muhammad himself
approved the change which 'Abdulla made in the verse, why
should Gabriel become angry at 'Abdulla and accuse him in
another verse? Muhammad used to say "oft-mighty, wise", and
he would write "oft-forgiving, compassionate", then he would
show it to Muhammad who would approve it. Therefore, he was
right when he said, "If God inspires Muhammad, he inspires me
also." Still, when 'Abdulla disclosed the matter, relinquished
Islam and departed, Muhammad uttered this verse (6:93) to
curse him, and issued 'Abdulla's death warrant.

Concerning this matter, Qadi (Judge) 'Ayyad, in his famous
book, "The Healing" (Shifa) remarks,

"'Abdulla ibn Sa'd said, 'I used to divert Muhammad the
way I wanted. He used to dictate to me "...oft-mighty,
wise" and I would say "oft-knowing, compassionate"
Then he would say, "Yes... It is correct". At the end, he
said to me, "Write as you wish!"'"

On page 184, the Imam Baydawi records another incident in
which 'Abdulla ibn Sa'd was involved. We quote it as it is
recorded. The Baydawi says (p. 184),

" 'Abdulla ibn Sa'd was one of the prophet's scribes when the verse, 'We have created man from scion of mud,' was revealed, and Muhammad continued until he uttered, '...and then we made a different creature.' 'Abdulla said with wonder, 'May God be blessed. Who is the best creator.' Muhammad said, 'Write it, this is how it was given to me.' 'Abdulla became suspicious and said, 'If Muhammad is true, then I receive the inspiration as he receives it, and if he is false, then I say as he says.'"

Thus, we have the verse recorded in chapter (Sura), "The Believers" (23:14), "This is how it has been inspired to Abdulla, not Muhammad! !"

Sa'd Ibn Moaz in the book, the Itqan (part I, p. 100), the Suyuti says,

"When Sa'd ibn Ma'adh heard what was said against Aisha, he said, 'Glory to Allah! This is a serious slander!' (Sura 24:16). It was set down as such in the Qur'an."

This verse was not revealed by Gabriel, but was uttered by Sa'd ibn Moaz when some of Muhammad's companions accused Aisha (Muhammad's wife) of adultery, among them Muhammad's cousin who was the sister of Zaynab, one of his other wives. On the same page, the Suyuti records verse 3:140, which was uttered by a woman, as well as verse 3:144, which was spoken by Mas'ab ibn al-Zubayr in the war of 'Uhud.

Women...Muhammad's wives

How Muhammad (I mean Gabriel) used to fulfill the desires of Muhammad's wives! In part I, p. 97, the Suyuti indicates in the Itqan that,

"Um Salma, Muhammad's wife, said to him, 'O, apostle of God, I do not hear that God has mentioned anything for the immigrant women.' Then God sent down, 'And their Lord has accepted of them and answered them, "Never will I suffer to be lost the work of any of you"' (Sura 3:195).' Um Salma also said, 'O apostle of God, you always mention men and ignore women.' Then the verse was sent down, 'For Muslim men and Muslim women....' (33:35)."

The Baydawi (pp. 100 and 558), the Zamakh-shari in the Kash-shaf (part I, p. 490), the Jalalan (p. 353) on the authority of Um 'Amara, and the Sahih al-Musnad (p. 120), confirm the exposition of these verses as they were interpreted by the Suyuti. On page 558, the Baydawi says,

> "The prophet's wives told him, 'O apostle of God, God has mentioned men with good things; do not we women have anything good in us to be mentioned?' Then the verse in the chapter of Parties was sent down—the above mentioned verse."

The same text is recorded in Asbab al-Nuzul by the Suyuti (pp. 69 and 219). There is a very significant question which we cannot ignore, neglect or avoid, "Did not God know that mentioning women in the Qur'an is very important until Muhammad's wives, such as Um Salma and Um 'Amara, complained? Why did Gabriel reveal these verses **only after the women complained** and after Muhammad's wives expressed the necessity for them?"

The question is very plain, and the answer is very clear also. The angel had nothing to do with these matters. Um Salma said to her husband Muhammad, 'I do not hear any mention of women.' Muhammad asked Gabriel to let her hear the mention of women, so the verses in Sura of the Parties: 35 and in Sura of the Family of Imran: 195, were given.

Aisha (Muhammad's most beloved wife whom he married when she was nine years old and he was 54 years old) had an influence on the inspiration of many verses. It is sufficient here to allude to one episode. Muhammad was on his way back from one of his raids, accompanied by Aisha. Aisha lost her necklace on the way. Now let Aisha relate the story,

"One of my necklaces fell in the desert while we were entering Medina. The apostle of God halted and made his camel kneel down. He alighted and rested his head on my lap, sleeping. Abu Bakr came and kicked me severely and told me, 'You delayed the people because of a necklace!' He also said, 'O daughter, in every journey you cause trouble to people.' When we woke up in the morning, we could not find water for ablution before the time of prayer. The verse in Sura of the Table was given in which permission was given to wash with sand instead of water when there is no water. Abu Bakr told me, 'You are a blessed woman.' Then Usayd ibn Hadir said, 'O, family of Abu Bakr, God has blessed people through you!'"

This episode is mentioned in "Asbab al Zuyul" (p. 101) by Suyuti. It is also recorded by al-Bukhari in his Sahih (part 4, p. 64) and the Commentary of the Jalalan (p. 89). This is a famous story. In order to justify Aisha's behavior, lest her father and the rest of the Muslims become angry because she delayed them in the desert (as well as the lack of water), Muhammad claimed that God told him that they can wash with sand instead of water before they pray. We don't know what type of ablution is this, when a person performs this ritual by using sand! It is common knowledge that Muhammad himself did this several times, as the Bukhari and the rest of the scholars indicate. The scholars say, "May God bless Aisha because for her sake, God allowed Muslims to use sand for ablution before prayer whenever they could not find water."

We would like to conclude this point by conveying a moving story as it is recorded in the "Biography of the Apostle" by ibn Hisham (part III, p. 23), as well as by the rest of the Muslim religious scholars such as al-Jalalan, al-Baydawi, and al-Bukhari. This episode is a famous one and is the reason behind the bestowing of a well-known verse. Ibn Hisham says,

"The (military) company of Abdulla ibn Jahsh and some Muslims who joined him, attacked some people from the tribe of Quraysh and killed them. They took their bounties. When they came to Muhammad, he told them, 'I did not command you to fight during a sacred month,' and he refused to take from the bounty the fifth of the mules and the two prisoners. Quraysh said, 'Muhammad and his followers made it lawful for themselves to shed blood, seize properties and capture men during the sacred months.' (The Arabs had previously agreed to abstain from fighting during certain months. When Muslims expressed their discontent for that, especially when Muhammad himself loathed that disgraceful thing and refused to take from the bounty, God spoke to His apostle saying, 'They ask you about the sacred month (if) fighting is allowable. Say in it there is a great fight.' The Muslim invaders rejoiced when this verse was given and Muhammad took the bounty."

We wonder how this happened. When Muhammad himself conquered Mecca, he commanded the Muslims to kill the infidel if they refused to believe, but **only after the elapse of the sacred months** (9:5). Yet here, when he saw that his followers were discontent and that might create a certain crisis among them, he was forced to claim that Gabriel had given him a verse which made war during the sacred months allowable, as if war were a good and necessary matter.

Verses Sent Down For Strange And Trivial Reasons

A puppy which entered the prophet's home: This episode is recorded in the Commentary of the Baydawi (p. 802); the "Itqan", by the Suyuti (part I, p. 92), and Asbab al-Nuzul (p. 299). This narrative is related to us because the infidel said that inspiration had departed from Muhammad, and his God had deserted him. The Suyuti says,

"Khawla, Muhammad's servant, said, 'A puppy entered under the bedstead in the prophet's home and died. For four days the inspiration ceased to descend on Muhammad. He said to me, (What happened in the house of the apostle of God to make Gabriel cease to come to me?' I told myself, 'What if I neatly prepared and swept the house?' I swept under the bedstead and brought out the puppy. The prophet came in with a trembling beard, for whenever inspiration descends on him, **he would be taken by a seizure.** God sent down at that time five verses from the Surah (chapter) of Duha."

It is well-known that the chapter of Duha is made up of only eleven verses. God sent half of it to assure Muhammad that He had not abandoned him. Infidels claimed that God had deserted Muhammad because inspiration ceased to descend upon him because a puppy entered his home and died under the bedstead. Gabriel, as the Bukhari recorded, had already told Muhammad that he would not enter a house which has a dog or a picture. The Suyuti stated that Muslim religious scholars (among them Abu Hajr) said that the story of Gabriel's hesitancy to enter Muhammad's house because of the puppy is very famous.

But the truth of the matter is that it is difficult to comment on these stories which **all Muslim scholars** confirm. What can a person say about such a story? Would God really delay His revelation to a prophet because of a dead puppy? Besides, did not Muhammad leave his home more than once during this period? Why then God did not give His revelation to Muhammad while he was away from his home?

There are many such stories in the Islamic episodes. I would like to relate to you three more distinctive ones.

The Red Velvet

In the Asbab-al-Zuyul (p. 65), the Suyuti says,

"Verse 161 of chapter 3, which states, 'No prophet could ever be false to his trust,' was given because a red velvet was missed after the War of Badr. Some people said, 'Maybe the apostle of God took it.' Thus, God revealed this verse to acquit the apostle... ibn 'Abbas said so."

The Baydawi in (page 94), the Zamakh-shari in the Kash-shaf (part I, p. 475) agree with the Suyuti and state the same reason. The Zamakh-shari adds,

> "Maybe this verse was sent down after the War of Uhud, when some worriers deserted their sites and came to him (Muhammad), requesting their booties. They said, 'Maybe the apostle would not divide the booties equally as he did in the Day of Badr.' The apostle told them, 'Did you think that we could be false to our trust and would not give you your share?'"

The Pretty Women Worshippers

In the reasons for the revelation of Qur'anic verses (Asbab al-Nuzul) (p. 159), the Suyuti says,

> "Ibn 'Abbas said, 'There was a woman who prayed behind the apostle of God. She was one of the prettiest women, thus some people stepped forward to be in the first row lest they see her; others lingered behind in back rows in order to look at her from under their armpits whenever they prostrated themselves.' So God sent down verse 24 of chapter 15: 'And verily we know the eager among you , and verily we know the laggards.' Someone asked Suhayl ibn Hanif about this verse if it was sent down in relation to fighting in the cause of Allah; he said, 'No, but it was sent down in relation to rows of prayer.'"

As usual the Baydawi (p. 342) confirms this interpretation and indicates that some Muslims lagged to gaze at the pretty woman, thus this verse was revealed. Also the Zamakh-shari in the Kash-shaf agrees with both the Suyuti and Baydawi. Many other scholars and chroniclers (on the authority of the ibn 'Abbas) such as Tirmadhi, Nisa'i, ibn Maja, and Imam al-Tabari assert this episode (refer to al-Kash-shaf, part 2, p. 576).

Give Room to Others, Says Gabriel.

On page 265 of Asbab al-Nuzul, the Suyuti says that whenever the Muslims saw a man coming to sit among them in the assembly of the apostle, they kept back their places and refused to make room for him, thus the verse was sent down,

"O, ye who believe! When it is said make room in assemblies, then make room" (58:11).

Indeed the Baydawi (page 722), along with the Zamakh-shari (part 4, p. 492 of the Kash-shaf), agree with the Suyuti in the interpretation of this verse.

The simple, but essential question which we would like to ask is, "Was it necessary for Gabriel to come down from heaven to reveal to Muhammad so many verses for such trivial things? Was not Muhammad himself able to teach Muslims to be unselfish and to make room for their brothers in the assemblies, so they can sit like the rest of them? Could not Muhammad exhort the Muslims not to stand behind pretty woman during the time of prayer to gaze at her? Or could not he say to the woman to go and pray in another place designated for women? Was this such as obtrusive problem that it required Gabriel to descend from heaven, bearing a revelation from God?"

Regarding the red velvet which was missed in the day of Badr, couldn't Muhammad tell the Muslims, "Shame on you! How could you accuse me of stealing and still claim that you believe in God and His apostle?"

Chapter Ten
The Abrogator and Abrogated Qur'anic Verses

In chapter 2:106, the Qur'an plainly indicates,

"Such of our revelation as we abrogate or cause to be forgotten, we bring (in place) one better or the like thereof."

In their interpretation of this verse (p. 16), the Jalalan say that God's intention for this verse is,

"To eliminate the ordinance of the verse, either with its wording, or to keep the wording and eliminate the ordinance, or we make you, O Muhammad, to forget it; namely, we will remove it from your heart" (p. 16).

The Baydawi says in p. 22,

"This verse was given because the Jews and the infidels said that Muhammad ordered his followers to do something, then He prohibited them from it and commanded them to do something opposite to it. Abrogation means eliminating reading it as an act of worship or eliminating the ordinance inferred from it, or both of them. To forget it means to remove it from hearts."

Refer also to the Zamakh-shari in "al-Kash-shaf" (part I, p. 303). In part 3, p. 59 the Suyuti says, "Abrogation means the

219

removal as it is mentioned in chapter Haj: 52, and it means alteration."

In his book, "The History of Islamic Law" (p. 115), Dr. Shalabi states,

> "The abrogation is to rescind something and replace it with something else, as ibn Hazm said. Muslims in general have consented that abrogation has taken place in the Qur'an, as it is clearly indicated in the sound verses."

This statement means that Muhammad was accustomed to stating something to his followers, with the claim that it was revealed to him through the angel Gabriel, then later (maybe after a few hours), he would tell them that God had invalidated it. Thus the infidels used to say, "Muhammad utters something today and abolishes it tomorrow" (refer to Zamakh-shari, part I, p. 303).

In Asbab al-Nuzul, p. 19, the Suyuti says that,

> "Ibn 'Abbas himself said, 'Sometimes the revelation used to descend on the prophet during the night and then he forgot it during daytime; thus God sent down this verse: 2:106."

Is it acceptable or sensible to think that God changes His mind during the night? Ibn 'Abbas is not the only one who insists on that, because ibn 'Umar says,

> "Two men read a Sura which the apostle of God had taught them, yet one night they rose up to pray, but they failed to remember one word of it. The next morning, they went to the apostle of God and related it to him. He told them, 'It is one of those which have been abrogated, thus, forget about it..'" (Refer to the Itqan, 3:74).

Such strange behavior led the infidels to say that Muhammad is a calumniator and he does not receive inspiration from God, for he changes his mind whenever he wishes or says, "I forgot the verse because God made me forget it and it was abrogated". Thus, a verse was written in the Qur'an referring to this debate which was waged between Muhammad and the infidel. The verse says,

> "And when we put one revelation in place of another revelation—and Allah knows best what He reveals— they say, 'To! thou art but inventing'" (16:101).

In his above mentioned book, Dr. Shalabi attempts to defend the concept of abrogation. He remarks,

> "God changes His ordinances according to the change of time and circumstances; therefore, the abrogation and the giving of one verse instead of the verses of the Qur'an, took place" (p. 116).

The reader can easily realize that this defense is meaningless and will not suffice, because circumstances do not change drastically in a few night hours as ibn 'Abbas has claimed when he said that the verse would be received during the night and abrogated in daytime. Dr. Shalabi, in the context of his defense, says,

> "Most of what was alluded to in the abrogated verses was intended to lighten (the ordinances)" (p. 117).

In part 3, p. 69 of the" Itqan", the Suyuti refers to the same reason. It is left to the reader to answer this question, "Did God not know the circumstances of His worshippers and their abilities so that He made it a habit to decree an ordinance or dictate an order, then change His mind and replace it immediately the next day with a lighter command or an easier commandment?" The fact is that **Muhammad** has failed to comprehend his followers circumstances; thus, he used to order something, then change it the next day whenever he found it too difficult to be implemented. For example, the Qur'an says,

> "O prophet! Exhort the believers to fight. If there be twenty steadfast among you, they shall overcome two hundred and if there be a hundred steadfast among you, they shall overcome a thousand of those who disbelieve. Now has Allah lightened your burden, for he knows that

there is weakness in you. So, if there is among you one
hundred who are steadfast, they shall overcome two
hundred."

This verse always confuses Muslims when they fight Israel in
their efforts to liberate Palestine and the mosque (Al Aqusa).

The verses say that Allah lightened your (task), for He knows
that there is a weak spot in you! Did God not know that each one
of them had a weak spot before He told them that "each one of
you can vanquish ten"? God had to change His mind and say
that "each one of you can vanquish two" only. The Suyuti says,

> "When God imposed on them that each one of them
> should fight ten, it became a burden and an unbearable
> (task) for them. Thus, God removed the burden from them
> and each one was (requested) to fight two men." (Asbab
> al-Nuzul, p. 134).

Both Baydawi (p. 244), and Dr. Shalabi (p. 117) agree with
him. Another illustration on this "lightening" is found in Sura
73:1,2,20.

> "O thou wrapped up in your raiment, keep vigil the night
> long save a little" (73:1,2). "Allah measures the night and
> the day. He knows that you count it not and turns unto you
> in mercy. Recite, then of the Qur'an why it is easy for
> you" (73:20).

On p. 117, 123, Dr. Shalabi along with Suyuti says,

> "The Qur'anic verse: 'Stand (to pray) by night, but not all
> night' was abrogated by the end of the Sura; then was
> abrogated again by (the implementation) of the five
> prayers."

The entire Sura is only 20 verses. Its beginning is abrogated
by its end, and its end is replaced by the injunction of the five
prayers; that is, the Abrogator has been abrogated. In relation to
this verse, the Jalalan say (p. 491),

> "When God imposed the night prayers, Muslims' feet
> swelled as they stood during the night (for prayer); thus,

God lightened it for them by saying, 'Pray as much as you are able.'"

Did God not know that this ordinance was going to be difficult for Muslims? Why did He not tell them that from the beginning, before their feet became swollen?

A third illustration relevant to this discussion is the Qur'anic saying, "Fear Allah as He should be feared" (3:102). This commandment is abrogated by His saying, "Fear God as much as you are able to do so" (64:16). This is the claim of the Muslim scholars (refer to Suyuti in Asbab al-Nuzul, p. 277; Jalalan pp. 53, 473, Dr. Shalabi, p. 122). On p. 53, the Jalalan say,

"On the authority of Sa'id ibn Jubayr, he said, when the verse 'Fear God as He should be feared' was sent down, it became very hard for the people to do so; therefore, God bestowed, in order to lighten on the people, 'Fear God as much as you can.'"

The question is now why did God send down this abrogating verse after Muslims said to the apostle of God, "Who can do that?" Why, **only after this objection**, was this easy verse was sent down to abrogate the first one?

I believe that these illustrations are sufficient to prove the points under discussion. If anyone is interested to know more about this subject, we would refer him to the books of Suyuti and many other authors. They are filled with such examples.

Two Reasons: Lightening And Forgetting

We believe that the reason behind the concept of abrogation is that Muhammad intended to make the performing of the Islamic rites and worship easier on his followers and to obtain their approval and satisfaction with his teachings. If he decreed something which later seemed to be too difficult for them to implement, and they remonstrated against it, he would "lighten" it immediately and claim that God had ordered him to rescind what he previously uttered, and all the verses he recited were replaced by new ones.

Whenever **he forgot** what he related to his followers, he spared himself the embarrassment by claiming that God had abrogated what he conveyed to them before. There is no doubt that Muhammad tended to forget. This is clear from the above illustrations and the incidents recorded in the Sahih of the Bukhari, (part 3, p. 223, and part 8, p. 91). The Bukhari says,

> "Aisha said, The prophet heard a man reciting in the mosque. He said, 'May God have mercy on him, he has reminded me of such and such verses which I dropped from Sura so and so.'"

So Muhammad sometimes used to forget some verses, and his friends had to remind him of them; but whenever he did not find anybody to remind him, he claimed that they had been abrogated. We saw this before when two of his followers came to him to help them to remember some of the verses which he had taught them. Muhammad told them these verses had "... been abrogated, forget about them." So abrogation in the Qur'an was the result of forgetfulness or to lighten the task for the Muslims.

Forgetfulness is plainly mentioned in the verse we quoted at the beginning of this discussion (Sura 2:106), and it was interpreted by Muslim religious scholars who affirmed that God used to make Muhammad forget and remove from his heart what he had revealed to him before, as ibn 'Abbas, who was among Muhammad's closest friends, admits to us.

Surely none of us believes that God suffers a wavering mind and changes his opinion in a few hours. We can believe that Muhammad himself was subject to forgetfulness and made it a habit to change his mind in order to please his followers.

Types of Abrogation

Without exception, all Muslim religious scholars state that abrogation not only includes the abolishing, dropping, or replacing of a verse by another verse, but it also includes abolishing a provision of the verse without eliminating its wording or text from the Qur'an. Refer to Shalabi (p. 119), the" Itqan" (part 3, p. 63), ibn Hazm in "The Nasikh and the Mansukh" and others. Throughout three pages, the Suyuti provides us with many examples; but Dr. Shalabi, who is the professor of Islamic history, tends not to agree with him on some of these examples. He says,

> "I have a personal inclination to say that not so many abrogations took place in the Qur'an" (p. 118).

We do not really care whether the abrogated verses are many or few; what we do care for is the concept itself. We wonder, if the provision of the verse is abrogated or abolished, why its text should continue to be placed in the Qur'an and to be read. The Suyuti attempts to answer this question by saying, "... so as Muslims will be rewarded whenever they read it" (part 3, p. 69). It is as if the rest of the Qur'an were not sufficient reading for obtaining the reward, or as if the reward is acquired by more reciting, even if they are verses whose provisions are abolished and are not in effect anymore.

We have already mentioned some examples pertaining to this type of abrogation, yet it is appropriate to allude to all the verses which call for peace and forgiveness of the infidel here. These verses are all abrogated by other verses which call for war. All religious Muslim scholars attest to this fact, as we mentioned in chapter one. Thus, no one should believe that the Qur'an calls for peace because all these 'peaceful' verses are recorded in it. All of them are abrogated, as all the Muslim scholars attest. The Suyuti says in this respect,

> "The order for Muslims to be patient and forgiving was issued when they were few and weak; but when they

became strong, they were ordered to fight and the previous verses were abrogated" (part 3, p. 61).

Ibn 'Arabi said, "The verse of the 'sword' has abrogated 124 verses" (p. 69).

What is the second type of abrogation? It is a very strange type of abrogation, stranger than the previous one, because it abrogates its recitation and **retains its provision**; that is, it keeps it in effect. If you wondered and asked what is the wisdom of that, you will find that the Suyuti himself asked the same logical question and endeavored to answer it. In part 3, p. 72, he says

> "The **recitation** of some verses is abrogated though their **provisions are retained**. Some people in this respect, asked a question, 'What is the wisdom in abolishing the recitation and retaining the provision? Why was not the recitation retained so that the implementation of the provision and the reward of reciting it will be combined?' Some have answered, 'That is to show the extent of this nation's obedience, without any preference to seek a determined path'" (Al Itqan. Refer also to Kishk legal opinions, part 4, p. 64. Sheik Kishk admitted this strange type of abrogation).

The Suyuti throughout these pages, presents many illustrations for this strange type of abrogation. It is obvious that it is utterly meaningless to abrogate and abolish a certain verse, and to retain its provisions. Concerning the subject of obedience, this could be manifested in many ways, apart from this strange matter. In his illustrations which the Suyuti quoted, he relied on 'Umar ibn al-Khattab's sayings.

Other Strange Things Related To Abrogation

1) The abrogator precedes the abrogated

In part 3, p. 69 the Suyuti remarks,

> "In the Qur'an there is no abrogator (verse) without being preceded by an abrogated (verse), except in two verses,

and some added a third one, while others added a fourth verse" (Al Itqan).

Then the Suyuti recorded these verses. We tell him that even if there is only one verse (not four), this matter is incomprehensible and unacceptable. Why should an abrogating verse (with which Muslims are to comply) **precede** the abrogated verse? How would an abrogating verse abolish something which is **not yet in existence**; then later, the abrogated verse is revealed and recorded in the Qur'an? Why should it be recorded if it is already abrogated?

2) In part 3, p. 70, the Suyuti himself admits to this odd and amazing situation. He indicates,

"One of the wonders of abrogation is a verse in which its beginning has been abrogated by its end. There is nothing like it. It is (placed) in the Sura of the Table 105."

This is Suyuti's statement which I quoted word for word.

3) Muhammad's traditions (sayings and deeds) abrogate the Qur'an. The majority of Muslim religious scholars confirm that this truly took place, and there is no room to deny it. One illustration would be the stoning of the married adulterer. The Qur'an talks only about scourging and exiling the adulterer, yet Muhammad himself stoned some adulterers. Thus, stoning the married adulterer (male or female), and not flogging them, has become Islamic law. The reason for that is that Muhammad said and did so. Therefore, the Suyuti (part 3, p. 60), as well as Dr. Shalabi (p. 121), has said that Muhammad's traditions abrogate the Qur'an. This is also the opinion of ibn Hazm and al-Shafi'i. In this regard Dr. Shalabi says (page 121),

"God is the source of the ideas whether they are included in the Qur'an or in one of Muhammad's Ahadith (traditions) which is inspired (by God) and not recorded in the Qur'an."

We believe that such things conform to sound Islamic thought because such events did take place as we mentioned before; but we cannot understand why these inspired traditions, which Muhammad received, have not been recorded in the Qur'an. Thus, such verses would abrogate other verses, especially since the Qur'an says, "We do not abrogate a verse without revealing a better one or something like it."

Nor do we understand the saying, "... we will reveal a better one," for is there better than the word of God? We understand that there could be something like it, but better? This is something we cannot comprehend or understand.

Before we conclude the subject of abrogation in the Qur'an there are two things which are worth mentioning:

First, the disagreement among Muslim religious scholars in regard to the abrogated verses despite the seriousness and importance of this matter. The Suyuti and Dr. Shalabi (along with all Muslim scholars and chroniclers) agree on a very significant dialogue which took place between 'Ali ibn Abi Talib and one of the jurisprudents which demonstrates the importance of knowing the abrogating and the abrogated verses. On page 120, Dr. Shalabi says,

> "Ibn Hazm talks about the necessity of knowing the abrogating and the abrogated (verses) in the Qur'an, and that this knowledge is a necessary condition of legal personal opinion (al-ijtihad). It was related that the Imam 'Ali saw Sa'id ibn al-Hasan presiding in his capacity as a judge in Kufa (Iraq). He asked him, 'Do you know the abrogating and the abrogated (verses)?' The judge answered, 'No.' He then told him, 'You have perished and make (others) to perish.'"

No doubt, that if the judge does not know the abrogating and the abrogated (verses), he may issue his sentence based on an abolished ordinance. A Muslim may ask what is wrong with that? The problem and the crux of the matter is that **no one knows exactly what the abrogating and the abrogated (verses) are.** Scholars disagree on pinpointing the abrogated (verses). In page 118, Dr. Shalabi says,

"Some scholars like ibn Hazm in his book, 'The Abrogating and Abrogator' (verses), have exaggerated (the issue of) abrogation to an extent which is unacceptable even to linguistic taste. He examined the Qur'an chapter by chapter and showed the abrogating and the abrogated in each of them. **We disagree with him** in this procedure."

Then, in the same book, "The History of Islamic Law", he says,

"**We have to pinpoint** the abrogating and the abrogated verses to be a ray of light for the students of the history of Islamic law. We will quote the Suyuti because he was sparing in his call for abrogation. He inclines toward rejecting excessive abrogation. Though the Suyuti believes that the abrogated verses are twenty, still we do not agree with him on all of them."

So what can the students of the Islamic law and the judges like the judge of Kufa do? Ibn Hazm has recorded many abrogating and abrogated verses, then the Suyuti came after him and eliminated many of them and ended with only twenty verses. Later, Dr. Shalabi indicated that he disagreed even with the Suyuti on some of them. The disagreement on this matter is not a simple issue. It is very serious because **knowing these verses is a basic condition in applying Islamic law** and in the science of jurisprudence, as Dr. Shalabi indicated. It is well-known that the "Ijtihad" (deduction of a legal opinion) is the third source of the Islamic law after the Qur'an and the tradition, according to all Muslim scholars (refer to p. 24). That was the trend during the time of Muhammad, the companions and the Caliphs—the Qur'an first, then tradition, then the Itjihad (refer to p. 156).

Secondly: God abrogates any desire Satan frames in the heart and the tongue of Muhammad. This means that Satan has the power to infuse certain verses in what Muhammad claims to be an inspiration from God. Satan was able to place on Muhammad's tongue certain words by which he praised the pagans' gods. This incident is confirmed and recorded by Suyuti, Jalalan, ibn Kathir (part 3, p. 229), Baydawi, Zamakhshari, ibn Hisham, and even ibn Abbas himself, along with the rest of the companions. It is all recorded in the Qur'an, chapter 22:52,

> "Never sent we a messenger or a prophet before you but when he recited the message Satan proposed (opposition) in respect of that which he recited thereof, but Allah abolishes that which Satan proposes."

The Suyuti says in Asbab of the Nuzul (p. 184),

> "Muhammad was in Mecca. He read the chapter of the Star. When he uttered, 'Have you seen the Lat, the 'Uzza, and the other third Manat?', Satan instilled in his tongue, 'These are the exulted idols (daughters of God) whose intercession is hoped.' The infidels said that Muhammad had mentioned their gods with good words. Then when he prostrated, they prostrated, too. Thus, the above verse 22:52 was not inspired."

On page 282 of the Commentary of the Jalalan, we read the same interpretation, and the Jalalan added,

> "Gabriel came to Muhammad after that and told him that Satan had thrust these words into his tongue. Muhammad became sad, then Gabriel delivered this verse to him to comfort him."

This verse, as the Jalalan remarked, comforted Muhammad because it revealed that all the prophets and the apostles who came before Muhammad had experienced this trial and not just Muhammad. It is obvious here that this is false and spurious because no one ever heard that any of the apostles or the prophets had been exposed to such trials in which Satan made them utter what they proclaimed to be a revelation from God, then they **later claimed it was Satan and not God who revealed it to them**. If we refer to the commentary of the Baydawi (p. 447), we find that he agrees with the Suyuti and Jalalan and adds,

"Muhammad desired that a Qur'an which brings his people closer to God and does alienate them, may be bestowed on him; thus, Satan ill-whispered these words to him."

In his book, "The Kash-shaf", the Zamakh-shari (part 3, pp. 164, 165), asserts that,

"This episode which Muhammad experienced is common knowledge and unquestionable, and is related to us by the companions of Muhammad."

Thank you, Mr. Zamakh-shari.

It is appropriate here to refer to ibn Hisham's statement in his book, "The Prophetic Biography". This book relies on the testimonies of Muhammad's companions. It is also the major source for all Muslims who always quote it. In part 2, p. 126, ibn Hisham says,

"When some Muslims immigrated to Ethiopia, they received the news that the inhabitants of Mecca had accepted them. They returned to find that it was false news The reason was that the apostle of God, as he was reading the chapter of Star (53:19, 20), mentioned the idols of Mecca. Satan instilled in his recitation their praises and he (Muhammad) acknowledged their intervention. The infidels were overjoyed and said, 'He mentioned our idols (gods) with good words.' Then God sent down this verse (22:52). Gabriel told Muhammad, 'I did not bring to you these verses (about the idols).'"

No one can accuse Salman Rushdi, in regard to the Satanic verses, of making false claims against Islam and the Qur'an because this incident is acknowledged by all Muslim scholars, along with Muhammad's companions and his relatives, especially ibn 'Abbas himself.

If we cannot comprehend how God abrogates what He Himself has inspired, we can easily understand that He abrogates what Satan utters, as is recorded in verse (22:52). Yet, we have here two important questions:

First, how was Satan able to distort the inspiration and to deceive Muhammad so that he told the people that these were God's words, then later he reversed himself and told them, "No, Satan was the one who ill-whispered to me with these words?" Muslims believe that prophets and apostles are infallible—in matters of inspiration, at least.

The second question is also very important. How was Satan able to imitate the Qur'anic text with its Arabic eloquence and profound diction? If the Arabic reader re-reads Satan's words to Muhammad, he should immediately realize that they possess the same Qur'anic literary characteristics, eloquence and style. It is impossible to distinguish them from the rest of the Qur'anic verses.

Chapter Eleven
The Contradictions of the Qur'an

Christian Orientalist researchers allude to dozens of Qur'anic contradictions. They indicate that there are many contradictory verses in the Qur'an. Maybe they are right. Yet, here we are going to examine only a few of these contradictions mentioned by these orientalists, mainly because we would like to quote Muslim scholars, as we agreed upon at the beginning of the book. It is sufficient that these Muslim scholars acknowledge the existence of these contradictions, even though they attempted to justify them. Their justifications proved to be feeble, as the reader will soon discover. Also, they completely ignored some other contradictions.

However, concerning the contradictions to which they produced some sensible justifications, we will accept what they offer since we are bound to recognize their interpretations of the Qur'an. Still, we believe that the refutations of the Orientalist researchers are more convincing in many cases. Nevertheless, we will continue to employ the same strategy we have been applying since the beginning of this study. We will cite Muslim scholars and refer the reader to their views.

The First Contradiction

In several verses the Qur'an indicates that it was revealed in the Arabic tongue; that is, in the Arabic language (refer to 14:4; 29:192-195; 13:37; 42 7; 39:28, and 43:3). Yet, in at least two plain verses, the Qur'an commands the deletion of any dialect other than the Arabic language in the Qur'anic text (16:103; 41:44). In his book, "al-Risala", edited by Ahmad Shakir (p. 41), the Shafi'i says,

> "It is said, 'What is the proof that the Book of God is in the Arabic language without being mixed with any (foreign words)?' The proof is the Book of God itself."

Then the Shafi'i quoted the above mentioned verses (16:103 and 41:44). The Shafi'i want to defend these verses, but he is not able to ignore the facts which all Muslim scholars verify, along with the companions and the legists, such as ibn 'Abbas, Mujahid, ibn Jubayr, 'Akrama, and 'Ata. Also, included in this group is the Suyuti, as well as other scholars like Dr. Muhammad Rajab, who expressed his views in "Solidarity" (al-Tadamun) magazine (April, 1989 issue). In his book, "The Itqan" (part 2, pp. 108-119), the Suyuti lists 118 non-Arabic words recorded in the Qur'an. Ibn 'Abbas, himself (along with other great Companions), asserts that some Qur'anic words are Persian, Ethiopian and Nabatean (p. 105). Dr. Bayyumi also confirms the Suyuti's opinions and views. Faced with these contradictions, what does the Suyuti say to justify them? He says in p. 106,

> "The existence of a few non-Arabic words does not make the Qur'an non-Arabic as the verses indicate."

And we say to Suyuti: "We know that the Qur'an is an Arabic book, but **the Qur'an denies** that it contains non-Arabic words (refer to verses 16:103; 41:44). It is obvious that this is a contradiction, especially since there are about 118 non-Arabic words—not just five or ten words. The simple explanation for this contradiction is that Muhammad himself did not know that the origin of the words he employed in the Qur'an were non-Arabic. He was not aware that some of them were Persian, Ethiopian, Berber, Turkish and Nabatean; thus, he claimed that **the entire Qur'an was revealed in pure Arabic language**.

The Second Contradiction

In part 3, p. 83 of "The Itqan", the Suyuti designated many pages under the title, "What is Mistaken For a Contradiction in the Qur'an." He remarks that there is something in the Qur'an to which ibn 'Abbas stopped short of giving any answer. A man told him that one verse in the Qur'an mentions that the length of the day of resurrection is one thousand years, and another verse says it is 50 thousand years (al-Sayda: 5 and al-Ma'arij: 4). Ibn 'Abbas said, "These are two days which God—may He be exalted—has mentioned in His book, and God knows best." This is an honest acknowledgment by ibn 'Abbas, without any attempt of justification.

When ibn Musayyib, one of the great companions, was asked about these two days and why they contradict each other, he said, "Ibn 'Abbas avoided talking about them, and he is more knowledgeable than me." Yet we find some contemporary scholars who endeavor to justify this contradiction and claim that they are more knowledgeable than ibn 'Abbas.

The Third Contradiction

In the same part (p. 79), the Suyuti says that the Qur'an states in chapter 6:22-23 that in the day of judgment, infidels attempt to conceal something from God, while in chapter 4:42 the Qur'an contradicts that and indicates that they do not conceal anything from God. The Suyuti tries to justify this contradiction by saying that ibn 'Abbas was asked about it and he answered that they conceal it by their tongues, but their hands and their limbs admit it. Yet the question is still without answer, because if their hands admit it in spite of themselves, it should not be said that they did not conceal any fact from God, because they did try to hide, but their hands gave it away, as ibn 'Abbas says.

The Fourth Contradiction

In chapter, "al Waqiha," the Qur'an talks about those who are destined to enter paradise. It states in verses 13 and 14 that the majority will be from the nations who came before Muhammad, and the minority will be from peoples who believed in Muhammad. But in the same chapter (verses 39 and 40), it is said that the majority will be from those people who came before and after Muhammad also. This is a contradiction in the same chapter. Verse 14 says, "... **a few of those of later time**", but in verse 40, the Qur'an says just the opposite, "... **a multitude** of those of later time."

I have tried to limit this discussion by quoting the interpretations of these verses by Muslim scholars, but they never presented any clear cut justification for this obvious contradiction (refer to the commentary of the Baydawi, p. 710; Zamakh-Shari in his Kash-Shaf, part 4, p. 458; and the Jalalan, p. 453). All of them just say that "... the formers are the nations from Adam to Muhammad and the latters are the people of Muhammad." Thus, one time the Qur'an remarks, "A minority from others," then it says "a majority or multitude from others." This is an obvious contradiction observed by many, and no one has found any refutation against it among Muslim scholars.

The Fifth Contradiction

Pertaining to marriages, it is clear that the Qur'an calls for the possibility of marrying four women at the same time. In Chapter 4:3,

> "But if ye fear that you shall not **treat them fairly**, then only one."

But in Chapter 4:129, we read,

"You will not **be able to deal equally** between your wives however much you wish to do so."

In his book, "The Itqan", the Suyuti says,

"In the first verse we understand that fairness is possible, while in the second, we perceive that fairness is not possible" (Itqan, part 3, page 85).

Actually, from the Qur'anic point of view, as well as according to Muhammad and the rest of the Muslims, "fairness is possible" to be practiced by the evidence that they got (and still get) married to four women. Even Muhammad's companions and his successors did so. Therefore, **"fairness" seemed to be possible** for them because it is not reasonable that all of them, including 'Umar, 'Ali, 'Uthman and Muhammad, violated the Qur'anic teaching.

Then why does the Qur'an say in chapter 4:129 that **"fairness" is not possible**? This is an obvious contradiction which Muslim scholars, among them the Suyuti, realized and comprehended. In order to solve the problem, the Suyuti argued,

"The first verse (meant) fairness in regard to fulfilling the pledges, while the second verse is related to the heart's inclination, and it is not within the ability of a man to be fair in this matter."

The Jalalan (page 82) and Baydawi (page 130) agree with him. The Baydawi reiterates the same statement and adds,

"Muhammad himself was fair with his women in the matter of human rights; but in the inclination of the heart, he used to say to God, 'Forgive me in regard to that over which I have no control.'"

Because Muhammad, according to all the scholars, favored A'isha over the rest, and he did not harbor any inclination toward Sawda bint Zamea. The Zamakh-shari asserts Muhammad's favoritism for A'isha, and states that some people have interpreted the second verse to mean that you cannot be fair in love. Sheik Kashkak indicates in his book of "Opinions" (part 5, page 52), that some favoritism is permissible. Yet, the Zamakh-shari gives another significant opinion when he explicitly says in the Kash-shaf (part 1, pages 568 and 69),

> "God has relieved you of (implementing) complete fairness to that which you are able to carry out because it is obligatory to treat the women equally in dividing their portions, expenses and pledges and many other things hardly uncountable. It is something which is beyond (human) ability, even if they all were beloved. How would the situation be if the heart inclined toward but some of them!"

Then the Zamakh-shari indicated, "The second verse, which indicated that you will not be able to be fair," could mean, "to be fair in love," as in what happened to Muhammad and A'isha. Yet, we understand from Zamakh-Shari's statement that "fairness" is not possible in division of portions, financial support, and pledges, even if they were all beloved. How much harder it would be if the man's heart was inclined to some of them more than others. He said what is really required is to abstain from being fully inclined toward one woman, which would be conducive to neglecting the rest of them. Zamakh-Shari's interpretation here is fully in congruence with the remainder of the verse.

Muslim scholars cited Muhammad as an example, and the issue became more complicated, for what would happen to the poor wife if her husband devoted his love to another wife? She cannot object because, based on the Qur'anic text and by the example set by Muhammad, her husband is innocent of any wrongdoing. The Qur'an asserts that you cannot, from an emotional point-of-view, treat women justly, and Muhammad himself has rejected the request of his daughter, Fatima, to treat all his wives alike and not to bestow on A'isha, his favorite spouse, more than the rest of them. He expressed his favoritism publicly several times. He planned to divorce Sauda (one of his other wives). Some said he already did, then he reinstated her when she agreed to relinquish her night for A'isha. What a pity for the Muslim women.

Western orientalists also say that the Qur'an contradicts itself when it alludes to the creation of earth and heaven by saying, on the one hand, that heaven was created after the earth (many verses); then on the other hand, in one verse, it says the earth was created after the heavens. We have not used this but have attempted, and continue to attempt, to quote only the Muslim scholars such as Suyuti, Baydawi, Jalalan, and Zamakh-Shari, who endeavor to explain these verses to negate any contradiction against the proper usage of the language, such as by saying the word 'after' means 'before'. Or, as we read in Sura 90:1, they said that God does not swear in the sacred land (that is, Mecca); then in Sura 95:3, we see Him swearing in Mecca, the sacred land. The contradiction between these two verses is evident, yet the Suyuti (along with other scholars) denied that there is any contradiction because the word 'no' in Chapter 90 is redundant. It is not intended to negate, but to affirm. The Suyuti mentioned this issue among many others, under the title, "What Was Mistaken to be Contradiction." He summarizes the opinions of the scholars in response to this criticism by saying:

> "The people did not reject what you rejected because the Arabs may use 'not' in the context of their conversation and abolish its meaning."

Chapter Twelve
The Perversion of Qur'an and the Loss of Many Parts of It

On page 131 of his book, "El-Sheaa and Correction", the contemporary Muslim scholar, Dr. Mosa-El-Mosawy, makes this frank confession,

> "Those who adopt the notion of the perversion of the Qur'an are present among all different Islamic groups, but the majority of them come from the El-Sheaa scholars."

Perversion of Qur'an is an unimaginable notion to the lay Muslim because the Scholars of Islam are hiding this truth from being published or becoming known.

Of course, we weren't just satisfied with what Dr. El-Mosawy has already mentioned, but we went back to the most popular ancient scholars, and to Muhammad's relatives and companions, to investigate this notion concerning the perversion and loss of several parts of the Qur'an because those are the trustworthy people regarding the history and development of Islam.

Upon examining the testimonies of these great companions, the answer was positive. They clearly stated that perversion and loss of large fragments of the Qur'an did occur. Let us scrutinize their testimony in order to present to deluded Muslims the truth as it is proclaimed by their trusted spiritual leaders and scholars.

241

The deceptive veil must be removed so people can see the true face of the Qur'an.

'Ibn Umar al–Khattab explicitly admits,

> "Let no one of you say that he has acquired the entire Qur'an, for how does he know that it is all? Much of the Qur'an has been lost; thus let him say, 'I have acquired of it what is available'" (Suyuti: Itan, part 3, page 72).

A'isha (also page 72) adds to the story of ibn Umar and says,

> "During the time of the prophet, the chapter of the Parties used to be two hundred verses when read. When Uthman edited the copies of the Qur'an, only the current (verses) were recorded" (73 verses).

The same statement is made by Ubay ibn Ka'b, one of the great companions. On page 72, part 3, the Suyuti says,

> "This famous companion asked one of the Muslims, 'How many verses in the chapter of the Parties?' He said, 'Seventy-two or seventy-three verses.' He (Ubay) told him, 'It used to be almost equal to the chapter of the Cow (about 286 verses) and included the verse of the stoning.' The man asked, 'What is the verse of the stoning?' He said, 'If an old man or woman committed adultery, stone them to death.'"

This same story and same dialogue which took place between the companion and one of the Muslims is recorded by Ibn Hazm (volume 8, part 11, pages 234 and 235). Then Ibn Hazm said,

> "'Ali Ibn Abi Talib said this has a reliable chain of authority (The Sweetest [Al Mohalla] vol. 8.)."

The Zamakh-shari also cited it in his book, "al-Kash-Shaf" (part 3, page 518).

These are unquestionable statements made by the pillars of the Islamic religion who transmitted Muhammad's sayings and biography, "The Tradition", and who interpreted the Qur'an— among them Ibn 'Umar, A'isha, Ubay Ibn Ka'b and 'Ali Ibn Abi

Talib. Ibn 'Umar states that a large part of the Qur'an was missed. A'isha and Ubay Ibn Ka'b assert that dozens of verses from the "Chapter of the Parties" have been lost. 'Ali confirms that, too. In regard to this particular verse, the following incident is recorded in "The Itqan" by Suyuti (part 1, page 168),

> "During the collection of the Qur'an, people used to come to Zayd Ibn Thabit (with the verses they memorized). He shunned recording any verse unless two witnesses attested to it. The last verse of chapter of Repentance was found only with Khuzayma Ibn Thabit. Zayd said, 'Record it because the apostle of God made the testimony of Khuzayma equal to the testimony of two men.' 'Umar came with the verse of the stoning but it was not recorded because he was the only witness to it."

One can only wonder and ask, "Does 'Umar need another witness to agree with him? Would he lie to God and the Qur'an? Because of that, 'Umar said after that, "If it were not that people would say, "Umar has added to the book of God', I would have recorded the verse of the stoning" (part 3, page 75 of the Itqan). Refer also to skiek Kishk's book (part 3, page 64). Another confession by A'isha:

> "Among the (verses) which were sent down, (the verse) of the ten breast feedings was abrogated by (a verse which calls for five breast feedings. The apostle of God died and this verse was still read as part of the Qur'an. This was related by Abu Bakr and 'Umar" (refer to Suyuti's qan, part 3, pages 62 and 63).

Events Which Led To The Loss Of Some Verses

A Domesticated Animal Eats Qur'anic Verses

In his book (volume 8, part II, pages 235 and 236), Ibn Hazm says plainly,

> "The verses of stoning and breast feeding were in the possession of A'isha in a (Qur'anic) copy. When

Muhammad died and people became busy in the burial
preparations, a domesticated animal entered in and ate it."

A'isha herself declared that, and she knew exactly what she
possessed. Also, Mustafa Husayn, who edited and reorganized
the book, "al-Kash-shaf" by the Zamakh-Shari, asserts this fact
in page 518 of part 3. He says that the ones who related this
incident and said that a domesticated animal ate the verses were
reliable persons, among them 'Abdulla Ibn Abi Bakr and A'isha
herself. This same story has been mentioned also by Dar-al-
Qutni, al-Bazzar and al Tabarani, on the authority of Muhammad
Ibn Ishaq who heard it from 'Abdulla, who himself heard it from
A'isha.

Professor Mustafa indicates that this does not negate that the
abrogation of these verses may have occurred before the
domesticated animal ate them. Why then did 'Umar want to
record the verse of the stoning in the Qur'an if its recitation was
abrogated? And why did people used to read the verses of the
breast feeding? And, if Muhammad died while these verses were
still recited, who abrogated them? Did the domesticated animal
abrogate them? It is evident that this really did occur according
to the witness of the companions, Muslim scholars, and A'isha
herself.

Other Matters Which Were Lost, Not Recorded And Altered

In part 3, page 73, the Suyuti said,

> "Hamida, the daughter of Abi Yunis, said, 'When my
> father was eighty years old, he read in the copy of A'isha,
> "God and His angels bless (literally pray for) the prophet.
> Oh ye who believe, bless him and those who pray in the
> first rows." Then she said, "That was before 'Uthman
> changed the Qur'anic copies."'"

On page 74, we read,

"Umar said to 'Abdul-Rahman Ibn 'Oaf, 'Didn't you find among the verses that we received one saying, "Strive as you strove at the first?" We do not locate it (any more).' 'Abdul-Rahman Ibn 'Oaf told him, 'This verse has been removed among those others which were removed from the Qur'an.'"

It is well-known that 'Abdul-Rahman Ibn 'Oaf was one of the great companions and was among those who were nominated for the caliphate.

Also, on the same page (74, of part 3) of "The Itqan", we read,

"Maslama al-Ansar said to the companions of Muhammad, 'Tell me about two verses which have not been recorded in the Qur'an which 'Uthman collected.' They failed to do so. Maslama said, 'Oh, ye who believed and immigrated and fought for the cause of God by (sacrificing) your properties and yourselves, you received the glad tidings, for you are prosperous. Also, those who sheltered them, aided them and defended them, against whom God (revealed) His wrath, no soul knows what is awaiting them as a reward for what they did.'"

Throughout pages 73 and 74 of part 3, the Suyuti records for us all the remarks made by Muhammad's companions in regard to the unpreserved Qur'anic verses which the readers failed to find in the Qur'an which 'Uthman collected and which is currently in vogue. It is worthwhile to notice that we only quote the testimonies of the most reliable authorities whose witness is highly regarded and cited by all the scholars and students of the Qur'an, such as 'Ali, 'Uthman, Abu Bakr, A'isha (Muhammad's wife), Ibn Mas'ud, and Ibn 'Abbas. In the context of expounding the Qur'an, these scholars are always quoted to shed light on the events which took place during the time of Muhammad. No one could interpret the tenets of Islam better than these scholars.

If we ponder the first part of "The Itqan", by the Suyuti, we read (page 184),

"Malik says that several verses from chapter 9 (Sura of Repentance) have been dropped from the beginning. Among them is, 'In the name of God the compassionate, the Merciful,' because it was proven that the length of Sura of Repentance was equal to the length of the Sura of the Cow."

This means that this chapter has lost 157 verses. Also (page 184), the Suyuti tells us that the words, "In the name of God, the compassionate, the merciful" were found in the chapter of Repentance in the Qur'anic copy which belonged to Ibn Mas'ud, which 'Uthman confiscated and burned when the current Qur'an was edited.

Not only verses have been dropped, but also entire chapters have been abolished from the 'Uthmanic copy, which is in the hands of all Muslims today. The Suyuti and other scholars testify that the Qur'anic copies of both Ubay and Ibn Mas'ud include two chapters called "The Hafad" and "the Khal'". They both are located after the chapter of "the 'Asr" (103) (refer to pp. 182 and 183 of part one of the gn).

He also indicates that the Qur'anic copy of 'Abdulla-Ibn Mas'ud does not contain the chapter of "The Hamd" and "The Mu'withatan" (Surah 113, 114). On page 184, the Suyuti tells us that Ubay ibn Abi Ka'b recorded in his Qur'anic copy two chapters that start with, "Oh God, we ask for your assistance," and "Oh God, you whom we worship." These are the two chapters of "The Hafad" and "The Khal'. " On page 185, the Suyuti assures us on the authority of the most famous companions of the prophet that 'Ali ibn Abi Talib was aware of these two chapters. 'Umar ibn al-Khattab was accustomed to read them after his prostration. The Suyuti records them in their entirety on page 185. They are available to any Arab who wishes to read them. Then, the Suyuti adds that the two chapters are found in the Qur'anic copy of ibn 'Abbas also. What more should we say after we heard the testimonies of ibn 'Abbas,

'Umar, 'Ali, ibn Mas'ud and ibn Abi Ka'b Talib? It is evident that the Qur'an once included these two chapters.

If the reader asks, "What do you mean by saying '...the Qur'anic copy of ibn 'Abbas', or '... the copy of ibn Mas'ud ... A'isha', etc.? Were there many different Qur'anic copies?' I will not supply the answer, but I leave that to the Muslim scholars and chroniclers as we examine how the Qur'anic copies were burned and only one universal copy was kept.

The Collection Of The Qur'an And The Fierce Dispute Among The Scholars And The Companions

Among the greatest events which took place during the reign of 'Uthman ibn 'Affan, third caliph after Muhammad, is the collection of the Qur'an. It is appropriate here to record briefly the story of the first collection of the Qur'an, which occurred during the time of Abu Bakr after the death of Muhammad. All chroniclers, without exception, have never questioned the authenticity of the incident (refer to "The Itqan" of Suyuti, part 1, page 165, Dr. Ahmad Shalabi, pp. 37 and 38, al-Bukhari, part 6, page 477). What did the Bukhari say in this regard?

> "'Umar said to Abu Bakr, 'I suggest you order that the Qur'an be collected.' Abu Bakr said to him, 'How can you do something which Allah's messenger did not do.' Then Abu Bakr accepted his proposal and came to Zayd and said to him, 'You are a wise young man and we do not have any doubts about you. So you should search for the fragments of the Qur'an and collect it.' Zayd said, 'By Allah, if they had ordered me to shift one of the mountains, it wouldn't have been heavier for me than this ordering me to collect the Qur'an.'"

The question which presents itself is, why did not Muhammad give orders to collect the Qur'an? Why did not the angel Gabriel suggest to him to do such an important task to avoid the disagreement, dispute, and the fight which spread among the people? He could have avoided the debate about the chapters and the verses of the Qur'an which raged among the great scholars.

Secondly, why did Zayd consider the task of collecting the verses of the Qur'an more difficult than removing a mountain? There is no answer for the first question. Of course, Gabriel was supposed to order Muhammad to collect the Qur'an while he was still alive, in order to save his people from the disputes and fights. The answer for the second question is evident because a great number of the reciters and the memorizers of the Qur'an had already been killed in the wars of the apostasies, especially in the battle of Yamama. So, how could Zayd collect the Qur'an thoroughly? Removing a mountain is much easier, as he said.

Now what happened during the time of 'Uthman? In his book "The History of Islamic Law" (page 38), Dr. Ahmad Shalabi says,

> "The Qur'an was collected and entrusted to Hafsa. It was not proclaimed among people until the era of 'Uthman ibn 'Affan. Huthayfa, one of Muhammad's companions, who fought in Armenia and Adharbijan, said to 'Uthman, 'The Muslims disagree on the (correct) reading of the Qur'an and they fight among themselves.' 'Uthman ordered Zayd ibn Thabit and the other three to collect the Qur'an in one copy. After they accomplished that, 'Uthman gave the order to bum the rest of the Qur'anic copies which were in the hands of Muhammad's companions. That was in the year 25 H."

All Muslim scholars concur—such as Al-Bukhari (part 6, page 225), Suyuti in "The Itqan" (part 1, page 170), and Ibn Kathir in "The Beginning and the End" (part 7, page 218) in which he remarks,

> "'Uthman burned the rest of the copies which were in the hands of the people because they disagreed on the (correct) reading and they fought among themselves.

> When they came to take ibn Mas'ud's copy to burn it, he
> told them, 'I know more than Zayd ibn Thabit (whom
> 'Uthman ordered to collect the copies of the Qur'an).'
> 'Uthman wrote to ibn Mas'ud asking him to submit his
> copy for burning."

When ibn Mas'ud said that he was more knowledgeable than
Zayd, his claim was not questioned because he was a very
reliable person. In part 7, page 162 of his book, "The Beginning
and the End", ibn Kathir said about him that he used to teach
people the Qur'an and the traditions. Some even thought that he
was a member of Muhammad's family because he had easy
access to Muhammad's assembly while Zayd was still young.
The Bukhari comments (part 6, page 229) that Muhammad
prompted his adherent to learn the Qur'an from four people; ibn
Mas'ud Zayd was not mentioned among them. Yet, when
'Uthman asked Zayd to collect the Qur'an, he did not add ibn
Mas'ud to the committee. A contemporary scholar, Sheikh
Kishk, remarks in his book, "Legal Opinions" (part 1, page 102),

> "The four most important commentators are ibn 'Abbas,
> ibn Mas'ud, 'Ali ibn Abi Talib and 'Ubay ibn Ka'bal-
> Ansari."

So ibn Mas'ud is one of the four great expounders of the
Qur'an and Zayd ibn Thabit did not enjoy the same prestige of
ibn Mas'ud.

It was common knowledge that both ibn Mas'ud and ibn Ali
Ka'b were accustomed to write the two chapters of the Hafad
and the Khal' which are now eliminated from the current Qur'an
which Zayd collected. Ibn Mas'ud asserts that the chapter of the
praise and the Mu'withatan are not part of the Qur'an (refer to
"The Itqan" by Suyuti, part 1, pp. 221, 222). Despite that, Zayd
recorded them.

It was a strange thing, 'Uthman's order to burn the
companions' copies. If we question that, we will be inclined to
believe that these copies differed from the Qur'anic copy which

Zayd edited and compiled, otherwise 'Uthman would not have burned them. This is not the conclusion of the author, but it is the opinion of many great contemporary Muslim scholars, among them Ibrahim al-Abyari, who expressed his view in his book, "The History of the Qur'an" (3rd print, 1982, page 107). He plainly says,

> "There were also other copies of the Qur'an such as the copy of Abi Musa al-Ash'ari, al-Maqdad ibn al-Aswad, and Salim, the client of Abi Huthayfa. There were differences between those copies, differences which Huthayka attested to it. That frightened 'Uthman; thus he issued an order to collect the Qur'an because the Kufis followed the copy of ibn Mas'ud; the Syrians the copy of ibn Abi Ka'b; the people of Basra, the copy of Musa al-Ash'ari; the Damascenes, the copy of ibn Maqdad."

On page 41, he adds:

> "Ibn Qutayba says that the differences between the recitations of the various Qur'anic copies may include the meaning also."

Also on page 109, he says:

> "When Abu Bakr and 'Umar assigned Zayd ibn Thabit to compile the Qur'an, there was a previous compilation of the Qur'an made by a group of the greatest companions, such as 'Ali ibn Abi Talib, ibn Mas'ud, ibn 'Abbas and others."

The Muslim has the right to wonder and to ask why Abu Bakr and 'Umar took the trouble to do that when ibn Mas'ud and ibn 'Abbas, who were (according to Muhammad) the most knowledgeable people in the Qur'an, had already accomplished it? Why did they not at least add them to the committee or solicit their opinions?

In regard to the copy of 'Ali ibn Abi Talib, the Imam Khu'i tells us in his book, "al-Bayan" (page 222), the following:

"The existence of Imam 'Ali's copy is an unquestionable matter. All scholars admit it and say that it contains additions which are not found in the current Qur'an. These additions are under the title of 'The Revelation of God for the Explanation of the Intended' (purpose)."

The Imam Khu'i is one of the greatest scholars among the Shi'ites. He drew his information from what the Imam al-Tabari had recorded in his book, "'al-Ihtijaj'" ("Apology") (refer to Dr. Musa, The Shi'ites and the Reformation, pp. 132,133).

Dr. Musa also indicates:

"Our scholars and legists infer from an episode recorded by the Tabari in the book of al-Ihtijaj about the existence of a Qur'anic copy compiled by the Imam 'Ali. This episode tells that 'Ali said to Talha (one of Muhammad's relatives and companions) that every verse God bestowed upon Muhammad is in my possession, dictated to me by the apostle of God and written by the script of my hand, along with exposition of every verse and all the lawful and unlawful (issues)."

Dr. Musa tells us, that despite the fact that he studied Islam and jurisprudence under the direction of the Imam al-Khu'i, he was involved in a fierce argument in regard to this serious matter. But we will tell Dr. Musa that all the Shi'ites and their scholars (whose total number is more than one hundred fifty million Muslims scattered all over the Islamic countries) believe this. Even Sheikh Kishk who was one of the Sunnis' scholars, repeats similar statements in his book, "Legal Opinions" (part 1, page 103). He says,

"'Ali remarked, 'Ask me about the book of God. I swear to God that there is no verse which I do not know whether it was sent down at night or during time, or on a plain or on a mountain.'"

He also states similar words about ibn Mas'ud. In spite of that, 'Ali ibn Mas'ud and ibn Abi Ka'b had been disqualified from contributing to the compilation of the Qur'an, and their copies were neglected, though they were the most important expounders of the Qur'an along with ibn 'Abbas.

It is 'Ali's copy which contains additional material lacked in the current Qur'an and includes revelations from God for explaining the intended purposes. This is what happened in the course of the compilation of the Qur'an during the time of 'Uthman ibn 'Affan. Thus, it is no wonder that ibn Kathir explicitly mentions that Muhammad ibn Abi Bakr, the righteous, and the brother of A'isha, Muhammad's wife, had participated with 'Ammar ibn Yasir, one of the famous companions, in the assassination of 'Uthman, reiterating, "You have altered God's book" (refer to the Bidaya and The Nihaya, part 7, page 185). On page 166, ibn Kathir records that a large number of the reciters of the Qur'an used to curse 'Uthman and encouraged people to revolt against him.

The question is, "Why do the reciters of the Qur'an do that, and why does ibn Kathir vow that ibn Abi Bakr said that to 'Uthman? Did 'Uthman really change the copies of the Qur'an as Hamida, daughter of Abi Yunis, testified along with the rest of the great companions whom we mentioned? Yes indeed.

The Dispute Among The Companions And The Seven Readings Of The Qur'an

On the authority of all the scholars, the Suyuti tells us that the most eminent companions disagreed on the number of chapters of the Qur'an and their verses. They disagreed on the order of the chapters. He listed for us the order of the chapters in 'Ali's and ibn Mas'ud's copies (refer to the Itqan, part 1, pp. 176 and 189). He tells us that the multitude of scholars said that the order of the chapters was the outcome of the companions' opinion and they disagreed about that among themselves. The Suyuti admits on this page that both 'Ali and ibn Mas'ud each owned his own copy. Also Ubay ibn Ka'b possessed his own, too.

He regarded the dispute over the verse, "In the name of God the Compassionate and Merciful", a striking example about the dispute between the most eminent companions and the scholars. Some said that it is not one of the Qur'anic verses, so ibn 'Abbas told them that they eliminated 114 verses from the Qur'an because it was repeated 114 times. The Zamakh-shari, who recorded this incident in the Kash-shaf (part 1, pp. 24-26), states that those who denied these verses were ibn Mas'ud himself, Abu Hanifa, Malik and all the reciters and legists of Medina, Basra and Syria.

Imam Malik used to say, "This verse should not be read aloud or privately because it is not part of the Qur'an. Sheikh Kishk agrees with the Zamakh-shari in this matter and confirms that a dispute has resulted among the greatest scholars because of this verse. Some famous scholars, such as the Qurtubi and ibn 'Arabi are of the same opinion as Malik, that this verse is not of the Qur'an (refer to "Legal Opinions" of the contemporary Egyptian scholar Sheikh Kishk, part 9, pp. 41-47).

Of course, this verse is included in all the chapters of the Qur'an except the chapter of the Repentance. The reason for that is a very significant story, which reveals that the compilation of the Qur'an and the order of the chapters are the product of human effort, in compliance with the order of 'Uthman. In his "Itqan" (part 1, pp. 172,173), the Suyuti tells us:

> "Ibn 'Abbas said to 'Uthman, 'What made you combine the chapter of the Anfal and the chapter of Tawba (repentance), without separating them by the verse, "In the name of God the compassionate, the Merciful"? (And why) did you put them among the seven long (chapters)?' 'Uthman said, 'The chapters used to be bestowed upon the apostle of God. The chapter of Anfal was among the early ones which were revealed in Medina, and the chapter of Repentance was among the last revealed. Its story was similar to the early story (of the Anfal), so I thought that it was part of it. Then the apostle of God died without showing us that it was part of the (Anfal); thus, I

combined them and did not write between them the verse,
"In the name of God the Compassionate, the Merciful",
and it is among the long ones."'

The order and organization of the Qur'an depended on
'Uthman's view as he admitted himself to ibn 'Abbas. This time
'Uthman's opinion was wrong. The Suyuti tells us in "The
Itqan" (part 1, page 195) that a dispute broke out among the
scholars because of this verse which was revealed in some of the
seven readings but not in all of them.

You may wonder what "the seven readings" are, and what we
mean when we say that the Qur'an was sent down in "seven
letters" (readings). We would briefly answer this question before
we move to the last subject in this chapter which is the religious
teachings, the mythical episodes and the meaning of the chapters
included in the contents of the Qur'an.

The Seven Letters (Readings) Of The Qur'an

Both former and latter Muslim scholars agree on this issue.
They all relied on Muhammad's famous statements which
Bukhari and others recorded, as well as an incident which is
frequently quoted by most of these scholars. The incident took
place between 'Umar ibn al-Khattab and one of the great
companions by the name of Hisham ibn al-Hakam in which
Muhammad was the arbitrator.

Muhammad's Statements

Muhammad said:

> "Gabriel made me read in (one dialect), I consulted with
> him again and continued asking for more (dialectical
> reading) and he continued to add to that until I finished
> with seven readings" (refer to Bukhari, part 6, page 227,
> and "The Itqan", part 1, page 131).

The Suyuti tells us that this admission is quoted in al-Bukhari, and Sahih of Muslim on the authority of ibn 'Abbas. Also, ibn 'Abbas indicated to us (part 1, page 132) that Muhammad said,

> "My Lord told me to read the Qur'an in one dialect. I sent back and asked Him to make it easy for my people. He answered me (saying), 'Read it in two dialects.' I requested of him again, thus he sent to me (saying), 'Read it in seven dialects.'"

> "Gabriel and Michael visited me. Gabriel sat at my right side and Michael at my left side. Gabriel said (to me), 'Read the Qur'an in one dialect.' Michael said, 'Add (more dialects)' until he reached seven dialects."

These are Muhammad's statements, but before we allude to the meaning of the seven letters (readings) as they were recorded by Muslim scholars, let us look at the incident which took place between 'Umar and Hisham (part 6, page 482 of al-Bukhari).

Umar ibn Al-Khattab said, "I heard Hisham ibn Hakim reciting Al-Furqan and I listened to his recitation and noticed that he recited in several different ways which Allah's messenger had not taught me. I was about to jump on him during his prayer and when he had completed his prayer, I put his upper garment around his neck and seized him by it and said, 'Who taught you this Surah which I heard you reciting?' He replied, 'Allah's Messenger taught it to me.' I said, 'You have lied for Allah's Messenger has taught it to me in a different way.' So I dragged him to Allah's Messenger and said to him, 'I heard this person reciting Surah Al-Furqan in a way which you haven't taught me.' Allah's Messenger said, 'It was revealed in both ways. This Qur'an has been revealed to be recited in seven different ways, so **recite out of it whichever way is easier for you**.'"

Refer also to Dr. Shalabi's book (page 40) along with other major sources, for all of them have recorded this story. It is very interesting to notice that Muhammad, the prophet, approved the readings of both of them in spite of the obvious differences between them, which provoked 'Umar and forced him to treat Hisham brutally and pull him by his clothes.

The Meaning Of The Seven Letters (Readings)

The Suyuti says in "The Itqan" (part 1, pp. 131-140), scholars have argued among themselves about the meaning of the seven letters. Some, like ibn Qutayba, said that there is a difference in the meaning, and not only in the usage of the vocabulary or the dialect. For some words, the meaning may change according to the vocalization of the word. The verb may be in the past tense or imperative, as we find in chapter Saba': 19; or it depends on the word's diacritical points which incur a change in the meaning; or whether a phrase was added or deleted from the verse; or if a word is replaced by another. These are the views of ibn Qutayba, who is one of the most famous scholars of his time.

Ibn al-Jazri agrees with him and admits that the meaning changes from one reading to another. The Suyuti states that Muslim scholars have said so because of the incident which occurred between 'Umar and Hisham ibn Hakeem, because both of them belonged to the same tribe of Quraysh and used the same dialect. It is impossible to say that 'Umar disapproved Hisham's dialect. This denotes that the Seven Letters do not mean mere difference in the dialect of the Arab tribes; otherwise 'Umar would not have objected to Hisham's reading (refer to Suyuti, part 1, page 136). Yet some other scholars, such as al-Tabari, argue that the difference is only in the vocabulary. One scholar agrees with the Tabari who said that ibn Mas'ud used to read:

> "'Every time the (lightning) shines, they walk therein' (chapter 2:20). Yet other times, he may read, 'Passed through or went forward'; that is, stating the same meaning but using different vocabularies."

It is obvious to the reader that the differences between the seven readings **include the meaning and the vocabulary** because both 'Umar and Hisham belonged to the same tribe, which speaks the same dialect. Yet they differed in their reading of the verses because the Qur'an was given without any vocalization or diacritical points, as the scholars indicated. In this case, it is inevitable that the meaning be exposed to change and disruption, as ibn Qutayba, ibn al-Jazri and others mentioned and demonstrated by definite examples.

It is evident then that there are seven different dialects in the Qur'anic text. That created a dilemma for Muslim scholars. Even Suyuti himself alluded (page 136) to the fact that this issue has created a doubt in the minds of the scholars because the seven dialects required Gabriel to deliver each verse seven times.

Scholars' Admission Of A Strange Thing

In his "Itqan" (paragraph 1, page 137), the Suyuti remarks,

"A great scholar, that is the Mawardi, said that Muhammad had permitted the reading (of the Qur'an) on the basis of any of the Seven Letters as it happened in the episodes of 'Umar. He also allowed replacing a letter with another letter."

The Suyuti also says on (pages 141,142),

"The multitude of the scholars and the legists said that the 'Uthmanic Qur'an was (written) in accordance to one letter (dialect) only."

On pages 170 and 171, the Suyuti adds:

"When the lads and their teachers fought against each other during the era of 'Uthman, due to the difference in reading (the Qur'anic text), he ('Uthman) standardized the reading and made people recite it accordingly because he was afraid of riots since the Iraqis and the Damascenes disagreed on the dialect. But before that, the Qur'anic copies (used to be read) on the basis of the Seven Letters in which the Qur'an was given."

Let us now examine what Dr. Shalabi said in this regard. In his book, "The History of Islamic Law" (pp. 40-41), he remarks:

> "'Uthman wanted to have a standardized text read by all Muslims, but, after the era of 'Uthman, Muslims began again to read the Qur'an based on the Seven Letters as they used to do before. Each country followed the dialect of a famous reciter whom it trusted. Then public opinion settled on the Seven Readings taken from the most eminent reciters, who were Nafi', Ibn Khathir, Abu 'Umar, Ibn 'Amir, 'Asim, Hamza and the Kisa'i. Egypt, for instance, followed the reading of Hafas, who learned it from 'Asim."

Such circumstances created a problem for many Muslims who were seeking a solution. One of the inquirers asked Sheikh Kishk a question which this scholar attempted to answer in his book, "Legal Opinions" (part 1, pp. 113 and 114). The question was, "I heard a reciter reading the Qur'anic text, 'O ye who would believe even if a godless messenger brought you news, be cautious.' He read it, 'Investigate' instead of, 'Be cautious'. I ask for a clarification for this reading and other similar verses."

Sheikh Kishk answers:

> "The reading of the reciter, 'Investigate', is a correct famous reading which has been handed down (to people). Hamza, Kasa'i and Khalaf followed it. These three were among the ten on whom the Muslims relied that their reading is correct. The Qur'anic copies to which the inquirer referred, do not contain this reading. Thus, the reading is correct because the Qur'anic copies with which (the inquirer) is acquainted have the diacritical points based on the recitation of Hafas. If the Qur'an, in our time, was written according to the recitation of Hamza or the reading of any of those who were with him, the diacritical points would be congruent with the reading of (Hafas).

> "Maybe, there are Qur'anic copies which are written in the same pattern as this reading, yet the point to be taken

into account is the authenticity of the chain of authority and its uninterrupted succession. All these readings proved to be correct and they were handed down uninterrupted. If the noble inquirer had pondered a little, he would have found that the formation of the word lends itself to be read in two ways, based on the difference in the diacritical points. This is one of the secrets of the 'Uthmanic copy, because during the era of the caliph 'Uthman ibn 'Affan, there was no vocalization or diacritical points."

Despite this answer, the question which is still without explanation is, "In which dialect was the Qur'an given to Muhammad? In which dialect were the tablets when it was still with God? Was there one Qur'an or seven Qur'ans with seven dialects? What did Sheikh Kishk (and his prophet Muhammad) mean when he said **all the dialects and all the meanings are correct**?"

Chapter Thirteen
The Content of the Qur'an

In this part, we are going to discuss two issues, the mythical episodes and the religious teachings. We will be brief, otherwise we would need to write another book to deal with the strange, unacceptable things contained in the Qur'an which no sensible person believes. Our main aim is to remove this deceptive veil from the face of the Qur'an.

First: Some Names Of Qur'anic Chapters And Mythical Episodes

We have already mentioned that there are some chapters in the Qur'an whose names have no meaning. These chapters are: 20, 36, 38, 50, and 68. No one knows what Taha, Yasin, Sad, Qaf, or Nun mean. Mostly, they are mere letters and not words, as to say, for instance, Chapter N, Chapter S, Chapter Y. Would that mean anything in English?

All the Muslim scholars have indicated that they do not know the meanings of the names of these chapters. God only knows (refer to the Jalalan). On the other hand, the meanings of the names of the rest of the chapters are understood and familiar, although there are very strange names linked to a mythical episode which is meaningless, as we will see.

261

It should be noted that some of the Qur'anic chapters carry the names of insects or animals such as the chapters of the Cow, Ants, Spider, Elephant, Bee and the Cattle. We do not find in the Bible, for example, books with such names as "The Book of the Lion" or "The Bat" or "The Buffalo" or "The Book of the Serpent". We also find in the Qur'an some chapters entitled, "Chapter of the Afternoon", or "The Dawn", or "The Night", or "Morning".

Moreover, there are strange stories which were the reasons behind these given names. Also, we are going to relate some stories recorded in the Qur'an which are only fit to be narrated by grandparents to children as part of folklore.

1. The Chapter Of The Ants (27:17-19)

In this chapter, the Qur'an says:

> "And there were gathered together unto Solomon his armies of the Jinn and humankind and of the birds and they were set in the battle order. Till, when they reached the valley of the Ants, an ant exclaimed, 'O Ants! Enter your dwellings lest Solomon and his armies crush you.' And Solomon smiled, laughing at her speech."

This is the reason why this chapter is entitled, "The Ant". All scholars (without exception) present this episode as it is recorded. They acknowledge that it is supernatural, yet it truly happened with Solomon, the Wise (refer to Baydawi, page 501; the Jalalan, p. 316,317).

When Qatada, one of Muhammad's companions, came to Iraq, he was surrounded by some Muslims who inquired of him about this episode. The Imam Abu Hanifa, who was still a lad, asked him, "Was the ant of Solomon male or female?" He answered, "It was a female." This is what Zamakh-shari has recorded. He even mentioned that the ant which warned its friends was called Tahina and Solomon heard her when he was still three miles away.

In order to have a fuller picture of the story, let us read the rest of the episode and see what happened to Solomon (chapter 27:20-22).

> "And Solomon sought among the birds and said, 'How is it that I see not the hoopoe, or is he among the absent? I verily will punish him with hard punishment or I verily will slay him or he verily shall give me a plain excuse.' But he was not long in coming and he (the hoopoe) said to Solomon, 'I have found out a thing that you apprehended not, and I come unto you from Sheba with sure tidings.'"

So Solomon sent the hoopoe to the Queen of Sheba and her people to preach to them about the oneness of God. Muslim commentators (without exception) confirm this interpretation. Of course, the Bible records for us that the Queen of Sheba came to visit Solomon. After she observed the wisdom of Solomon and of his servants, she believed in the God of Israel; but there is no mention of a military battle between Solomon's soldiers of vultures and Jinn, and the kingdom of ants, or of the hoopoe, the teacher and the preacher.

2. The Chapter Of The Prophets (21:81, 82)

> "And unto Solomon we subdued the wind in its raging. It set by his command toward the land which we had blessed. And of the evil ones (demons) subdued we unto him some who dived for pearls for him and did other works."

All scholars agree on the interpretations of these verses. God utilized the winds to obey Solomon's orders. Thus, they sometimes blew smoothly and sometimes they raged like a strong storm whenever he wanted them to carry him fast for a long distance. God even utilized the demons to dive deep in the sea to bring forth treasures of precious stones. They were sometimes ordered to construct cities and palaces, and to invent some progressive handicrafts. These same words are recorded also in another place in the Qur'an. The expounders presented the same interpretation for these verses (refer to Baydawi, page 435;

Jalalan, page 274; Zamakh-shari in The Kash-shaf, part 3, page 130).

Of course, the Azhar scholars along with the Saudi scholars, agree with the former scholars concerning the subject of the ants, the hoopoe, and the exploitation of the wind and demons to serve Solomon. For example, Sheikh Sha'rawi (the most famous preacher in the Islamic world today) asserts that this story undoubtedly happened and that God subjected the Jinn to Solomon in order to refurbish the earth and for the benefit of the people (refer to the "Legal Opinions", page 422).

3. The Chapter Of The Jinn Or Jan (17:1)

Since we have mentioned the Jinn, it is inevitable that we allude to the chapter of the Jinn.

> "Say, O Muhammad, it is revealed unto me that a company of the Jinn gave ear and they said, 'Lo, it is a marvelous Qur'an.'"

All Muslim scholars, in the context of their exposition of those verses, say that God foretold this matter to Muhammad which was invisible to the eyes of Muhammad. As Muhammad was praying the morning prayer and reading the Qur'an beside a palm tree near Mecca, a party of Jinn (who were Satan's soldiers) heard him. When they returned to their own people, they told them, "We have heard eloquent, well-styled words, and we have to repent and believe and never worship Satan again or be subservient to him." They were between three and ten persons.

The Baydawi says that the Jinn are beings which are made mostly of fire or wind, or else they are mere spirits or human souls which departed from their bodies (refer to Baydawi, page 763; Jalalan, page 488; Zamakh-shari, part 4, page 623). The Bukhari assures us that they were demons who listened to the Qur'an being recited by Muhammad during the dawn prayer while he was on his way to Suq 'Ukadh. They were moved by what they heard, and recanted. This is the testimony of ibn 'Abbas himself (refer to the Sahih of the Bukhari, part 6, page 200).

This same story of the Jinn listening to Muhammad and repenting is found in the chapter of the Ahqaf. Both Kishk and Sheikh Sha'rawi agree with the former scholars and do not question their interpretation (refer to the "Legal Opinions" by Sheikh Kishk, part 1, page 20).

4. Chapter Of The Elephant

This chapter could have been called the chapter of the gravel or the vultures, but it was called the chapter of the Elephant simply because the vultures carried the gravel and threw it at the elephants and their riders who marched towards Mecca to invade the Ka'ba. We read in the Qur'an the following:

> "Hast thou not seen how your lord dealt with the owners of the elephants? Did he not bring their stratagem to naught, and send against them swarms of flying creatures which pelted them with stones of baked clay."

All Muslim scholars affirm that this event took place many years before the proclamation of Muhammad's prophethood. Some said maybe during the time of his birth. What really happened was that Abraha, king of Yemen, constructed a church in San'a. An Arab man came and defiled the church and did some damage to it. Abraha decided to demolish the Ka'ba, which was a sacred site for the heathen people of Quraysh and the site of their annual pilgrimage before Islam.

Abraha headed the invasion operation along with his generals who rode on elephants. It was said that there was a huge, strong elephant called Mahmud. God sent black or green birds to attack the invading army. Each bird carried one piece of gravel in his beak and two in his claws and hit the owners of the elephants. They claim that each piece of gravel penetrated the head of a man and exited from the backside (anus - lower opening of the rectum). On each piece of gravel was written the name of the victim. Abraha suffered a violent death (refer to the Zamakh-shari in the Kash-shaf, part 4, page 797; Baydawi, page 811;Jalalan, page 519; also the "Prophet's Biography" by ibn Hisham, part 1, pages 38 and 39).

The Qur'an does not tell us why God sent these vultures to assist the heathens against the Christians. The Qur'an was content to record the episode of this battle between the vultures and the elephants. Thus, a chapter in the Qur'an was inspired under the title of Chapter of the Elephant.

5. The Chapter Of The Cave

Why was it called by this strange name? The answer is simple. Some lads (accompanied by their dog) entered a cave and slept for three hundred and nine years. The story is recorded in the Qur'an in seventeen verses (18:9-25).

The Qur'an clearly relates this story, and all Muslim scholars agree on its interpretation. They said that God forbade the sun to hurt them, and he used to turn them from one side to the other so the ground would not erode their flesh. Their dog, whose name was Qatmir, laid down stretching its legs. The lads who entered the cave were seven. Their names were Yamlikha, Makshalmina, Mashilmina, Martush, Darnush, Shadhinush, along with a shepherd. They were from the city of Ephesus. (This information is related to us by the Baydawi, page 390; Jalalan, pp. 244, 245, and the Zamakh-shari in the "Kash-shaf", part 2, page 703.) Contemporary scholars verify this information.

Before we conclude the episode of the chapter of the Cave, it is appropriate to allude to the story of Moses, the Whale, the ship and the lad. This strange story is also recorded in the chapter of the cave (18:60-82). The gist of the story, as it is stated in the Qur'an, is that God disagreed with Moses who claimed that he was the most knowledgeable person. He told him that he has a servant "whose name is Khadr who is more knowledgeable than you. Take with you a whale and go to the confluence of the two seas. When the whale departs from you, you will find him (the man)."

Moses did so and found the man. Moses told him, "I will be submissive and obedient to you." The Khadr took Moses and sailed in a ship which belonged to some poor people who toiled hard in the sea. This man, Khadr, caused the boat to spring a leak big enough to sink it. When Moses complained, the Khadr told him, "We had agreed that you would never complain. I will show you in the end that I am more knowledgeable than you are." Moses kept silence.

Then they met a young boy who was playing with his friends. The Khadr seized him and violently killed him by smashing his head against the wall, the Zamakh-shari remarked. Moses objected to that, then he apologized to the Khadr. Later, the Khadr started to explain to Moses the implication of his behavior. He said, "I sank the ship because there was a wicked king who was intending to confiscate it by force. And I killed the lad because he was going to cause his righteous parents much hardship by his atheism."

This strange story is meaningless, because this poor lad was guilty of no crime that he should be brutally killed by a man of whom God boasted. God said to Moses that the Khadr was "my righteous servant and he is more knowledgeable than you". Did he foretell the future and know that this lad was going to create a lot of problems for his devout parents? Would this be a justification for his death, or should it be a cause for his guidance and repentance?

This baffling issue made some people ask ibn 'Abbas, "Is it permissible for the Khadr to do that to the lad?" He answered that the apostle of God himself said, "Yes." He also added that this is lawful to anyone if he can foretell what this lad is going to do in the future (refer to Baydawi, page 396; Bukhari, part 6, pp. 111, 112; Jalalan, page 250; and the Zamakh-shari in the "Kash-shaf", part 2, page 736). The Bukhari insists that the Khadr seized the lad and pulled his head off, separating it from his body.

We have already discussed the story of Alexander the Great who had located the sun's setting place which is recorded in this same chapter (the Cave).

6. The Chapter Of The Cow

In this lengthy chapter, there arc at least four mythical stories recorded. We will briefly examine them as evidence of the lack of authenticity of the Qur'an.

A. *Jews Transformed Into Apes*

God transformed these Jews into apes because they disobeyed His commandment and went to catch fish on a Saturday. These Jews inhabited a coastal city (refer to Chapter 2:65). The Qur'an says:

> "And you know of those of you who broke the Sabbath,
> how we said unto them, 'Be apes, despised and hated!'"

The interpretation of the expositors of the Qur'an is in full agreement with the content of these verses (refer to the Baydawi, page 14; Jalalan, pages 10, 11; Zamakh-shari, part 1, page 286). We also read the same incident in chapter 7:163-166 and in chapter 5:60, in which these Jews were transformed into apes and swine.

B. *Two Angels Teach People Magic*

This story is among the strangest episodes recorded in chapter 2. Who would believe that God would send two angels in order to tempt people to see whether they would be seduced into learning magic or not? Muslim scholars indicate that these two angels were called Harut and Marut and the incident took place in Babylon. They used to warn people not to learn magic "... because it is ungodly, but if this is your desire, then we will teach you." Thus, people started to learn how to cause separation between a husband and wife by employing magic (refer to the commentary of the Jalalan, page 15; The Baydawi, page 21; Zamakh-shari in the "Kash-shaf", part 1, page 301).

Contemporary scholar Sheikh Sha'rawi states in his "Legal Opinions" (part 1, page 42) that this incident of separation between a husband and wife really happened by the power of magic performed by these two angels. Sha'rawi says:

> "One of the characteristics of the Jinn is the ability of transformation. It is possible for a Jinn to take the image of an ape (and superimpose) himself on the face of a woman. Thus, her husband would hate her. Also, Satan can transform himself into a beast (and superimpose) himself on the face of a husband, which would make her turn against her husband."

C. Should Angels Prostrate Themselves Before Man?

The Qur'an says yes, and God Himself commanded them to do so; therefore, they all prostrate themselves before man except Satan who refused to obey. We read in the Qur'an (2:34),

> "And when we said unto the angels, 'Prostrate yourselves before Adam,' they fell prostrate, all save Iblis (Satan). He demurred through pride, and so became a disbeliever."

The reason for all that is an obscure, meaningless story recorded in chapter 2:30-34:

> "And he taught Adam all the names, then showed them to the angels saying, 'Inform me of the names of these, if you are truthful.' They said, 'Be glorified! We have no knowledge saving that which Thou has taught us. Lo! Thou, only thou, are the Knower, the wise'" (2:3 1 -32).

We wonder why it would be a crime if the angels did not know the names of the animals. What merit does Adam have if God secretly taught him these names? Does this justify God's command to the angels to prostrate themselves to Adam? It is well-known that the Bible teaches us that such worship should be only to God.

We do not believe this story and this dialogue between God and the angels, especially since the angels' words proved to be true and they manifested their knowledge of the future. Man defiled the earth and shed blood since the time of Cain, son of Adam, who killed his brother. Adam himself disobeyed his Lord and did not deserve worship from the holy angels—no respect or adoration, but only reproach, even though he knew all the names.

D. The Cow And The Dead Man.

This episode is clearly taught in the Qur'an (2:67-73). Muslim commentators indicate that a righteous Israeli old man had a son who was assassinated by his cousins in order to get his inheritance. They dumped his corpse at the city gate. No one knew who had killed him. God told Moses, "Slay a cow and hit the dead man by a part of it (its tongue, or thigh, or ear) as the scholars say." When Moses did so, the deceased rose up and told them who had killed him, then he immediately died again (refer to the commentary of the Baydawi, pp. 14,15; the "Kash-shaf" by the Zamakh-shari, part 1, page 289; and the Jalalan, page 11). Indeed, we do not find this story in the biblical records of the Old Testament.

7. Chapter Of al-Hujarat (The Private Apartment)

There is no mythical story in this chapter, but the reason for naming it is somewhat amusing and does not entail the need to receive an inspired chapter under this title. Those who translated the Qur'an into English indicate that this name was given to this chapter because of the following verse:

> "Lo those who call you (Muhammad) from behind the private apartments, most of them have no sense" (49:4).

Now, what is the interpretation of this verse? The Baydawi says (page 683),

> "What is meant by 'Private rooms,' is 'the women of the prophet Muhammad.' It is tantamount to his being in

seclusion with the women and their calling to him from within their private quarters. Either they came into them (private rooms) room by room, or they (the women) scattered themselves among these rooms calling for him."

We read the same words in the "Kash-shaf" of the Zamakh-shari (part 4, page 357), also in the commentary of the Jalalan (page 435). They said,

"Each one of his women called from behind (inside) her room in a voice filled with harshness and estrangement."

These are the statements of the scholars who interpreted this verse. Does this personal, private, insignificant matter require that Gabriel inspire a chapter under the title, "The Private Rooms"; that is, the private rooms of Muhammad's wives?

8. The Chapter Of Yunis

It is sufficient to quote verses 90 and 91 of this chapter. The

Pharaoh, while he was sinking in the sea, said, "I have believed in God," but God did not accept his repentance, and told him, "Do you say this now because you are drowning?" The commentators tell us that Muhammad's companions, such as ibn 'Umar and ibn 'Abbas, have said that Muhammad himself told them:

"Gabriel told me, 'I wish you had seen me taking mud from the sea to close up Pharaoh's mouth lest he believe and be reached by God's mercy' (refer to Jalalan, page 179; Zamakh-shari, part 2, page 368, and others).

Undoubtedly, this story is mythical, because if Pharaoh intended to believe, God would have accepted his repentance immediately; and there is no need for the angel Gabriel to hasten to take a handful of sea mud to close Pharaoh's mouth so that he would not make a confession of faith and be pardoned. God does not send his angels to do such wicked things.

We believe Muhammad's companions and ibn 'Abbas, who claimed that Muhammad related that to them. They cannot lie in

such matters, especially since Muhammad warned them that
whoever "lies and claims things which I do not do, or says things
which I did not say, will occupy his seat in hell". We believe the
companions in all that they convey to us on the authority of
Muhammad, but we cannot believe Muhammad's claim that
Gabriel had told him that he closed Pharaoh's mouth. The one
who prevents people from believing is Satan—not an angel of
God.

Second: God In The Qur'an

God in the Qur'an is not the God of love, the God of the
Christian revelation and the Holy Gospel. It is as if God (six
hundred years after the birth of Christ) has deteriorated. After He
had been full of love and affection, He has become a relentless,
wrathful God. You can search the heart of this God of Islam, but
you will never find the flowing, loving feelings which were
clearly manifest in Jesus Christ.

Let us now probe the most significant characteristics of God
as they are revealed in the Qur'an. There is no doubt, the
Qur'anic God differs from the God of the Gospel. The Gospel's
God is real while the other is illusive, non-existent. We have
already alluded to God's command recorded in the Qur'an when
we discussed human rights and women's status, non-Muslims
classification and the enslavement of man to his fellow man.

Yet, here we would like to magnify a very salient concept;
that is, the concept of love. The God of the Qur'an lacks the
element of love. The Qur'an records ninety-nine attributes of
God which do not include the attribute of love, although among
these attributes are some which repeatedly contain the same
inference, but love is not one of them. Indeed, some of these
attributes indicate that God is merciful, yet you do not find
mercy expressed on the pages of the Qur'an, in the life of
Muhammad, or among his companions. If mercy had ever been
practiced in Muhammad's life or in the life of his companions,

this would have been the exception and not the rule. The rule was the application of relentless brutality and barbarism.

There is no substitute for the word love. Love is stronger and richer than mercy. We do not say that a husband bestows mercy on his wife. We say he loves her. Likewise, we do not say (even when it is fitting to say) that a mother bestows her mercy on her children, but rather that she loves them. Love is a word rich with the meanings of sacrifice and giving. Love is a warm expression elevating human relationships to the highest summit of healthy growth. The Qur'an is empty of this word, whether in its relationship to man or in the area of human relationships.

God (in the Qur'an) does not liken himself to a Father who loves His spiritual children, the believers, as stated in the Gospel, but rather as a fearful master. People are but mere slaves who must always live in fear of Him.

Now let us survey some Qur'anic verses and vivid samples from the lives of the most devout Muslim believers.

1. In chapter "The Believers" (: 60), we read the following:

> "And those who give that which they give with hearts
> afraid because they are about to return unto their lord."

Muhammad himself spared us the trouble of interpreting this verse because he himself explained it. In Baydawi (page 457), Jalalan (page 288), and in the "Kash-shaf" of the Zamakh-shari (part 3, page 192), we read:

> "A'isha said, 'O, apostle of God, is the one who is afraid
> of God the one who commits adultery, steals, drinks wine,
> thus he is afraid of punishment?' Muhammad told her,
> 'No, O daughter of Sedik, he is the one who prays, fasts
> and gives alms, thus he is afraid that God may not accept
> these things from him.'"

We wonder where then is the sense of security and peace of mind. Where is the assurance and the guarantee concerning eternal life? How can peace fill the Muslim's heart? How can his soul rejoice and his spirit be filled with joy if he does not know whether God is going to accept his acts of fasting, praying and his almsgiving or not? Therefore, all Muslims suffer from fear because whatever they do of good deeds, their hearts will constantly be subjected to fear, according to the Qur'anic text and the interpretation of Muhammad himself.

We do not find among the chapters of the Qur'an and their verses one clear verse which offers a life of joy. There is no love and joy. Of course, we do not hear melodies of rejoicing bursting out of the hearts and mouths of the Muslim worshippers who gather in the mosques, but rather you see grim faces, especially those who are the most devout and those who are the most acquainted with the fundamentals of their religion, the interpretation of the Qur'anic verses and Muhammad's expositions. The reason is because they are not sure of what to expect after death. The future of their eternal life is obscure and their God does not guarantee them anything.

The first person we quote is Abu Bakr Al Sedik, who said that there is no certainty with God. Abu Bakr (the first Caliph) is regarded by all Muslims as one of the best Muslims if not the best. Even Muhammad acknowledged that Abu Bakr Al Sedik was the closest to him. Therefore, the Muslims elected him as caliph after the death of Muhammad. Abu Bakr always believed in Muhammad and in all that he uttered. He used to obey him blindly. When Muhammad suffered from a sickness which caused his death, he ordered Abu Bakr to lead the Muslims in prayer. What did Abu Bakr Al Sedik say about God?

> "I swear to God that I do not feel safe from God's cunning (deceitfulness) even if one of my feet is already inside paradise" (refer to the successors of the Apostle, bu Khalid Muhammad Khalid, page 114).

What a striking acknowledgment uttered by Abu Bakr the caliph of the Muslims and the father of A'isha, wife of Muhammad! "I do not feel safe from God's cunning even if one of my feet is already inside paradise". Maybe God would deceive him and push that foot outside of paradise because He changed His mind. There is no other meaning of this statement. This is not surprising, O, Abu Bakr, because the God of Islam and Muhammad as well as of the Qur'an, as you well know, does not bestow on the believer any assurance concerning eternity. He is not at all the God of the Christian revelation whom we know and experience, enjoying His love—with whom we have a personal relationship based on spiritual love because He is our heavenly father.

When we ponder the life of both Rabi'a al-'Adawiyya and Hasan al-Basri who both are renowned among Muslim circles so that students used to come from all of the Islamic world to learn from them and to receive instruction, we find that both of them lived in fear of God. Dr. Su'ad 'Abdul-Razzak says:

> "Rabi'a al-'Adawiyya asked al-Hasan al-Basri and said to him, 'What does a scholar say when asked, "If I die and the people are called in the day of resurrection (to be divided in two groups), one group to go to paradise and the other to be sent to hell, in which group will I be?" He said to her, "This is concealed, and nobody knows what is concealed except God"'" (p. 44).

On page 87, we also read that whenever death was mentioned in the presence of Rabi'a al-'Adawiyya, she would shiver and faint. On pages 84 and 85 of the same book, we read:

> "Rabi'a al-'Adawiyya's life bore the stamp of sadness and fear; and Hasan al-Basri was heading the group of the fearful devout. Sadness dominated his life. He increasingly (spent his time) in mourning. He made mourning a norm for all people. He used to believe that the Qur'an is the key to permanent sadness. He was accustomed to saying, 'O, son of Adam, I swear to God, if you had read the Qur'an and believed in it, your sadness would have been prolonged, and your fear would have been stronger. You mourning in the world would have been excessive.' The people of Basra said about him,

'Every time we see him, he looks as if calamity has recently befallen him.'"

We have to remember that al-Hasan al-Basri received his religious education from the companions (refer to "Itqan", part 4, page 211). Those people understood Islam, and they knew that the Qur'an is the key to abiding sadness. Whoever reads it and believes it will be subject to ever-increasing sadness, fear and mourning.

On the other hand, the word Gospel, which we will discuss later, means "glad tidings" and "good news," which makes people full of joy, happiness and abiding peace.

These are living examples drawn from the lives of Rabea al-'Adawiyya, al-Hasan al-Basri and Abu Bakr Al Sedik, who said when resurrection, paradise, and hell were mentioned in his presence, "I wish I were a tree eaten by an animal; I wish I had never been born" (refer to Jalalan, page 45 1). This is the same Abu Bakr who remarked, "I do not feel safe from God's cunning."

But, there is more than that about God in the Qur'an. God is depicted in the Qur'an as if He purposed the destruction of all people. He says, for example, "I indeed will fill hell with both people and jinn." In another verse, He indicates:

"And if your lord willed, all who are in the earth would have believed together" (Yunis: 99).

On the other hand, the Gospel declares clearly that **God does will that all people be saved**. God is not the cause for the eternal damnation of any man. He does not will that. God forbid! The only reason for man's eternal damnation, is his own rebellious will and his unrepentant heart. This fact is repeated dozens of times in the Gospel.

This is contrary to the Qur'an, which indicates that God does not will the salvation of all people. Had He willed it, then all who inhabited the earth would have believed in Him. Such a God is not the God whom Jesus Christ proclaimed to us.

In addition to the above, the Qur'an presents God to us a God who plots against man to destroy him. If you do not believe it, turn with me to the Qur'an to read a quotation from the "Chapter of the Isra" ("The Night Journey") 17:16:

> "And when we would destroy a township, we send commandment to its folk who live a life of ease and afterwards they commit abomination therein, and so the word of doom has its effect and we annihilate with complete annihilation."

The reader should notice that God did not eradicate the town because it was filled with so much wickedness that He found himself obliged to destroy it against His will. Rather the Compassionate, the Merciful God purposed and **determined to annihilate it**. Therefore, He laid down a very well-planned plot. He ordered its sumptuous residents to live a licentious life, thus it becomes subject to damnation. He **ordered** its affluent residents to commit debauchery. What a holy order!

Lastly, we say that God has disclosed his heart's desire when He referred to hell in the chapter Mariam: 71. He said, "Not one of you but will pass through it." People asked whether this verse refers to the wicked or includes all men; and what does the phrase 'passing through it' mean? In "Itqan" (part 4, page 237), the Suyuti tells us that Muhammad himself has answered this question and said:

> "There is no **righteous or debaucher** who would not enter hell."

We do not understand the reasoning which causes God to send even the righteous to hell. Then the verse continues, "But we (God) shall save those who guarded against evil."

Sheikh Kishk asserts Suyuti's claim that Muhammad said that all people (the righteous and the debaucher) will "pass through it" or "enter it" (refer to "Legal Opinions", part 6, page 41). This is the God of the Qur'an, my dear reader. He is indeed a fearful God who cannot be trusted, who wills and plans to annihilate people to fill hell with them. He is a God with whom nobody can feel safe, even the most devout person (like Abu Bakr), lest He does not accept him as Muhammad said. This is the acknowledgment of many great Muslims who experience this fear in their relationship with God and according to what they understood from Muhammad and the Qur'an.

What a difference between this God and the God of the Gospel which was said of Him:

> **"God demonstrates His own love toward us, in that while we were still sinners, Christ died for us"** (Romans 5:8).

Third: Content of Paradise

Since we have alluded to eternal life, it is appropriate to examine the image of paradise in the Qur'an. What did Muhammad say about Paradise? How it was depicted in the Qur'an in clear verses? Paradise in the Qur'an is a place full of beautiful women and seducing virgins, grapes, and pomegranates. Yes, it is a place filled with fruits, meats, wine and honey for everlasting feasts. Also, its inhabitants wear silk and splendid clothes. This is the picture of paradise which is presented to us by the Qur'an, Muhammad, and most of the former and later Muslim scholars.

It is feasible here to cite one example from among the dozens of Qur'anic verses which give us an accurate description of the Qur'anic paradise (refer to the following chapters and verses: 47:15, 87:31-33, 56:35-37, 56:22-23, 36:55-56, 55:56, 37:41-49).

Of course, the expounders agree on the interpretation of these verses. Refer, for instance, to the Jalalan (page 328), or any other commentary you like. In chapters 68:31-33 and 55:56, we are presented with the houris, who are assigned to fulfill men's sexual pleasures. These houris are always virgins. Their sexual relationship with men does not affect their virginity. Every time men approach them, they find them always virgins. Their breasts are not hanging down loose. They are always firm. They do not age beyond thirty-three years of age. They are white with black, wide, charming eyes. Their skin is smooth. Women who died old on earth will be re-created virgins for the enjoyment of men. Read the following commentaries—Al Glalan (p. 328, pp. 451-453, p. 499), Al Baydawy (pp. 710, 711, 781), Al Zumakhary (part 4, pp. 690,453, 459-462).

This is Muhammad' s own description of Paradise (refer to the commentary of the Baydawi, pp. 710, 711 and 781; the Zamakh-shari in 'Kash-shaf', part 4, pp. 453, 459-462, and 690; and the Jalalan, pp. 451-453, 499). You may also refer to any other major commentary because all Muslim expositors re-iterate the same thing. But as we read chapter Yasin: 55-56, we encounter some strange and shameful matters:

> "Lo, those who merit Paradise this day are happily employed (working), they and their wives, in pleasant shade, on thrones reclining."

Ibn 'Abbas himself acknowledged that their 'business' is to deflower the virgins (refer to Zamakh-shari, part 4, page 21; Jalalan, page 372, and "Women of the Paradise" by Muhammad Abu al-'Abbas, page 54). **This is the mission of the believers in paradise**.

Is it any wonder that many people embrace Islam, seeking to enjoy this imaginary paradise by which Muhammad deceived the Arabs; thus they entered God's religion by groups? Arabs sought this alluring life in the desert. They missed the fruit, pure water, fresh milk, beautiful white women whose skin is not browned by the heat of the desert sun. This is paradise as it is depicted in the Qur'an.

In his book, "Legal Opinions", Sheikh Sha'rawi exposed Islam and Muhammad when he said on page 36:

"The apostle of God was asked, 'Will we have sexual intercourse in paradise?' He said, 'Yes, I swear by the One who holds my soul in His hand that it will be a vigorous intercourse, and as soon as the man departs from her (the houri), she will again become immaculate and virgin.'"

On page 148, the Sha'rawi says:

"The apostle of God, Muhammad, said, 'Every morning one hundred virgins will be (the portion) of each man.'"

On page 448, he states that:

"The houris in paradise are white with big eyes."

He also indicates on pp. 265 and 266:

"Her (the houri, the virgin) two breasts are like the cone; that is, they are not hanging loose."

On page 191, the Sha'rawi says that if a woman got married to more than one man, either because her husband died or she was divorced, she would be given the right in paradise to choose one of them. Yet a man in paradise has the right to have dozens of the houris. It is not a secret that the Lord Christ (to Him be all glory), when He was asked the same question, said:

"You are mistaken, not knowing the Scriptures nor the power of God. For in the resurrection they neither marry nor are given in marriage, but are like angels of God in heaven" (Matthew 22).

In his "Legal Opinions" (part 6, page 42), Sheikh Kishk remarks:

But in the case of the houris, they are a blessed favor from God, bestowed on his servants who sincerely worshipped Him. They are added to the man's believing women for his enjoyment, as the texts record. But concerning women, Muhammad said, 'Any woman who believed in God and died before she was married, God will marry her to the best of the devout.'"

When I singled out both Sheikh Sha'rawi and Sheikh Kishk, I did so because of their reputation as famous scholars whose knowledge in the fundamentals of Islam is highly recognized and trusted by millions of Muslims all around the world.

In his famous book, "The Women of The People of Paradise; their Classifications, and Beauty", Muhammad 'Ali Abu al-'Abbas (a contemporary Muslim scholar) wrote about one-hundred pages in which he specified these matters in detail. This book is a current book published in 1987. The author encourages young men to be practicing Muslims in order to acquire all the available women in paradise, food, drinks, and clothes. On page 33, he himself says,

"We pray to God that He may grant us the pleasure of virgin women of paradise because the virgin has a sweeter mouth, **and is more desirable in bed, than the deflowered woman.**"

On page 41, he says that Muhammad, the apostle of God, said:

"Every man of the people of paradise is given the power of a hundred men for eating, drinking, intercourse and sexual desire" (The Qurtubi in his book al-Tadhkira).

He also said that the apostle of God indicated that:

"Whoever wears silk on earth will never wear it in eternity; and whoever drinks wine on earth will never drink it in eternity" (page 40, also al-Qurtubi in the al-Tadhkira).

The Tirmadhi also mentioned (part 7, page 161 of his book) that the apostle of God said:

"The martyr will be married to seventy-two wives of the houris. He has the right to intercede for seventy of his relatives" (page 44).

Muhammad, the apostle of God, was asked about the meaning of the Qur'ans words, "good dwellings in paradise of Eden." Muhammad replied, "The dwellings are palaces made of pearl.

In each palace there are seventy mansions. In each mansion there are seventy houses. In each house there is a bed. On each bed there are seventy sheets of different colors. On each sheet there is a nymph wife (houri) and in each house there are seventy tables, and on each table there are seventy kinds of food" (Volume 4, page 537 of "The Revival of Religious Science"— The Ghazali).

These are quotations from Muhammad's sayings and interpretations. No wonder, then, a Muslim wishes to fight against Christians and Jews (infidels) and die as a martyr in order to get married to seventy-two women.

In his Sahih (part 4, page 142; part 7, page 47, and part 9, page 50), the Bukhari records this incident in which Muhammad related to the Muslims that when he ascended to Paradise on the back of the Buraq, he saw a beautiful, young girl beside a palace. When he asked the angel about it, the angel answered, "The palace and the girl are for 'Umar ibn al-Khattab." Muhammad turned away because he remembered 'Umar's jealousy toward his women. When Muhammad related this incident to his companions, 'Umar started to cry, saying, "Would I feel jealous of you, 0, the apostle of God!" This is Muhammad who deceived his Arab people and promised them they would be rewarded with houris (refer also to Sahih of Muslim, volume 5).

Chapter Fourteen
Some Ordinances and Laws of the Qur'an and Islam

Pilgrimage Is A Pagan Practice

All Muslims agree that the practice of pilgrimage existed before the rise of Muhammad by hundreds of years. The people of Quraysh (along with pagan Arabs) were accustomed to celebrating the pilgrimage. Even Muhammad himself did so before he claimed to be a prophet. After he installed himself as the apostle of God, he and his followers continued to perform the pilgrimage's rites with the polytheistic pagans. He did not change many things (refer to Jawami' al-Sira al-Nabawiyya "Prophet's Biography" by ibn Hazm, page 14. Also "Islam: A Creed and A Law" by the Imam Mahmud Shaltut, pp. 113-115).

Almost every major Islamic history book documents these facts. Even after the conquest of Mecca, the pilgrimage has become one of the pillars of Islam. Muhammad banned the Arab polytheists from the Hajj after the year of the conquest. They were given four months either to embrace Islam or be killed, as we stated in chapter one. After that, Muhammad made very slight changes in the ceremonial rituals of the pilgrimage although he destroyed all the idols of the Ka'ba. Yet Muhammad himself continued to practice many paganistic rituals. He did not abolish them nor reject them. That created some consternation among his followers who expected him to uproot these idolatrous rudiments.

Some Pagan Rituals

Muslims continued to practice some of the pre-Islamic, pagan rituals, such as running between the two hills of Safa and Marwa or kissing the Black Stone. In the first case, Arab polytheists were accustomed to running between the two hills to glorify the idols which they erected and called them Isaf and Na'ila. When Muhammad destroyed the idols, Muslims were ashamed to continue this practice, and asked Muhammad about it. Soon, he claimed that a Qur'anic verse was given to him in which this practice was re-ordained. On page 33, of his commentary, the Baydawi says this in the course of his interpretation of chapter 2:158. Muslim scholars generally agree with the Baydawi (the Jalalan, page 22, Zamakh-shari in his "Kash-shaf", part 1). The Bukhari, for instance, remarks:

> "One of the companions said to Anas ibn Malik, 'Did you use to hate running between the Safa and Marwa?' He said, 'Yes, because it was part of the pre-Islamic rituals, until God gave Muhammad this verse and proclaimed that it was also one of God's ceremonial rites'" (refer to Sahih of al-Bukhari, volume 2, page 195).

We also read in the Sahih of Muslim:

> "Adherents of the prophet, (when) they were still in the pre-Islamic period, used to come up to visit two idols, Isaf and Na'ila; then they would go and run between Safa and Marwa; then they would have their hair cut. When Islam was established, they hated to run between them, but God sent down this verse (2:158), thus they ran (between them)" (refer to Sahih of Muslim, volume 3, page 411).

Ibn 'Abbas himself said:

> "The demons in the Jahiliyya used to circumnavigate all night around these two mountains. The idols (were

crectcd) bctwccn thcm. Whcn Islam camc, thcy (Muslims) said, 'O, apostle of God, we would never run between the Safa and Marwa because this is an unfavorable matter which we were accustomed to do in the Jahiliyya.' Thus, God gave this verse" (refer to Asbab al-Nuzul by Suyuti, page 27).

So, this "unfavorable matter" was strongly related to idolatry, but even so, Muhammad refused to abolish it, and several Qur'anic verses were given to confirm it. Muhammad himself performed it, and Muslims are still practicing it today.

The Kissing of the Black Stone

This famous meteorite is one of the Ka'ba's stones. The idolatrous were accustomed to worshipping it and kissing it. When Islam was established, Muhammad did not abolish this practice, but rather he himself performed it and commanded his followers to do so, in spite of their surprise and objection. In his Sahih (part 2, page 183), al-Bukhari records a famous statement made by 'Umar ibn al-Khattab, which demonstrates the confusion of the Muslims. The Bukhari says:

"When 'Umar ibn al-Khattab reached the Black Stone, he kissed it and said, 'I know that you are a stone that does not hurt or benefit. If I had not seen the prophet kiss you, I would have not kissed you.'"

All scholars (ancient and contemporary) confirm that this statement is uttered by 'Umar (refer to Sahih of Muslim, volume 3, page 406, and "Islam: A creed and a Law" by Imam Shaltut, page 122). It is well-known that Muslim pilgrims jostle around to kiss it, as Muhammad and his companions did before them. Because of such crowding, the pilgrims suffer a large number of serious casualties. Sheikh Sha'rawi says:

'The kissing of the meteorite is a firm practice in Islamic law because Muhammad did it. You must not ask about the wisdom behind that because this rite is (an expression) of worship in spite of the obscurity of its wisdom" (refer to "Legal Opinions", part 3, page 167).

This was his answer to the Muslim youths who asked, "What is the wisdom of kissing the meteorite?"

Other Rituals Of Pilgrimage

To be brief, we state that in addition to the kissing of the meteorite and running between the Safa and Marwa, the Muslim pilgrim has to make the trip to mount 'Arafa. Hundreds of thousands attempt to climb this mountain, but many suffer hardship which results in many casualties, because they hasten toward it in a disorderly manner as they do when they jostle around the meteorite. Climbing this mountain is one of the most important rituals of the pilgrimage. Even Muhammad used to say, "'Arafa **is** the Hajj (pilgrimage)." After that, they go to another mountain called the Muzdalifa. Then, on the tenth day of the pilgrimage, they go to Mina and they start casting pebbles. They also have their hair cut or shortened (having it cut is better), provided that the barber starts from the right side of the head, because Muhammad did so. After that, they slay their sheep. Some prefer to offer these sacrifices before the day of Mina, because these sacrifices pile up in Mina. Some are forced to donate money instead of sacrificing sheep, contrary to the advice of Muslim scholars who believe that such acts abolish one of the rudiments of the pilgrimage and create a dispute among Muslims. (Refer to "Rudiments of the Hajj" by Imam Shaltute; Sahih of the Bukhari, part 2, Sahih of Muslim, volume 3, and any other source about the rudiments of the Hajj.)

The Hajj (Pilgrimage) by Substitution

This may invoke the surprise of the reader, yet it is true and confirmed by Muslim scholars who assert that Muhammad himself allowed the Hajj by substitution. In the Bukhari (part 2, page 163), it is recorded that a Muslim asked Muhammad if it is possible to make the pilgrimage in lieu of his father. He said to him, "Yes, make the pilgrimage in lieu of your father." In "Legal

Opinions" of the Sheikh al-Sha'rawi, page 188, we read:

> "A woman asked Muhammad the prophet if she could make the pilgrimage in lieu of her mother who died before she was able to make the pilgrimage. He said to her, 'Yes, do so.' He also allowed another man to make the pilgrimage in place of his relative whose name was Bashrama."

When Sheikh Kishk was asked plaintively (part 3, page 113 of his "Legal Opinions"), "Is it admissible for (a man) to make the pilgrimage in lieu of either a dead or a living person?" He answered, "Yes, it is admissible." Therefore, the pilgrimage is not a personal worship, but an ordinance which a Muslim has to perform, or (in some cases) have performed for him. It is worthwhile to note that fasting, like pilgrimage, can be performed by substitution. Ibn 'Abbas relates that to us:

> "A man came to the prophet and told him this story: 'O apostle of God, my mother died without fulfilling her fasting; can I perform it in her place?' The apostle of God asked him, 'In your view, if your mother had a debt, would you pay it for her?' He said, 'Yes.' The prophet told him, 'The debt of God is more deserving of payment'" (refer to ibn 'Abbas, by 'Abdul-'Aziz al-Sha nnawi, page 133).

Fasting, then, is a **mere ritual** which a Muslim has to perform even after death.

In the above-mentioned book, Muhammad said that:

> "The Black Stone was whiter than milk when it descended (from heaven) but, the sins of children of Adam have blackened it" (refer to page 142).

The Rewards Of Pilgrimage

In the same previous source, ibn 'Abbas asserts that Muhammad used to say that the pilgrim who rides his animal on his way to Mecca, gains seventy merits for every step his animal makes. But, if he comes walking, he will gain seven hundred merits of the Sacred Mosque for every step he makes. It was asked of him, "What are the merits of the Sacred Mosque?" He answered, "Every merit is equal to one hundred thousand merits." We need not be surprised to see Muslims strive to perform the pilgrimage and compete to kiss the black stone, or climb the mount of 'Arafa, or to circumnavigate around the sacred sites of Mecca, in order to obtain hundreds of thousands of merits which will wipe out their misdeeds.

Ablution and Prayer

It is well-known that every Muslim has to pray five times a day. These are memorized prayers and must be uttered in Arabic. Originally, according to the Islamic Hadith and the testimony of Muhammad himself, God intended to impose on Muhammad and his followers praying fifty times a day instead of five, but Moses warned him and urged him to go back and negotiate with God to reduce the number to five. God approved that in the end. This incident took place during the time of the Night Journey and the Ascension. Muhammad claimed that Gabriel the angel came to him and made him ride an animal called the Buraq (an animal between a donkey and a mule). It took him first to Jerusalem, then to heaven, where he experienced many things, among them the reduction of the number of prayers.

Most Muslim scholars, early and late, believe that Muhammad experienced this supernatural event in flesh. A whole chapter was inspired in which the entire story was recorded. It tells us how Muhammad traveled from Mecca to Jerusalem in a few hours, where he met all the prophets and led them in prayer; then he ascended to heaven on the back of this animal. Our main concern is to re-examine the story of the reduction of the number of daily prayers. This incident is recorded in all the reliable Islamic sources, among them, "The Prophetic Biography" by ibn Hisham (part 2, page 9), Al-Sira al-Halabiyya (volume 2, page 132), also in the Sahih of the Bukhari (part 1, page 98). The story tells us:

"The apostle of God said, 'Then I came back and passed by Moses who asked me, "How many times a day does God require you to pray?" I said fifty prayers a day. He said, "Prayers are a heavy (task) and your people are still weak. Go back to your Lord and ask Him to lighten for you and for your people." I returned and asked my Lord (to do so). This matter was repeated several times until (God) imposed five prayers a day. Then I went back to Moses who told me the same as before. I said to him, "I have already returned to Him (several times) and asked that. I am embarrassed before Him, thus I am not going to (go back to Him)." So anyone who performs these five prayers will have the reward of fifty prayers'" (refer to ibn Hisham).

Ablution With Water Or Sand

The Qur'an says:

"If you find not water, then go to clean high ground and rub your faces and your hands with some of it" (5:6).

Before every prayer, each Muslim has to perform his ablution with water; that is, he has to wash his hands, feet, face and ears. If he does not find water, he must use sand ... yes, the sand of the desert. Don't think this is a printing error. Without exception, all Muslim scholars confirm this because of that very famous incident which happened to A'isha, wife of Muhammad and led the angel to deliver verse 6 of chapter 5. We spoke of this story earlier.

We do not understand this command. Is it cleansing or dirtying? Is this the religion of purification, as they claim? Yet, this practice is acknowledged by all Muslims, even a clear Qur'anic verse alluding to it. The Bukhari set aside an entire chapter to discuss it (refer to part 1, page 91). The prophet, as the Bukhari, tells us, used to plunge his hands in the sand or wipe his face and palms with it (refer to part 1, page 93), and ordered his followers to do the same. The same statement is found in the Sahih of Muslim (volume 1, page 663).

Indeed, ablution results in great reward, no matter if the ablution is performed with water or sand. Muhammad said:

> "Whoever performs the ablution, his sins will depart from his body, they even come out from under his nails, and his former and later iniquities are forgiven" (refer to the "Riyad of the Salihin" by Imam al-Nawawi as quoted from Sahih of Muslim, chapter "The Merits of Ablution," page 312).

The Ablution Spoiled and The Prayer Made Void

This is a very important matter because it shows that prayer in Islam is not a personal relationship and a loving conversation between man and his God, as is manifested in Christianity. It is a mere ritual and the fulfillment of an order.

Would the reader imagine that if a Muslim has performed the rites of ablution and bathing, and is almost through with his prayer, that this prayer will be nullified and his remuneration will be taken away, if a donkey, or a dog or a woman passes in front of him? He has to bathe or to perform the ablution anew and to repeat the prayers. We wonder and ask, "What does it mean to have the prayer invalidated? Has his conversation with God been erased? Are not prayers a conversation with God, being in His holy presence in full submission of the heart and mind? What does it mean that he has to repeat his prayer? Are prayers just uttering memorized words, or are they heartfelt fellowship? What effect does a dog or a donkey or a woman have if any of them passes in front of the worshipper?"

Muhammad says that the prayer will be defiled and invalidated. We have already alluded in chapter two of this book to the references related to this subject in the context of our discussion of the status of women in Islam. We also stated A'isha's answer to the prophet's companions when they pointed to this issue, after they vowed that they heard those words from the lips of Muhammad. She told them, "You have equated us with a dog and a donkey." Yet, what is significant for us here, is that prayers in Islam are **external practice and not internal worship. They are outward bearing**, not **essence**.

Muhammad assures us that there is another reason for nullifying the ablution; that is breaking wind. Can the reader imagine that? In his Sahih, the Bukhari assures us that Muhammad made these statements while he was talking about ablution (refer to part 1, page 46). He said:

> "The Apostle of God said, 'God does not accept the prayer of one who breaks wind, until he performs the ablution anew.'"

We don't see why some gases nullify ablution and prayer.

We have already mentioned that anyone who touches a woman's hand after ablution, has to perform it again, even if he spent five minutes in carrying out this ritual.

Certain Times In Which Prayer Is Forbidden

Muhammad forbade Muslims from praying to God at sunrise or sunset, that is, from dawn until sunrise or afternoon until sunset. If you ask for the reason, the prophet of the Muslims tells you, "Satan at this time brings his head closer to the sun so those prostrate to it become infidels." All these strange things are confirmed by Muhammad's followers (refer to Sahih of Muslim, volume 2, pp. 476-486 under the title, "The Times in which Praying is Forbidden").

We do not understand these things because Christ taught us in the Gospel that we ought to pray all the time. Also we read, "Pray without ceasing." It is permissible for the believer to pray anytime he wishes. He can enter his own room and close the door to pray to his Heavenly Father, as Christ commanded us. Yet, Muhammad forbade the Muslims to pray at particular times, such as sunrise or sunset, because Satan brings his head close to the sun during these times.

Reward And Punishment Regarding Friday Praying

One Friday, Muhammad was addressing the Muslims. A caravan of camels arrived from Syria and most of the audience left him, except for twelve men. Thus, a Qur'anic verse was given which says, "Whenever they had (an opportunity) for trade or entertainment, they hastened to it and left you standing alone" (refer to Sahih of Muslim, volume 2, page 514). Thus, Muhammad promised many great rewards for those who pray the Friday prayer. Ibn 'Abbas quotes Muhammad as saying:

> "Bathing on Friday atones for sins, and walking to the mosque (on Friday) is like working twenty years. If the Muslim completes the Friday prayer, he will receive a reward equal to one hundred years of work" (refer to ibn 'Abbas by 'Abdul-'Aziz al-Shannawi, page 121).

What a strange claim !

It is also recorded in Sahih of Muslim, volume 2, page 510:

> "Whoever performed the ablution, then attended the Friday prayers and listened (to the sermon), all his sins he would commit between that Friday and the following Friday would be forgiven, including three more days."

What an easy way to obtain forgiveness!

But the one who neglects prayers is regarded as an apostate, and must be killed if he does not repent, as we mentioned in chapter one. This is related to us by Muslim scholars such as ibn Hazm, ibn Timiyya, Imam al-Shafi'i and Malik, on the authority of Muhammad who said so. But Imam Abu Hanifa, who was more merciful than the rest, said, "He must not be killed, but should be beaten and thrown in jail until he prays; otherwise, he must be continuously beaten until he prays, even if his beating results in his unintentional death." In regard to this subject, the Azhar scholars have published many important statements ascribed to Muhammad in the Egyptian Magazine, "The Liwa' al-Islami", issue of 12/31/1987. They claim that Muhammad said:

"The one who neglects to pray will die thirsty, hungry, humiliated and his grave will become so narrow that it will press his ribs tight until they break. A snake called the 'Bald Brave' will be set on him to beat him in the grave until he plunges into the ground seventy cubits. Then, (the snake) will pull him by his face to the fire of hell."

Are these not meaningless words uttered by Muhammad?

The irony is that these great scholars have believed and accepted these claims. Yet, what makes it worse is that the one who abandons his prayers is subject to death, or in the best case, he will be beaten and jailed. Some scholars quoted Muhammad, saying:

"Whoever neglects part of the prayer will complete them after his death on a mountain of fire."

Some Statutes And Penalties Of Islamic Law

The Penalty Of The Thief

Islamic law is very clear about this crime. It says that a thief's hand must be cut off. This sentence is based on an explicit Qur'anic text which says:

"As for the thief, both male and female, cut off their hands. It is the reward of their own deeds, an exemplary punishment from Allah." (Refer to chapter "The Table": 38.)

All legists confirm that Muhammad has endorsed this penalty. They all quote his statement:

"A hand is cut off if he steals (anything) that costs one-fourth of a dinar and over. May God curse the thief. If he steals an egg, his hand must be cut off, or if he steals a rope, his hand must be cut off" (refer to Sahih of the Bukhari, part 8, pp. 199-201).

On these same pages, the Bukhari assures us that A'isha, Muhammad's wife, and the rest of his companions have said that

Muhammad used to cut off a thief's hand if he stole a shield which cost three dirhams (refer to Sahih of Muslim, volume 4, page 258 and on; ibn Timiyya, volume 8, page 331, ibn Qayyim al-Jawziyya in Zad of al-Ma'ad, part 5, page 49; The Baydawi, page 149; The Jalalan, page 93, and the Zamakh-shari in the Kash-shaf, part 1, page 612).

The Azhar scholars have been very explicit about this. In "The Statute of Legal Penalties", we turn to page 5 to read:

> "A person found guilty of theft shall be punishable as follows: 1 - amputation of the right hand for the first offense, 2 - amputation of the left foot for the second offense, 3 -imprisonment till the time of evident repentance for subsequent offenses."

On the same page, the Azhar scholars remark that there are cases in which the penalty is not to be carried out. These cases are:

> "When theft occurs in a public place during its hours of activity or in a place to which the culprit had free access, unless stolen property is found in his possession."

In his book, "Zad of the Ma'ad" (part S, page 50), ibn Qayyim al-Jawziyya says that the embezzler and the thief who steals fruit are not subject to the penalty of the Islamic law. He adds that Muhammad had commanded that they drop the penalty against them.

There are **two illogical elements** in this Islamic law concerning the penalty of the thief.

Muhammad's claim that the embezzler or the thief who robs public property, are not subject to the penalty, is meaningless. There is no law in any country of the world which endorses such an unjust, irrational, and illogical statement. Why should an embezzler not be punished? We do not find any answer for that.

Why should a father not be punished if he robs his son? It is possible that the son is a diligent person who is responsible for his wife and children, while his father is a reckless and extravagant man who wastes his money on his own pleasures. Why then should he and other relatives who rob their own kin, not be punished? When Muhammad said to someone, "You and your property belong to your father," he was stating a meaningless verdict because each person lives an independent life and has his own distinctive entity.

What about the larceny of the public property? It is evident that the thief must be punished. This is the opinion of the Imam Malik, but all other scholars disagree with him on the basis of Muhammad's deeds and sayings. Ibn Qayyim al-Jawziyya tells us that Muhammad issued an order in which he dropped the penalty against the plunderer, the embezzler, and the traitor of the trust (refer to part 5, page 50).

Obviously, the relentlessness of Islamic law and Muhammad's attitude are evident. Is it reasonable that a man's hand is not worth more than a quarter of a dinar, or three dirhams, or an egg? Would it not be more fair that the punishment be in proportion to the crime? Should Muhammad cut off the hand of a man whether he steals an egg or a shield? What logic or sensible person would accept that? Is it fair that a person be disabled to work or to be productive and inflicted with a permanent handicap because of such a simple matter? Also, does he have the right to replace it with an artificial hand or not? Contemporary scholars disagree on this problem.

More than that, it was Muhammad's habit to cut off the thief's hand and to hang it around his neck to make an example of him, to humiliate him, and as a warning to other people (refer to ibn Qayyim al-Jawziyya in Zad of al-Ma'ad, part 5, pp. 52, 56). Ibn al-Jawziyya also mentioned that Muhammad ordered the death of a thief after he stole for the fifth time (part 5, page 56).

Moving Stories

The following famous moving stories are recorded by most Muslim scholars. One is a story of a woman who was accustomed to borrowing things and failing to return them. So, Muhammad cut off her hand in spite of the intercession of his companions (refer to the Bukhari, part 8, page 199). Another story related by the majority of the scholars who said:

> "A man stole the gown of Safwan while he was in the mosque. Safwan, who was one of Muhammad's famous companions, arrested him and brought him to Muhammad. Muhammad ordered his hand to be cut off. Safwan shouted with surprise, 'Because of my gown you cut off his hand? I give it to him free.' Muhammad said to him, 'That would only have been possible before you brought him to me.' Muhammad ordered his hand to be cut off immediately" (refer to ibn Timiyya, volume 28, page 311; ibn Qayyim al-Jawziyya, part 5, page 51 of Zad of the Ma'ad).

Is it fair, then, after Safwan has given up his gown and presented it to the thief as a gift, that Muhammad still cut off the thief's hand, instead of reducing his punishment? What does it matter if Safwan did that before he brought the thief to Muhammad, or afterward? He waived his right, what more is needed? If someone claims that this is God's right and the cutting off of the hand is a must, then the question is, why did Muhammad tell Safwan that waiving of punishment would have been possible before he brought him before Muhammad? What eccentric behavior!

If somebody steals a gown or an egg, they cut off his hand; but the one who loots public property and embezzles the state's treasury is not subjected to the punishment. This is iniquitous law devoid of rationale and fairness.

Other Strange Things

Islam allows the beating of the accused, if he acts suspiciously. Muhammad himself whipped and jailed a defendant before the charge was proven true against him (refer to ibn Qayyim al-Jawziyya, part 5, page 56). Such a practice is left in the hands of the plaintiff, who decides whether to request the whipping of the suspect or not. But if the plaintiff demanded the beating of the suspect and it was proven that he was innocent, then the plaintiff (the owner of the stolen property) would be beaten. Muhammad himself did so and told the accusers, "If you wish me to beat them (the suspects), I will do so; and if your property is found with them, then let it be. Otherwise, I will flog your backs as I flogged their backs." They asked him, "Is this your verdict?" He said, "(It is) God's verdict and His apostle's" (refer to ibn Qayyim al-Jawziyya, part 5, pp. 52, 53, under the title, "Testing the Suspect by Beating Him').

We do not believe that this is God's decree, as Muhammad claims, because God does not punish a man before he is proven guilty. Neither God nor a free, just society would accept this. Such abuse is the reason behind the torture inflicted on the defendants in the Arabic and Islamic countries, in order to force them to confess to crimes they never committed. What an intolerant law, an unforgiving religion ... and an unmerciful prophet!

The Drunkard

The punishment of the drunkard is to be flogged forty times, and to be killed if he is arrested drunk for the fourth time. This is according to Islamic law and to actions and sayings of Muhammad. In the book of "A Proposal For The Law Of Legal Penalties," which was published by the Azhar (page 27), we read:

"Whipping is approved by a saying of the prophet, peace be on him, narrated by Abu Daud and others, 'Whip those who drink wine.'"

This same book describes (page 8) the flogging procedure as follows:

"The punishment of whipping shall be inflicted by means of a knotless whip of medium length and a single tip after stripping the convict of such clothing as may prevent pain to the body. Strokes must be divided all over the body;

regarding women, the strokes may only be on her back
and shoulders."

It is very evident that the Islamic Tradition has a significant
role in the implementation of Islamic Law since it records all the
sayings and the deeds of Muhammad. It explained, interpreted
and demonstrated some essential elements of worship which the
Qur'an either did not deal with, or was brief. Because of its role,
the Hadith's books (Sahih of Bukhari, Sahih of Muslim and
other books which collected or recorded the Islamic Tradition)
occupy a very important place in Islam. Most of these traditions
are handed down to us by Muhammad's companions, his
wives—A'isha in particular—as well as others who lived around
Muhammad. Without the information we obtain from the
Traditions, it would be impossible to construct a detailed system
of worship, procedure of pilgrimage, list of unlawful food, or
laws of inheritance. Many of the religious penalties, such as the
punishment of the drunkard, the punishment of the married
adulterer, are not mentioned in the Qur'an, but uttered by
Muhammad (refer to the "History of the Islamic Law" by Dr.
Ahmad Shalabi, pp. 142-153). Dr. Shalabi asserts that the
Islamic Tradition is a basic source of Islamic law, not because it
explains new ordinances which are not mentioned in the Qur'an
only, but also because in it Muhammad expounded the Qur'anic
verses and the reasons for their revelation. All contemporary
scholars agree with Dr. Shalabi.

Let us now examine the implementation of the penal code on
the drunkard as it is recorded in the Sahih of the Bukhari, which
is regarded by all scholars as the most important book about
Islamic Tradition.

Beating with Brutality and Savagery

In his book, part 8, pp. 196, 197, the Bukhari says:

"The prophet's custom was to beat the drunkard with palm
branches and sandals. When a drunkard was brought to
him, he ordered his companions to beat him with their

hands, sandals and robes. One of Muhammad's companions by the name of al-Sa'ib ibn Yazid says, 'We used to bring the drunkard before the apostle of God, and during the caliphate of Abu Bakr, and in the first stage of the caliphate of 'Umar, and we would beat him with our hands, sandals and robes. During the last part of 'Umar's caliphate, he ordered us to flog him eighty times'" (refer to ibn Timiyya, volume 28, page 336; and the book of the Sunna and its Significance, by Dr. M. Yusuf, page 29).

What brutality to see Muhammad and his followers rise against the drunkard, to beat him altogether at the same time with their sandals and hands, with the poor man agonizing in the middle. Later, during the last days of 'Umar, the penalty of the drunkard was eighty lashes and not forty. Likewise, 'Ali ibn Abi Talib sometimes used to lash the drunkard either forty times or eighty. It is no secret that Muhammad really did whip anyone who drank even a drop of any intoxicating drink. Yes, even one drop! This was confirmed by all the scholars when Muhammad was asked about wine as a medicine. He said, "No, it is its own malady and can never be a remedy" (refer to ibn Timiyya, volume 28, page 339, and Sahih of Muslim, volume 4, page 666).

More Than Flogging

This is true, because Muhammad said, "If someone drinks wine, lash him; if he drinks again, lash him; if he drinks for the third time; lash him; but if he drinks for the fourth time, kill him" (refer to ibn Timiyya, volume 28, page 336).

On page 347, ibn Timiyya tells us that:

"Some people came to Muhammad and told him, 'We use a drink made of wheat to protect us against the cold of our country.' Muhammad said, 'If it intoxicates (you), shun it.' He was told that the people would not relinquish it. Muhammad said, 'If they do not relinquish it, then kill them.'"

So, the penalty was (and still is) to lash and even kill anyone who drinks any intoxicating drink, even if it is used moderately or in a small amount as a protection against cold.

What a law! If somebody steals an egg or anything which costs a quarter of a dinar, they cut off his hand. If that is repeated for five times, they kill him. If someone drinks even one drop of wine, they brutally beat him with sandals, palm branches, and hands. If he repeats that four times, they kill him.

Despite that, they tell us this is **the justice and the wisdom of Islamic law**. They also tell us that Islam is the religion of forgiveness, and **Muhammad is the prophet of mercy**. Can we believe that the one who hangs the amputated hand of the thief around his neck, then orders his followers to parade him around, is **the prophet of mercy**? Such an act makes our bodies quiver, our souls feel disgusted and our free consciences rebel, especially if the defendant was punished before he was proven guilty as Muhammad said and did.

Section Four

Facts About Christianity

One God, The Holy Trinity

A Christian is one who believes in one God who has no equal in glory or in authority.

It is natural to believe in one God since the universe itself has no need except for one, almighty, omniscient God, the God of love and justice. In fact, Christ confirmed that God is one God, and so did all the disciples and apostles who wrote the New Testament books as they were moved by God's Holy Spirit. Christ said, "The Lord is one" in Mark 12:29. James, the apostle, said, "You believe that there is one God. You do well" (James 2:19), and Paul, the apostle, said, "For there is one God" (I Tim. 2:5). There are clear evidences of the oneness of God in Christianity.

As to the subject of the Trinity, it is a different issue that does not contradict or disprove the fact of the absolute oneness of God since the Trinity explains and clarifies *the nature* of this oneness of God. It is impossible to believe that the oneness of God is an abstract, as is the oneness of material things such as a pen or a chair. It is certain that the oneness of God is a universal, comprehensive oneness.

Regarding the number, it is absolutely sure that our God is one with no partner and no one equal to Him. God can never be three gods or the third of three gods, God forbid. This one God is alive in His Holy Spirit and not dead. He is speaking in His Word (Logos) and reasoning in His Wisdom. Christ is called, "The Word of God" (John 1) and "The Wisdom of God" (Proverbs 8). The fact that man himself is a body, a reasoning soul, and a spirit, does not disprove that he is one and not three. Just so, God is one, but He has a Spirit and a mind; i.e., understanding and wisdom.

In fact, the existence of this one God is of His own doing; i.e., spontaneous—that is why we call him "The Father". He is alive in His own Spirit who is called "The Holy Spirit". This great one

God is reasoning in His Wisdom and speaking in His Word who is called "The Son." "The Trinity" is 1 x 1 x 1 and not 1 + 1 + 1.

What Does The Term " Son Of God" Mean?

As Christians, we say that Christ is God the Son and this expression has a simple, spiritual meaning (not a carnal, physical one) since it is impossible to conceive that God has a wife. God chose to incarnate Himself in Jesus who said, "A body You have prepared for Me" (Heb. 10:5). The expression, "Son of God", means that Christ shares the spiritual nature and character of God.

It is obvious that Christ led an absolutely perfect life, which is why no one can object to the statement that Christ has the character and nature of God. As evidenced early, Christ never sinned, has never yielded to the temptations of Satan, nor has God ever said to Him, "I have taken away your sins that have bent your back," as Muhammad claimed that God said to him.

In addition to that, He was born of a virgin and He ascended to heaven as the living Lord. What a wonderful life is His! Moreover, His life was unusually great and His miracles were amazingly wrought. His authority extended even to the realm of nature, as it was claimed in the Qur'an in the Table Surah 5:110 (Al-Maeda) that Christ created birds out of clay; i.e., a living creature. Here, Muhammad inadvertently witnesses to the deity of Christ, for who can create but God Himself? This is a special characteristic limited to God alone, since God is the only creator. This is Christ, and this is the meaning of Christ, the "Son of God."

New Birth and Highest Moral Standard for Life

In Christianity, you will discover wonderful doctrines and principles that at first seem to be unusual and difficult to understand; yet you will discover later on how simple and practical they are. One who believes in these precious doctrines and principles and submits himself completely into the hands of God, will have a wonderful, exciting experience called, "being born again" (John 3 :1-18). His heart will also be filled with inner power, as well as real joy and peace, and consequently he will experience a personal, living relationship with God as he discovers the meaning of his own life. No longer will he need to be frightened of eternity that comes after this short life is over now. Death becomes "gain" as Paul the Apostle said in Philippians 1:21.

Referring to Christ, the Gospel says,

> "But as many as received Him, to them He gave the right to become children of God, to those who believe in His name" (John 1:12).

Christianity teaches that when one becomes a child of God, he experiences the new birth and the indwelling of the Holy Spirit. So, in the new birth, God implants anew nature into the inner being of man, a nature which man has never had before. In addition, God sends His Spirit to indwell man's heart as he receives Christ into his life. In fact, one needs to accept Christ as the incarnate Word of God who died on the cross to save him from sins and ascended to heaven. Such a relationship with God is man's dire need.

In order to have spiritual union, fellowship and love between man and his God, we must have God's Holy Spirit, who is the agent of the new birth. Moreover, the Holy Spirit gives us inner power and leads us into a life of joy and happiness, as well as a life of knowing God personally, not as a master but as a father. Assurance of eternal life after death is a gift of the Holy Spirit to the believing heart. It is difficult to describe all the spiritual and psychological blessings which one will experience as a result of belief in the God of Christian revelation—accepting Christ as personal Savior. May the reader experience all these blessings.

In Christianity, God gives man everything. His indwelling Holy Spirit embraces him in a wonderful way, even to the extent of total union between God and man in the person of our Lord Jesus Christ (John 17). As a matter of fact, God in Christianity is not a remote, silent God, but He is a caring, loving God who united Himself with us through Jesus Christ. Christ is known as the Son of God as well as the Son of Man. In taking on "the likeness of men" (Phil 2:7), He became fully man and fully God. Through His Spirit, man is able to experience a glorious life and every day, he can enjoy personal, inner fellowship with God, man's heavenly Father.

Day after day as he grows in grace and knowledge, the Christian experiences more power in his life and becomes able to express and convey love to all those around him. The life of holiness and purity becomes his normal pattern of life as well as having genuine love and inexpressible joy, even amidst all situations and hardships (II Peter 1:3,4).

The Cross

In fact, the cross is not merely a historic event, but it is the purpose for which Christ came to our world, as He mentioned frequently, "The Son of Man did not come to be served, but to serve, and to give His life a ransom for many" (Matt. 20:28). So, the cross is the key to understanding the books of the Old Testament which are full of prophecies about the cross which were written thousands of years BC—such as Psalm 23 and Isaiah 53.

It is well known that David's psalms and the Pentateuch were available to many people in different parts of the world long before the coming of Christ. In Christ, the prophecies were fulfilled, including all those concerning His crucifixion.

"But God demonstrates His own love toward us, in that while we were still sinners, Christ died for us" (Rom. 5:8)

> "For God so loved the world that He gave His only Son,
> that whoever believes in Him should not perish but have
> everlasting life" (John 3:16).

The cross is the evidence that God loves us; and without the cross, we would not have comprehended the meaning of love or recognized its standard, which is to sacrifice for those whom we love (Gal. 5:22-25). Without the cross, there would be no perfect example to teach us the great meaning of sacrificial living.

Not only do we have forgiveness for our sins in the cross, since Christ redeemed us and was punished for us, but we also have power to enable us to lead a life of wonderful ideals. The Bible says,

> "Knowing this that our old man was crucified with Him,
> that the body of sin might be done away with, that we
> should no longer be slaves of sin" (Rom. 6:6).

The "old man" is that sinful nature within us which is inclined to selfishness, egocentricity as well as deviation from God's love. It is only in the cross that one can experience victory over this "old man", a corrupted heart and a sin-driven soul.

Because He is God and man, our old nature was crucified with Him, and we are enabled to experience victory. Jesus was crucified as a man like us for He had identified Himself with our humanity. So we died in Him and we rose with Him as the Bible says.

Moreover, the Bible teaches us that we are seated with Him in heavenly places. What a wonderful high position it is! Therefore, our behavior and conduct must be heavenly (Col. 3:1-10).

These are profound truths of Christianity which proclaim that the loving God indwells us and empowers us in our daily life. Thus, our spiritual desires are fulfilled as a result of our union with God (Eph. 5:18, Gal. 5:16). What more does one need than union with God, receiving God's Holy Spirit, and being filled with Him?

My fricnds, in Christianity God has given us everything, even His own Spirit (II Pcter 1:3,4). We need only to open our hearts to God's wonderful love which was manifested to us when He came to our world in the person of Jesus Christ, accomplished our redemption; indwelling, enabling, and empowering us through His Holy Spirit, equipping us through His Word. Anyone who knows who God really is, will offer himself to God to enjoy being present in the bosom of the loving Father—the God of love, tenderness and compassion

Verses From the Bible

It is time now for us to conclude this book with verses from the Bible so that the reader may realize that there is no other book deeper or sweeter than the Bible. The Bible is the sole and only revelation of God in our world. Unlike all other books, the Bible has spread to all parts of the world in all the languages of mankind.

"All have sinned and fall short of the glory of God" (Rom. 3:23).

"For the wages of sin is death, but the gift of God is eternal life in Jesus Christ our Lord" (Rom. 6:23).

"For God demonstrates His own love toward us, in that while we were still sinners, Christ died for us" (Rom. 5:8).

"That if you confess with your mouth the Lord Jesus and believe in your heart that God has raised Him from the dead, you will be saved" (Rom. 10:9).

Peace, Joy and Pleasure Are Found in God

"In Your presence is fullness of joy; At Your right hand are pleasures forevermore" (Ps. 16:11).

"I will greatly rejoice in the Lord, My soul shall be joyful in my God; for He has clothed me with the garments of salvation, He has covered me with the robe of righteousness" (Isa. 61:10).

"Rejoice in the Lord always. Again I will say, rejoice! Let your gentleness be known to all men. The Lord is at hand. Be anxious for nothing, but in everything by prayer and supplication, with thanksgiving, let your requests be made known to God; and the peace of God which surpasses all understanding, will guard your hearts and minds through Christ Jesus" (Phil. 4:4-7).

"My brethren, count it all joy when you fall into various trials" (James 1:2).

A Life of Love

"You have heard that it was said, 'You shall love your neighbor and hate your enemy.' But I say to you, love your enemies, bless those who hate you, and pray for those who spitefully use you and persecute you, that you may be sons of your Father in heaven" (Matt. 5:43-45)-

"By this we know love, because He laid down His life for us. And we also ought to lay down our lives for the brethren. My little children, let us not love in word or in tongue, but in deed and in truth" (I Jn. 3:16, 18).

Prayer and Fasting

"And when you pray, you shall not be like the hypocrites. For they love to pray standing in the synagogues and on the comers of the streets, that they may be seen by men. Assuredly, they have their reward. But you, when you pray, go into your room, and when you have shut your door. pray to your Father who is in the secret place; and your Father who sees in secret will reward you openly" (Matt. 6:5,6).

"When you fast, do not be like the hypocrites, with a sad countenance. For they disfigure their faces that they may appear to men to be fasting" (Matt. 6:16).

A Life of Holiness

"As He who called you is holy, you also be holy in all your conduct, because it is written, 'Be holy for I am holy'" (I Peter 1:15,16).

"And do not be drunk with wine, in which is dissipation; but be filled with the Spirit" (Eph. 5:18).

"Whoever looks at a woman to lust for her has already committed adultery with her in his heart" (Matt. 5:28).

"The women adorn themselves in modest apparel, with propriety and moderation" (I Tim. 2:9).

God's Providence

"The very hairs of your head are all numbered" (Matt. 10:30).

"The Lord is my shepherd; I shall not want. He makes me to lie down in green pastures; He leads me beside the still waters, He restores my soul; He leads me in the paths of righteousness For His name's sake" Psalm 23: 1-3).

With these words of this beautiful psalm, we conclude this book. May God bless you.

Bibliography

<u>Contemporary and Ancient Muslim Scholars</u>

Interpretation and Background of Verses from the Qur'an:

1. Commentary of al-Baydawi, The Lights of Revelation, Dar Al Geel (The Generation)

2. Brief Commentary of Al Emam Al Tabari, Dar Al Shorok (Sunrise)

3. Commentary of Al Galaleen, Al Azhar, supervision 1983

4. Commentary of Al Zama Khsharie, 4 volumes Al Kasshaf, Dar (The Arabic Book)

5. The Right in Qur'an's Science (Al Itkan) Al Siewtie, Dar Al Torth (The Tradition) Abo-AI-Fadl

6. The Reasons of the Verses of the Qur'an (Asbab Al-Nuzul) Al Seiewtie, Nosair Library, Azhar scholars, supervision

7. Al Sahih Al Mosnad (The Reasons of Qur'anic Verses) Dar Al Arkam

8. Al Wahedy (The Reasons of Qur'anic Verses) including the Abrogator and the Abrogated verses concerning the law of Islam (Sharia)

9. The Bill of Legalistic Penalties, Azhar scholars

10. Ibn Teimiyya (36 volumes) Al Fatawy, Saudi Arabian scholars

11. The Ordinances (Akham) of the Qur'an, The Imam, Alshari'i, Dar (The Scientific Books in 2 volumes)

12. The Sweetest (2 volumes) (Al Mohalla) Ibn Hazm (dozens of volumes), corrected version, Beirut, Lebanon

13. Zad-Al-Maad, Ibn Qayyim-al-Jawziyya, Library of 'Manara al-Isalmiyya 1984 and the 5th volume 1981, 2nd version

14. The Spirit of Islamic Religion - Afify Abdel Fatah, review Azhar scholars

15. The History of Islamic Legislation (shariaa) Dr. Ahmad Shalabi, 2nd version

16. Islamic Nation State - Taky Al Dean Akl Banahani, The Liberty Part, Al Kods (Israel)

17. The Main Issues (Kadaya) in Islam, Abdel Al Motal Al Seidi-Al Azhar University

18. The Shita and the Correction, Dr. Mosa Al Mosawy, 1978

19. The Opinions (Al Fatawy) 1-10, Mohamad Mutwaly Al Sharawy (Egypt)

20. You Ask and Islam Answers - Al Sharawy, Dar Al Muslim, 1982

21. Islam - A Dogma and A Law (Sharia) Al Imam Muhamad Shaltout (12 versions)

22. Islam in the Face of Modern Challenges, Abu al-ala al Mawdudi, 1983, 5th version)

23. The Rights of Non-Muslims in the Islamic State, Al Mawdudi

24. You Ask and Islam Answers, Abdul latif Mushtahari

25. Women of Paradise (1) Muhamad Ali Abul Alabbas, 1987, Qur'an's Library

26. The Revival of Religion's Science, Al Ghazali, Dar (The Knowledge) for printing and publishing, Beirut

Concerning the History of Islam/the Biography of Muhammad, His Disciples, His Relatives and Wives:

27. The Biography of the Apostle, Ibn Hisham, Dar Al Tawfikie Al Azhar

28. The Biography of Myhammad and the Wars (Maghazy) Ibn Isaac, Dr. Sohaul Zakkar, Dar Al Fekr

29. Al Rod Al Anf, Al Sohaily, Dar Al Fekr, 1971 30. The Biography of Muhammad, Al Halabbya, Dar (The Knowledge), Beirut

31. The History by Tabari, Dar (The Scientific Books), Beirut

32. The Biography of the Prophet, Ibn Kathir, Dar Al Knowledge, Beirut

33. The Beginning and the End, Ibn Kathir, Library of Maaref, Beirut

34. The Perfect in History, Ibn Al Athir, 1967, Dar Al Arabic Book

35. The History by Ibn Khaldon, Al Aaelmy, Beirut, 1971

36. The History of the Kholafa (Successor of Muhammad) Al Sweitie

37. The Prophetic Biography (Gawameh) Ibn Ham, Mecca Mokarrama

38. Al Gameh Kerawany, Islamic Tradition -17

39. The Light of Certainty "Nur Al Yaqin" Al Khodary, 24th version

40. The Life of Muhamma, Muhammad Heikal, Dar Al Knowledge (Maaref), 17th version

41. Jurisprudence of Muhammad's Biography, Dr. Buti, Al Azhar, 7th version

42. Al Isaba (Life History of Muhammad's Friend) Ibn Hagar, Dar, The Arabid Book, Beirut

43. The Lion of the Forest (Asad Al Ghaba) Ibn Al Athir, Dar Al Shaab (People)

44. The History of the Arabic Nation, Dr. Abdul Fattah Shehata, Al Azhar, 1972

45. The Successor of the Prophet, Khalid Muhammad Khalid, Dar thabet. 1986

46. The Guided Caliphs, Dr. Abu Zeid Shalaby, Al Azhar, 1967

47. The Jurisprudence of Muhammad's Friends, Ibn Abbas, Abdel Aziz Al Shennawy, 1989

48. Explanation of Nahg Al Balagha, Ibn Al Hadid

49. Muhammad's Wives, Aisha Abdul Rahman

50. Muhammad's Daughters, Aisha Abdul Rahman, Dar The Arabic Book, Beirut (Bent Al Shati)

51. Ali and His Enemies, Dr. Nory Gafar, 1982, Beirut

52. Ali and His Sons, Taha Husain

53. The Big Division, Taha Husain

54. The Two Elders, Taha Husain

55. About the Biography of Muhammad, Taha Husain

56. The Roots of Divisions in Islamic Parties, Hason Sadek, Madboly Library

57. Before the Fall, 1985, Dr. Farag Fouda

58. The Ignored (Neglected) Fact, 1986, Dr. Farag Fouda (NOTE: Dr. Fouda was killed by fanatic Muslims in 1992)

59. Three Books About Muhammad's Successors, Abu Bakr Omar and Ali, (Abbas Mahmoud Al Akkad).

(NOTE: Dr. Fouda, Taha and Al Akkad are not Muslim scholars, of course, but they depend totally upon all ancient Muslim scholars with accuracy and complete honesty and no Muslim scholar can object to that.)

The Sayings of Muhammad (Sunnah) (NOTE: these are the most popular and important books among all Muslims.)

60. Sahih Al Bukhary

61. Sahih Muslim- Mawawy

62. Riad Al Salehen (Imam Al Mawawy)

63. Al ahadeth Al Kodsia

In addition to these reference books, many Muslim magazines, newspapers and pamphlets were used.